Application of Artificial Intelligence to Assessment

A volume in
The MARCES Book Series
Hong Jiao, and Robert W. Lissitz, *Series Editors*

Application of Artificial Intelligence to Assessment

edited by

Hong Jiao
University of Maryland

Robert W. Lissitz
University of Maryland

INFORMATION AGE PUBLISHING, INC.
Charlotte, NC • www.infoagepub.com

Library of Congress Cataloging-in-Publication Data

A CIP record for this book is available from the Library of Congress
http://www.loc.gov

ISBN: 978-1-64113-951-9 (Paperback)
        978-1-64113-952-6 (Hardcover)
        978-1-64113-953-3 (E-Book)

CONTENTS

CHAPTER 1

AUGMENTED INTELLIGENCE AND THE FUTURE OF ITEM DEVELOPMENT

Mark J. Gierl
University of Alberta

Hollis Lai
University of Alberta

Donna Matovinovic
ACT Inc.

Testing organizations require large numbers of diverse, high-quality, content-specific items to support their current test delivery and test design initiatives. But the demand for test items far exceeds the supply. Conventional item development is a manual process that is both time consuming and expensive because each item is written individually by a subject-matter expert (SME) and then reviewed, edited, and revised by groups of SMEs to ensure every item meets quality control standards. As a result, item development serves as a critical bottleneck in our current approach to content

Application of Artificial Intelligence to Assessment, pages 1–24
Copyright © 2020 by Information Age Publishing
All rights of reproduction in any form reserved.

development for testing. One way to address this problem is to *augment* the conventional approach with computer algorithms to improve the efficiency and increase the scalability of the item development process. Automatic item generation (AIG) is the process of using models to produce items using computer technology. With AIG a single model can be used to produce hundreds of new test items. The purpose of our chapter is to describe and illustrate how augmented intelligence in item development can be achieved with the use of AIG. The chapter contains three sections. In the first section, we describe the conventional approach to item development. We also explain why this approach cannot be used to meet the growing demand for new test items. In the second section, we introduce augmented intelligence in item development and we describe how AIG can be used to support the human-machine interactions needed for efficient and scalable content production. In the third section, we provide a summary and we highlight directions for future research.

CONTEMPORARY ITEM DEVELOPMENT AND THE PROBLEM OF SCALABILITY

The conventional approach to item development is a manual process where SMEs use their experiences and expertise to produce new test items. It relies on a method where the SME creates each test item individually. Then, after each item is created, it is edited, reviewed, and revised until the item meets the required standards of quality (Haladyna & Rodriguez, 2013; Lane, Raymond, Haladyna, & Downing, 2016; Schmeiser & Welch, 2006). The SME is responsible for the entire process which involves identifying, organizing, and evaluating the content required for creating new items. This approach relies on human judgment acquired through training and experience. As a result, item development has often been described as an "art" because it depends on the knowledge, experience, and insight of the SME (Haladyna & Rodriguez, 2013; Schmeiser & Welch, 2006). Conventional item development is also a standardized process that requires iterative refinements to address quality control (Lane, Raymond, Haladyna, & Downing, 2016; Schmeiser & Welch, 2006). The item development process is standardized through the use of guidelines where SMEs are provided with information to structure their task in a consistent manner that produces reliable and valid test items (Haladyna & Downing, 1998; Haladayna, Dowing, & Rodriguez, 2002; Haladyna & Rodriguez, 2013). Standardization helps control for the potentially diverse outcomes that can be produced when different SMEs perform the same item development task. Guidelines provide a summary of best practices, common mistakes, and general expectations that help ensure the SMEs have a shared understanding of their tasks and responsibilities. Iterative refinement supports the practice of item development through the use of a structured and systematic item review. That is, once an item has been written, it is then reviewed to evaluate whether it has met important outcomes described in the guidelines. Typically, reviews are conducted by committees of SMEs. Reviews can focus on a range of standards and objectives related to item content (e.g., does the item match the test specifications), fairness (e.g., does the item illicit construct-irrelevant variance due to subgroup differences), cognitive complexity (e.g., is the linguistic complexity of the item aligned to grade-level expectations), and presentation (e.g., is the item grammatically correct; Perie & Huff, 2016; Schmeiser & Welch, 2006). The review yields feedback on different standards of item quality that, in turn, can be used by the SME to revise and improve the original item.

The conventional approach has two noteworthy limitations. First, conventional item development is inefficient. It is both time consuming and expensive because it relies on the item as the unit of analysis (Dragsow, Luecht, & Bennett, 2006). That is, each item in the process is unique and therefore each item must be individually written, edited, reviewed, and revised. Many different components of item quality can be identified. For example, item quality can be determined, as noted in the previous paragraph, by the item content, fairness, cognitive complexity, and presentation. Because each item is unique, each component of item quality must be reviewed and, if necessary, each item must be revised. Because writing and reviewing is conducted by highly-qualified SMEs, the conventional approach is expensive.[1]

Second, conventional item development is challenging to scale in an economical way. The scalability of the conventional approach is again linked to the item as the unit of analysis. When one item is required, one item is written and reviewed by the SME. When 100 items are required, 100 items must be written and reviewed by the SMEs. Hence, a large number of SMEs who can write and review items is needed to scale the process. Conventional item development can result in an increase in item production when large numbers of SMEs are available. But item writing and reviewing is a time-consuming and expensive process due to the human effort needed to create, review, edit, and revise large numbers of new items.

These two limitations highlight the importance of establishing an efficient and scalable approach to item development. These limitations are also amplified in the modern era of educational assessment where test delivery and design are rapidly evolving to support different forms of on-demand testing. Test delivery marks the most important shift. Researchers and practitioners now recognize that educational testing is neither feasible nor desirable using the paper-based format. The cost of printing, scoring, and reporting paper-based tests requires tremendous time, effort, and expense. Computer-based testing (CBT) provides a viable alternative to paper-based testing that helps reduce delivery costs while providing important benefits for examinees. CBT permits testing on-demand thereby allowing examinees to take the test at any time during instruction. Items on CBT are scored immediately thereby providing examinees with instant feedback. CBT allows for continuous administration thereby allowing examinees to have more choice about when they write their tests.

A second important change, made possible with the implementation of CBT, is the rapid expansion of test design. Many innovative test designs are now being used to create new types of computerized tests. For instance, computerized tests can be designed to identify examinee's cognitive problem-solving strengths and weaknesses (e.g., Hoijtink, Béland, & Vermeulen, 2014; van der Kleij, Eggen, Timmers, & Veldkamp, 2012; van der Kleij, Vermeulen, Schildkamp, & Eggen, 2015). Computerized tests can be paired with computer "agents" to engage examinees in conversational dialogues (Graesser, Li, & Forsyth, 2014). Computerized tests can be designed to score examinee's written and spoken responses and then to provide examinees with feedback on their responses using dynamic multimedia score reports (Shermis, Burstein, Brew, Higgins, & Zechner, 2016). These designs require computerized delivery. These designs must also be supported with large banks of items to permit frequent administration and to provide examinees with continuous feedback. A bank is a repository of items. Banks must be initially created with a set of items and then constantly replenished with new items to ensure that examinees receive a continuous supply of diverse, high-quality, content-specific items while limiting exposure to maintain test security. With a paper-based test designed to support summative test score inferences, a relatively small number of items was sufficient because the test was delivered in fixed length format across a small number of administrations in order to meet a specific purpose. Modern CBTs that incorporate innovative test design, by way of comparison, require large numbers of items because tests are delivered in variable length forms or with multiple forms at many times during the year in order to meet multiple purposes (e.g., examinees receive their summative score as well as detailed formative feedback on their problem-solving strengths and weaknesses). Unfortunately, the large banks required for modern educational testing are not readily available. Moreover, the means by which large numbers of items can quickly be developed using the conventional approach to satisfy these new banking requirements are unclear.

AUGMENTED INTELLIGENCE IN EDUCATIONAL TESTING

Artificial intelligence is a term for describing the theory and the application of computer systems that perform tasks and solve problems that normally require human intelligence (Russell & Norvig, 2010). Human-in-the-loop hybrid-augmented intelligence or augmented intelligence, for short is an area within artificial intelligence that deals with how computer systems can emulate and extend human cognitive abilities thereby helping to improve human task performance and to enhance human problem-solving (Zheng et al., 2017). It requires the interaction between a computer system and a human in order for the system to produce an output or solution. Augmented intelligence combines the strength of modern computing using computational analysis and data storage with the human capacity for judgment to solve complex and, often, unstructured problems. Augmented intelligence can therefore be used to characterize any process or system that improves the human capacity for solving complex problems by relying on a partnership between a human and a machine (Pan, 2016).

While conventional item development relies entirely on the knowledge, experience, and insight of the SME, AIG is a process where models are first created by SMEs and then these models are used by a computer system to generate items (AIG; Gierl & Haladyna, 2013; Irvine & Kyllonen, 2002). Hence, AIG can be characterized as an augmented intelligence approach in educational testing because large numbers of new items can readily be manufactured using the coordinated inputs created by humans with outputs produced from computers. Gierl and Lai (2013, 2016a) described AIG as a three-step approach. First, the content for item generation is identified by the SME. This content is specified using principles and guidelines that highlight the knowledge, skills, and abilities required to solve problems and perform tasks in a specific content area. Second, an item model is developed by the SME to stipulate where the content must be placed to generate new items. Item models (LaDuca, Staples, Templeton, & Holzman, 1986) identify which parts of the assessment task can be manipulated for item generation. Third, computer algorithms place the content into the item model subject to rules. Assembly is conducted with algorithms because constraint programming is required to ensure that the content in the models is combined is a way that yields meaningful test items.

THE ROLE OF HUMAN EXPERTISE IN AIG

Content Definition

To begin, the content of interest must be identified for item development. Currently, the items for most educational tests are developed using test specifications. These specifications are created by SMEs, often, as a two-way matrix, where the rows represent content areas and/or learning outcomes and the columns represent cognitive skills (Haladyna & Rodriguez, 2013; Perie & Huff, 2016; Schmeiser & Welch, 2006). The content domain is organized by the structure of the topics and the content included within each topic. Mathematics, for example, is often structured in a hierarchy of topics that range from simple to complex. The topics in mathematics also require the integration of simple concepts (e.g., simple addition and subtraction) to produce more complex concepts (e.g., application of addition and subtraction in factoring) as the topics increase in complexity. Alternatively, language arts is often structured using a list of key topics. But instead of developing the topics in a hierarchy like mathematics, language arts uses the same topic (e.g., vocabulary) but in different contexts (e.g., sentence structure). The topics in the content areas are then organized using descriptions of knowledge, skills, and abilities. The most widely used taxonomy for identifying these skills is Bloom's Taxonomy of Educational Objectives: Cognitive Domain (Bloom, Englehart, Furst, Hill, & Krathwohl, 1956) or some variation of Bloom's approach (e.g., Anderson & Krathwohl, 2001). The taxonomy ranges from the simplest level, knowledge (i.e., recall of specific information), to the most complex level, evaluation (i.e., the ability to judge the value of materials and methods for given purposes). Because SMEs have extensive knowledge and experience with the examinees, curriculum, and learning environment, they develop items for each cell in the test specifications by anticipating the cognitive skills that examinees will use to answer items correctly for topics in each content area.

A construct map can be used to identify the content required for item development. A construct map is a description of different knowledge and performance skills that are ordered from easy to complex on a score scale (Wilson, 2005). These skills are expressed as proficiency claims. The claims include statements about the knowledge and skills that examinees who score at different points on the scale should exhibit for a specific content area. Hence, the purpose of a construct map is to describe how a scale can be created that links test scores to test performance using specific claims about examinees' knowledge and skills in a content area. Construct maps can be used to guide item development because the proficiency claims include a description of the cognitive mechanisms within a content area for each task (Luecht, 2013; Mislevy, Steinberg, & Almond, 2003). Items are designed by SMEs to measure these claims.

The content for item development can also be identifying using cognitive models. A cognitive model specifies the thinking processes that underlie test performance (Leighton & Gierl, 2007). Gierl, Lai, and Turner (2012) described the development and use of a cognitive model, specifically, for AIG. This model highlights the knowledge, skills, and abilities required to solve a problem in a specific domain by organizing the cognitive- and content-specific information into a structured representation of how the SME expects examinees to think about and solve test items. The knowledge and skills specified in a cognitive model are identified using an inductive process by asking the SME to review an existing item and then to identify and describe information that could be used to create new items. A cognitive model can be used to guide item development because it outlines the knowledge, skills, and abilities required to solve a problem in specific content areas. Items are designed by SMEs to measure these content-specific knowledge and skills.

Content Definition for AIG Reading Comprehension Example

To demonstrate how the content definition is used to guide item development, we provide an example from the domain of reading comprehension as measured on the ACT assessment. Reading comprehension on the ACT assessment requires examinees to

> derive meaning from several texts by (1) referring to what is explicitly stated and (2) reasoning to determine implicit meanings. Specifically, questions will ask you to use referring and reasoning skills to determine main ideas; locate and interpret significant details; understand sequences of events; make comparisons; comprehend cause-effect relationships; determine the meaning of context-dependent words, phrases, and statements; draw generalizations; and analyze the author's or narrator's voice and method. (ACT Inc., 2017)

An example of a section of a short prose passage from a released version of the ACT assessment is presented in Figure 1.1. After reading the passage, examinees are presented with a series of selected-response items about the

---

At Home in a Language

When I was a child growing up in Delhi, India. My parents and I will have spent our summers in Calcutta, India, visiting my grandparents, aunts, uncles, and cousins. We took the train over eight hundred miles from Delhi to Calcutta, which I considered a treat as itself. I loved the dining car, the cozy sleeping berth in our cabin, and the gentle rocking motion of the train that would lull me to sleep at night. As an adult, I prefer to travel by car. When we arrived at the Calcutta station the next morning, we were welcomed announcing train arrivals and departures over the intercom by the sound of the Bengali language.

Back in Delhi, the language most people commonly spoke was Hindi. Though I spoke Hindi fluently, it wasn't my first language. My parents were born in Calcutta, when most people spoke Bengali. They had lived there for many years before they go married and moved to Delhi, where Hindi was widely spoken. Because my parents had grown up speaking Bengali, we spoke Bengali, not Hindi, in our house. It was not surprising, then, that hearing Bengali on the streets of Calcutta made me feel right at home.

Figure 1.1 A section of a short prose passage taken from the released June 2011 administration of the ACT.

content in the passage. Each item is designed to measure one of three different skills: key ideas and details, craft and structure, and integration of knowledge and ideas (see ACT Inc., 2017, p. 7 for details). For the purpose of our chapter, the skill we will use to illustrate AIG is called "correcting inappropriate shifts in verb tense and aspect" which is found in the craft and structure category.

Item Model Design

After the content is identified, a test item that can be used to measure the content is created. Using a conventional approach, items are created individually to measure the content. Using AIG, the goal is to create many items simultaneously to measure the content. To achieve this goal, an item model for AIG must be designed. An item model specifies the components in a test item that can be manipulated to produce new items (Bejar et al., 2003; LaDuca et al., 1986). These components include the stem, options, and auxiliary information. The stem contains context, content, item, and/or the question the examinee is required to answer. The options include a set of alternative answers with one correct option and one or more incorrect options or distracters. Both stem and options are required for selected-response item models. Only the stem is created for constructed-response item models. Auxiliary information includes any additional content, in either the stem or option, required to generate an item, including text, images, tables, graphs, diagrams, audio, and/or video. Each component contain variables. Each variable, in turn, can have one or more integer and/or string values (i.e., values nested within variables for each component of the item model).

Often, item model design begins by identifying a parent item. The parent can be found by reviewing items from previous administrations or by drawing on a bank of existing test items. A decade ago, Gierl, Zhou, and Alves (2008) presented a list of 20 item models derived from existing parent items across a range of content areas that could be used for AIG. The parent item provides a starting point for item model design because it highlights the underlying structure for a potential model thereby providing a point-of-reference for creating alternative items. The statistical characteristics can also be used to identify well-functioning parents and, by implication, high-quality, content-specific test items. The SME creates a model using the parent by identifying variables within each component of the item that can be manipulated to produce new items. Hence, the parent serves as a template that can be used for item design. Alternatively, design can proceed by creating the item model from scratch without the use of a parent.

In addition to the model, the SME must also specify the values, which can be formatted as integer and/or string, for each variable in the model.

Item Model for AIG Reading Comprehension Example

An example of the parent item and the associated model derived from the short passage in Figure 1.1 is presented at the top of Figure 1.2. The item is: When I was a child growing up in Delhi, India. My parents and I will have spent our summers in Calcutta, India, visiting my grandparents, aunts, uncles, and cousins. The item contains the underlined phrase "I will have spent." The correct answer is "I would have spent." The model presented below the parent item in Figure 1.2 can be expressed using variables in the sentence as: [Variable 1, Part 1] [Variable 2, Part 1] [Variable 3] [Variable 1, Part 2] [Variable 4] [Variable 2, Part 2] [Variable 5]. The key feature in this model required to measure the content specification "correcting inappropriate shifts in verb tense" is that [Variable 1, Part 1] must contain the key determiner and [Variable 1, Part 2] must contain the cue. Our example also contains feasible alternative content strings for each variable in the model. For instance, the string options for the cue (i.e., Variable 1, Part 2) has six values: "spent," "will have spent," "spending," "will spend," "will be spending," and "have spent."

Summary

The SME is responsible for identifying, organizing, and evaluating the content and designing the models used for item generation. The content used for item development can be found in many different sources of information, including test specifications, construct maps, and cognitive models. These sources all provide different types of descriptions for the types of cognitive skills required to solve problems in specific content areas. Once the content is identified, item models are designed to measure the content. Item modeling is a method for scaling production by specifying the variables and the integer and/or string values that can be manipulated to produce new items. Because an item model serves as an expression of the SME's understanding of how examinees use their knowledge and skill to solve problems in a specific content area, many different item models can be created to capture this understanding. Hence, each model is distinct for each SME meaning different models can be produced by different SMEs. For this reason, defining content and designing models are considered to be creative tasks that rely on the knowledge and judgement of the SMEs acquired through their training and experience.

[Variable 1, Part 1][Variable 2, Part 1][Variable 3][Variable 1, Part 2][Variable 4][Variable 2, Part 2][Variable 5]

Variable 1, Part 1	Variable 2, Part 1	Variable 3		Variable 1, Part 2		Variable 4		Variable 2, Part 2		Variable 5
When I was a child growing up in	Delhi, India,	my parents	and	I would spend	our	summers	in	Calcutta, India,	visiting my	grandparents, aunts, uncles, and cousins.
During the year we lived in	Buffalo, United States,	my family		I spent		weekends		Boston, United States,		grandparents
By the time I leave	Cologne, Germany,	my siblings		I will have spent		holidays		Berlin, Germany,		aunts and uncles
Were I to have stayed in	Tel Aviv, Israel,	my cousins		I would have spent		vacations		Jerusalem, Israel,		cousins
				I spending						
				I will spend						
				I will be spending						
				I have spent						
				NO CHANGE						

Figure 1.2 Item model and the string value for each variable in the model.

THE ROLE OF COMPUTER TECHNOLOGY IN AIG

The third step for item generation requires computer systems to place the content into the item model. Assembly is conducted with algorithms because it is a constraint logic programming task. Iterations assemble all possible combinations of the integer and/or string values for each of the variables, *subject to rules*. The rules are created using constraints applied to each integer and/or string value across all variables in the model. Without the use of constraints, all of the values in each of the variables would be iteratively combined to create new items. However, many of these combinations do not produce items that are sensible or useful. For instance, the city–country combination of [Variable 2, Part 1] in Figure 1.2 must be constrained so it corresponds with the appropriate city–country combination in [Variable 2, Part 2]. For example, Cologne, Germany must be matched with Berlin, Germany. It would not be reasonable to match Cologne, Germany with Boston, United States, particularly when [Variable 4] used the string "weekends." Constraints serve as restrictions that described the rules that must be applied during the assembly task so that meaningful items are generated. When the goal is to produce large banks containing many similar items, a relatively small number of constraints are applied to the variables in the item model. Alternatively, when the goal is to produce small banks containing different items, a relatively large number of constraints are applied to the variables in the item model. Hence, constraint coding is considered to be the source of "intelligence" in AIG. It is the method by which AIG captures the specific decisions, judgments, and rules used by SMEs to produce diverse, high-quality, content-specific test items. Constraint coding also yields *every* plausible combination of the values within the variables. As a result, both plausible content combinations that would be anticipated by the SME, and some that would possibly be unanticipated, are produced during generation.

The Logic of Constraint Coding for Item Generation

To generate items, conditions are expressed as constraints in the item model. Constraints initially expressed as Boolean logic conditions (see Gierl, Zhou, & Alves, 2008 for details) are now expressed as a binary, element-by-element, matrix to guide the generation process. The process of defining constraints begins by selecting a pair of variables in the item model. This selection results in the creation of a vector that specifies all element (i.e., integer and/or string value) combinations for the two selected variables. Next, constraints between the two variables for each value element are defined in binary, with 0 being non-permissible and 1 being permissible.

The constraints required for all variable pairing is then defined for every value element in the item model. Each constraint of a variable pair contributes a vector. Finally, all of the vectors from the constraint coding are combined to create a matrix that defines the permissible content combinations for the entire model. This matrix, in turn, guides the generation process by providing a detailed rule-based map where the product of each binary element define all permissible content combinations and where each permissible content combination is an individual test item. Large item models, which are common in operational AIG applications, often contain 8–12 integer and string values nested within 5–7 variables producing millions of content combinations, prior to the application of the constraints. Then, when the constraints are applied, the majority of the content combinations are eliminated because they produced infeasible combinations that would result in meaningless or inaccurate items. The combinations that remain are meaningful items produced by assembling specific combinations of integers and/or string values across the variables in the item model. Gierl, Lai, Hogan, and Matovinovic (2016) described a mathematics AIG example used for operational item development in a large testing company. They presented the results from 18 math item models that generated over 109,300 items. The largest model in their study contained seven variables. The string and/or integer values ranged from 3 to 12 across the seven variables in the model resulting in 1,270,080 generated items before the application of the constraint codes. The final bank for this model contained 11,145 items after the use of the constraints demonstrating that 99% of the content combinations were eliminated after the constraints were applied.

Item Generation with IGOR

Different types of computer systems have been written to generate test items (e.g., Gütl, Lankmayr, Weinhofer, & Höfler, 2011; Higgins, 2007; Higgins, Futagi, & Deane, 2005; Singley & Bennett, 2002). Gierl et al. (2008) created the IGOR computer system to conduct the assembly task. IGOR, which is the acronym for **Item GeneratOR**, is a JAVA-based program that assembles test items using the integer and string values specified for each variable in the item model. That is, once the content is defined and the item model is created, IGOR systematically places the content into the model subject to the constraints to produce new items. To begin, the item model is entered in IGOR. The Item Model Editor window has a clearly structured interface that allows the user to input and structure each model. The editor has three panels corresponding to the components of either a selected- or constructed-response test item. The stem panel is where the stem for the item model is specified. The item model presented in Figure 1.2 is presented in the stem panel in Figure 1.3. The variables panel is used to add and manipulate the integer and/or string values as well as to apply the constraints between variables. The options panel is used to specify the correct and incorrect alternatives. The options are classified as either a key or distractor. An example of constraint coding is provided in Figure 1.4. The city–country combination of [Variable 2, Part 1] in Figure 1.2 is constrained so it corresponds with the appropriate city–country combination in [Variable 2, Part 2]. Buffalo, United States is matched to Boston, United States for our reading comprehension AIG example. To generate items from a model, the Test Item Generator dialogue box is presented where the user specifies the size of the generated item bank and the location where the generated items will be saved. A full test bank with no IGOR coding can be generated or a portfolio which contains the item bank along with a list of the IGOR input can be produced. The user is also required to specify the

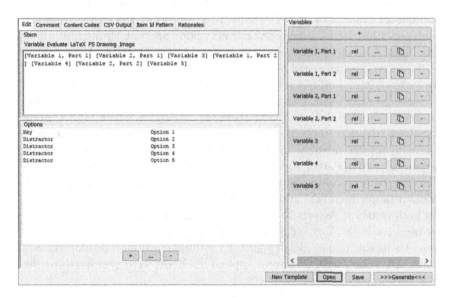

Figure 1.3   The Item Model Editor window in IGOR.

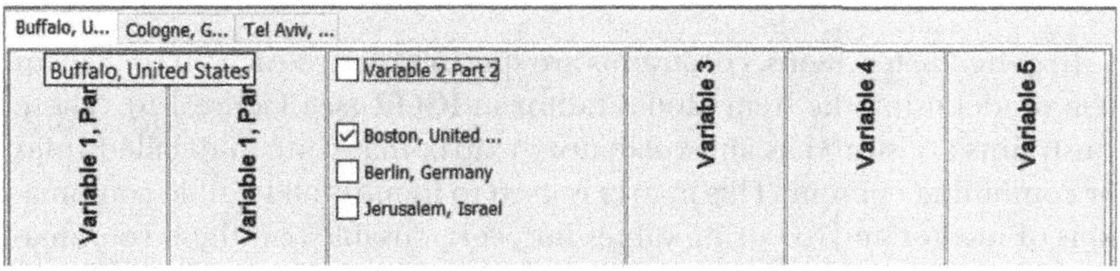

Figure 1.4   An example of a constraint in IGOR.

generation options. These options include the size of the generated item bank, the order of the options, the number of options for each generated item, and the format (i.e., with or without key; raw or formatted).

Generation Using the Reading Comprehension Item Model

In our example, constraint coding is required to generate the stem, the correct option, and the distractors for the item model in Figure 1.2. Four different sets of constraints are defined. The first set of constraints specify the relationship between [Variable 1, Part 1], which contains the key determiner, and [Variable 1, Part 2], which contains the cue, for the correct option. This constraint is used to align the appropriate key determiner and cue to produce the correct option. The second set of constraints define how the content for [Variable 1, Part 2] will be used to produce the distractors. Each multiple-choice item contains one correct option and four distractors, where one of the distractors will always be the option "NO CHANGE." Hence, three of the seven distractors will be selected with the constraint that each distractor for each item is unique for every generated item. One of the options must include "NO CHANGE." The third set of constraints define the relationship between [Variable 2, Part 1] and [Variable 2, Part 2], which both contain locations. In our example, the country variables India, the United States, and Germany for Part 1 will be matched with Part 2 for [Variable 2] so the same country is used in Parts 1 and 2 (see Figure 1.4). The fourth set of constraints describe the relationship between [Variable 3] and [Variable 5], which both contain family members and/or relatives. In our example, cousins is used for both variables. As a result, a constraint is specified so that cousins cannot be used for both [Variable 3] and [Variable 5] in the same generated test item. Using the item model in Figure 1.2 without constraints produced 5,832 items. After the constraints were applied, 83 items were generated for the reading comprehension example.

Summary

To generate test items, constraints are specified across each variable in an item model using the Item Model Editor in IGOR (see Figure 1.5). These constraints are stored as an explanatory matrix that contain detailed rules for combining content. This matrix is used to identify all feasible combinations of integer and/or string values for every variable and these combinations, in turn, are assembled to produce a bank of generated items. Large

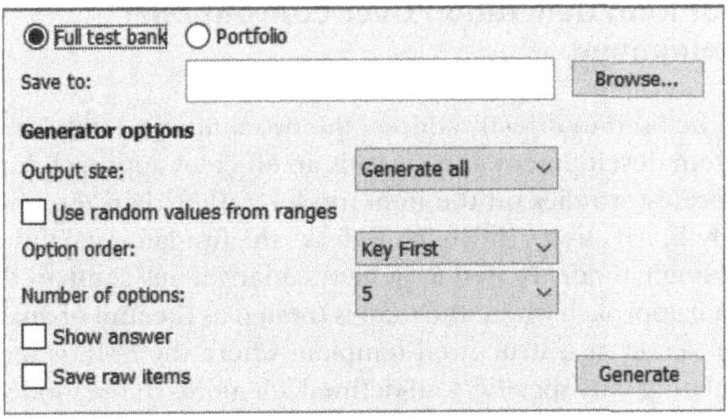

Figure 1.5 The Test Item Generator dialogue box in IGOR.

item models, initially producing millions of content combinations, are reduced to a relatively small number of meaningful integer and/or string combinations after the application of the constraints. The generation process on a modern high-speed computer requires only seconds to complete.

SUMMARY AND DIRECTIONS FOR FUTURE RESEARCH

In their 2006 chapter on "Test Development" in the 4th edition of the handbook *Educational Measurement*, Cynthia Schmeiser and Catherine Welch begin with this provocative question—Test Development: art or science? When augmented intelligence is applied to educational testing using AIG the answer is art *and* science. AIG is a process where the content required for testing is first identified by the SME and then the model required to process this content is created by the SME. Content specification and item model design require human expertise, experience, and judgment. These models, in turn, are used to generate large numbers of high-quality, content-specific test items using the algorithmic power of modern computing and the logic of constraint programming. Computational power, constraint coding, and data storage are features of a computer system. By merging the outcomes from the content-based creative task with the technology-based generative task, automated processes can be used to create a new approach to item development. AIG, therefore, represents a merger between the art and science of item development where well-defined responsibilities that adhere to specialized skills and the appropriate task assignments contribute to the production of diverse, high-quality, content-specific items using an approach that is both efficient and scalable.

Benefits of Item Generation Over Conventional Item Development

AIG can be used to directly address the two limitations inherent to conventional item development. First, AIG is an efficient approach for content creation because it relies on the item model, rather than the item, as the unit of analysis. AIG treats the item model as the fundamental unit of analysis where a single model is used to generate many items compared with the conventional approach where the item is treated as the unit of analysis. The item model serves as a structured template where the SME is responsible for manipulating only specific, well-defined, elements in the model. The remaining elements are not altered during the AIG process. Because the item model can be used to yield many test items compared with developing each item individually, quality is easier to monitor and maintain. The view of an item model as a template with both fixed and variable content contrasts with the conventional view of a single item where every element is unique, both within and across items.

Second, AIG is a process that is easily scaled, unlike conventional item development. AIG permits the SME to create a single item model that, in turn, yields many test items. Hence, AIG is scalable because one item model can generate many test items. When one item is required, one item model is written by the SME. But when 40 items are required, one item model may be sufficient, depending on the content specification. As a result, the number of required items is no longer tied to the number of SMEs who can write and review items. Rather, production is linked to the number of available item models, where a small number of SMEs can create the models that produce large numbers of new items. Because of this unit of analysis shift, the cost per item will decrease because SMEs are producing item models that yield multiple items rather than producing single unique items. As a result, building banks using SMEs who implement AIG could be an efficient and sustainable approach to item development.

DIRECTIONS FOR FUTURE RESEARCH

Scaling Item Production

Expanding Output Within and Between Item Models

Once the content has been identified and the item model has been structured, as outlined in Figure 1.2, the content for each of the variables can easily be expanded in order to increase the generative capacity for each model. For instance, new phrases can be added for [Variable 1, Part 1], new cities and countries can be added for [Variable 2, Part 1] and [Variable 2, Part 2], and new family and extended family members can be added [Variable 3] and [Variable 5]. An expanded list of relationships between the key determiner and the cue can also be specified. New key determiners and cues can be identified within an existing sentence or in new sentences in the passage.

In the model presented in our example, relationships between cities and countries, immediate and extended family members, and tenses for verbs was used to generate items. These value and variables combinations could be used to create a database library of cities and countries, family members, and verb tenses. Subsequent models that require one or more of these variables could use the information in the library to generate content. For example, once the cities and countries database is complete, that list could be used for *any* model that includes a cities and country variable. Or, new models could be designed that intentionally include a cities and country variable to make use of the generative capacity that exists when using content in the database. These types of AIG content libraries do not currently exist.

Implementing n-Layer Item Modeling

The goal of item generation using the item model is to produce new test items by manipulating the values within the variables using rules garnered from the constraints. The example in our chapter is described as a 1-layer item model because a relatively small number of values and variables were used. But a limitation of using a 1-layer item model is that relatively few variables can be manipulated because the number of potential manipulations is fixed to the total number of words in the stem. As an alterative, *n*-layer item models can be created (Gierl & Lai, 2012). The goal of AIG using the *n*-layer item model is to produce items by manipulating the variables at two or more levels in the model. Unlike the 1-layer model where the manipulations are constrained to a linear set of generative operations using the variables at a single level, the *n*-layer model permits manipulations of a nonlinear set of generative operations using variables at multiple levels. As a result, the generative capacity of the *n*-layer model is comparatively high. The concept of *n* layer item generation is based on a hierarchical structure of content meaning that values are often embedded within one another. This hierarchical organization can also be used as a guiding principle to generate large numbers of meaningful test items. The use of an *n*-layer item model is therefore a flexible template for expressing different structures thereby permitting the development of many different but feasible combinations of embedded variables. The *n*-layer structure can be described as a model with multiple layers of variables, where each variable can be varied simultaneously at different levels to produce different items.

A comparison of the 1-layer and *n*-layer item model is presented in Figure 1.6. For this example, the 1-layer model can provide a maximum of four different values for Variable A. Conversely, the *n*-layer model can provide

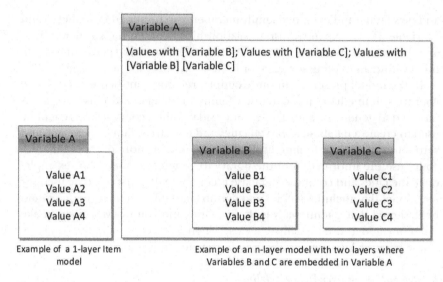

Example of a 1-layer Item model   Example of an n-layer model with two layers where Variables B and C are embedded in Variable A

Figure 1.6   A comparison between a 1- and *n*-layer item model.

up to 64 different values by embedding the same four values for Variables B and C within Variable A. Because the maximum generative capacity of an item model is the product of the ranges in each element (Lai, Gierl, & Alves, 2010), the use of an *n*-layer item model will always increase the number of items that can be generated relative to a 1-layer structure. To date, the application of *n*-layer item modeling has been limited (for an example, see Gierl et al., 2015). However, the potential for *n*-layering to increase the generative capacity of an item model is significant.

Refining and Expanding the AIG Process

Quality Control

The SME is responsible for creating the content and the logic specified in the item model. This logic should be evaluated by another SME as part of the AIG quality control process necessary for any operational item development system. Using conventional item development, SMEs evaluate new items individually using guidelines and standards for quality. But with AIG, the item model is a structured template where the SME is responsible for manipulating specific, well-defined, elements in the model. The remaining elements are not altered during the AIG process. As a result, costly yet common errors in item development (e.g., including or excluding words, phrases, or expressions along with spelling, grammatical, punctuation, capitalization, typeface, and formatting problems) can be avoided because only specific elements in the stem and options are manipulated across a large number of items. In other words, the item model serves as a template for which the SME manipulates only a small number of clearly-defined elements. The remaining elements are not altered during development.

One other important consequence of creating item models is that the unit of analysis in quality control moves from the item to the model level. The SME is responsible for identifying the content and specifying the logic for each item model. If the model is correctly specified, then the generated items will reflect the correct combination of the content and logic. Hence, quality control is focused on the more manageable task of evaluating the quality of a small number of AIG models rather than reviewing large numbers of individual test items. Gierl and Lai (2016b) described how the content and the logic specified in the item models could be evaluated using a standardized rating scale. The outcome of the rating would, in turn, serve as feedback for improving the model thereby ensuring the generated items meet high standards of quality. The effectiveness of using rating scales to improve the quality of the models and the generated items has not yet been evaluated.

Creating Item Development Ecosystems
Educational testing is now in a constant and unprecedented state of change. As noted earlier, significant change is occurring in how educational tests are delivered and designed. In addition to delivery and design, educators are also beginning to change the purpose and the longstanding conventions associated with educational testing. In 2015, ACT Inc. released a report called "Beyond Academics: A Holistic Framework for Enhancing Education and Workplace Success" (Camara, O'Connor, Mattern, & Hanson, 2015). The authors claim that accountability systems of the past have focused exclusively on measures of academic achievement when attempting to understand college and career readiness. This limited construct definition, they claim, is far too narrow for understanding the complex factors that affect the school to work transition for today's students. To expand the construct, ACT developed a holistic framework that includes a comprehensive list of the knowledge, skills, behaviors, and competencies across four areas related to college and work readiness as well as a description of how these skills change as students progress from kindergarten to career:

> Development of this the framework is based on a comprehensive review of relevant theory, education and work standards, empirical research, input from experts in the field, and a variety of other sources for each of four broad domains [core academic skills; cross-cutting capabilities; behavioral skills; education and career navigation skills]. The framework spans the K–Career continuum, since the precursors of success emerge very early in life and development continues well beyond the confines of traditional secondary and

postsecondary education. To describe what people need to know and be able to do across this continuum, both the education and work readiness framework and the associated model of success are defined in terms of critical transitions. These transitions differ slightly across the four broad domains, but some major transitions are relevant to all four ... For each of these transitions, the framework describes what individuals need to know and be able to do to be successful. A hierarchical taxonomy within each broad domain organizes the more specific dimensions and the knowledge and skills and provides a common language for describing the precursors of success. The focus is ultimately on knowledge, behaviors, and skills because these are amenable to change. Thus, the taxonomy is well positioned to inform education and other interventions aimed at helping people achieve education and workplace success. Because the taxonomy is holistic and comprehensive, it can be used to identify new ways to assess and improve education and workplace readiness. (Mattern & Hanson, 2015, p. 9)

This description demonstrates how educators are beginning to radically change the scope and purpose of their tests. AIG is an example of how augmented intelligence can be used to increase the efficiency and scalability of item production for any testing scope. But when the purpose of the test is also questioned, a more complex problem must be addressed: How do we create large numbers of new test items in an efficient and cost-effective manner to measure complex, dynamic, and, potentially, ill-structured tasks characteristic of new and evolving constructs such as college and career readiness?

One way to address this problem is by drawing on the benefits of a *problem-solving ecosystem*. Crowdsourcing is one example of a problem-solving ecosystem. In this ecosystem, large complex tasks are decomposed into smaller more simple tasks. Participants drawn from a broad range of content areas and backgrounds then contribute to solving the tasks. The tasks are embedded in a workflow which ensures that the participants in each step of the process use and augment solutions provided by participants from the previous step. This workflow, in turn, is embedded in the problem-solving ecosystem which is designed to systematically address a larger more complex multi-faceted problem.[2]

In an *item development ecosystem*, the cognitive capabilities of the participants could be used to create diverse item models for measuring complex task performance in a unique construct such as "studying and learning" (ACT cross-cutting capabilities; O'Connor, Gambrell, & Pulvermacher, 2015) or "maintaining composure" (ACT behavioral framework; Casillas, Way, & Burrus, 2015). These cognitive outputs, in turn, could then be supplied as inputs for an AIG computer system that uses the information from the models to produce large numbers of new items to measure these novel constructs. The ecosystem requires an online workspace where participants can connect, contribute, combine, revise, evaluate, and integrate their ideas and data using a common framework (Michelucci & Dickenson, 2016). The workspace also includes a well-designed user interface so participants can easily and readily interact with the AIG computer system. An item development ecosystem must include strategies for scaling the item development process and for monitoring the quality of the generated content. But most of all, the ecosystem needs a broad range of human participants who have diverse backgrounds and experiences. Recall that the "art" of item modeling yields an expression of the SME's understanding of how students use their knowledge and skill to solve problems in a specific content area. But different item models can be created from many diverse perspectives to capture this understanding. In this chapter, we demonstrated how this understanding is expressed in a well-defined content area like English language arts. Presumably, it can also be expressed in an ill-defined content area like "studying and learning" and "maintaining composure." Each item model is distinct for each participant meaning that different but equally valid models can be produced by different participants in the ecosystem. Some of the models will be characteristic of the SME perspective. This perspective is predictable and expected because SMEs are content experts who have item development experience. But the item development ecosystem is not just composed of SMEs. Other models will be characteristic of a different and possibly unanticipated perspective. For instance, the item models designed by a developmental psychologist to capture critical education and workplace transitions may differ from the models created by the English language arts SME. Finally, interactions between participants (e.g., the developmental psychologist and the English language arts SME) may lead to yet a different outcome. In sum, problem-solving ecosystems where the unique contextual knowledge and rich cognitive capabilities of humans interact seamlessly with powerful computing systems to produce both predictable and novel outcomes may provide the most promising environment for solving the complex item development challenges that await researchers and practitioners in educational testing. An item development ecosystem has yet to emerge. But the conceptual foundation, the item development methods, and computational tools now exist to make this type of ecosystem possible.

NOTES

1. Rudner (2010) estimated that the cost of developing *one operational item* for a large-scale test using the conventional item development approach ranged from $1,500 to $2,500 USD (p. 157).
2. In our view, creating large numbers of new test items to measure many evolving concepts and constructs related to college and career readiness that begin in kindergarten is an example of a complex multi-faceted problem.

REFERENCES

ACT Inc. (2017). *Preparing for the ACT test.* Iowa City, IA: Author.

Anderson, L. W., & Krathwohl, D. (2001). *A taxonomy for learning, teaching, and assessing: A revision of Bloom's taxonomy of educational objectives.* New York, NY: Longman.

Bejar, I. I., Lawless, R., Morley, M. E., Wagner, M. E., Bennett, R. E., & Revuelta, J. (2003). A feasibility study of on-the-fly item generation in adaptive testing. *Journal of Technology, Learning, and Assessment, 2*(3). Retrieved from https://ejournals.bc.edu/index.php/jtla/article/view/1663

Bloom, B., Englehart, M., Furst, E., Hill, W., & Krathwohl, D. (1956). *Taxonomy of educational objectives: The classification of educational goals. Handbook I: Cognitive domain.* New York, NY: Longman.

Camara, W., O'Connor, R., Mattern, K., & Hanson, M. (2015). *Beyond academics: A holistic framework for enhancing education and workplace success* (ACT Research Report Series Vol. 4). Iowa City, IA: ACT.

Casillas, A., Way, J., & Burrus, J. (2015). Behavioral skills. In W. Camara, R. O'Connor, K. Mattern, & M. Hanson (Eds.), *Beyond academics: A holistic framework for enhancing education and workplace success* (pp. 25–38). Iowa City, IA: ACT.

Drasgow, F., Luecht, R. M., & Bennett, R. (2006). Technology and testing. In R. L. Brennan (Ed.), *Educational measurement* (4th ed., pp. 471–516). Washington, DC: American Council on Education.

Gierl, M. J., & Haladyna, T. (2013). *Automatic item generation: Theory and practice.* New York, NY: Routledge.

Gierl, M. J., & Lai, H. (2016a). Automatic item generation. In S. Lane, M. Raymond, & T. Haladyna (Eds.), *Handbook of test development* (2nd edition; pp. 410–429). New York, NY: Routledge.

Gierl, M. J., & Lai, H. (2016b). A process for reviewing and evaluating generated test items. *Educational Measurement: Issues and Practice, 35*, 6–20.

Gierl, M. J., & Lai, H. (2012). Using automatic item generation to create items for medical licensure exams. In K. Becker (Chair), *Beyond essay scoring: Test development through natural language processing.* Paper presented at the annual meeting of the National Council on Measurement in Education, Vancouver, BC.

Gierl, M. J., & Lai, H. (2013). Using automated processes to generate test items. *Educational Measurement: Issues and Practice, 32*, 36–50.

Gierl, M. J., Lai, H., Hogan, J., & Matovinovic, D. (2015). A method for generating test items that are aligned to the Common Core State Standards. *Journal of Applied Testing Technology, 16*, 1–18.

Gierl, M. J., Lai, H., & Turner, S. (2012). Using automatic item generation to create multiple-choice items for assessments in medical education. *Medical Education, 46*, 757–765.

Gierl, M. J., Zhou, J., & Alves, C. (2008). Developing a taxonomy of item model types to promote assessment engineering. *Journal of Technology, Learning, and Assessment, 7*(2). Retrieved from https://ejournals.bc.edu/index.php/jtla/article/view/1629

Graesser, A., Li, H. I., & Forsyth, C. (2014). Learning by communicating in natural language with conversational agents. *Current Directions in Psychological Science, 23*, 374–380.

Gütl, C., Lankmayr, K., Weinhofer, J., & Höfler, M. (2011). Enhanced Automatic Question Creator – EAQC: Concept, development and evaluation of an automatic test item creation tool to foster modern e-education. *Electronic Journal of e-Learning, 9*, 23–38.

Haladyna, T. M., & Downing, S. M. (1989). Validity of a taxonomy of multiple-choice item-writing rules. *Applied Measurement in Education, 2*, 37–50.

Haladyna, T. M., Downing, S. M., & Rodriguez, M. C. (2002). A review of multiple-choice item-writing guidelines for classroom assessment. *Applied Measurement in Education, 15*, 309–333.

Haladyna, T. M., & Rodriguez, M. C. (2013). *Developing and validating test ttems.* New York, NY: Routledge.

Hoijtink, H., Béland, S., & Vermeulen, J. (2014). Cognitive diagnostic assessment via Bayesian evaluation of informative diagnostic hypotheses. *Psychological Methods, 19*, 21–38.

Higgins, D. (2007). *Item distiller: Text retrieval for computer-assisted test item creation* (RM-07-05). Princeton, NJ: Educational Testing Service.

Higgins, D., Futagi, Y, & Deane, P. (2005). *Multilingual generalization of the Model Creator software for math item generation* (RR-05-02). Princeton, NJ: Educational Testing Service.

Irvine, S. H., & Kyllonen, P. C. (2002). *Item generation for test development.* Hillsdale, NJ: Erlbaum.

LaDuca, A., Staples, W. I., Templeton, B., & Holzman, G. B. (1986). Item modeling procedures for constructing content-equivalent multiple-choice questions. *Medical Education, 20*, 53–56.

Lai, H., Gierl. M. J., & Alves, C. (2010, April). Using item templates and automated item generation principles for assessment engineering. In R. M. Luecht (Chair), *Application of assessment engineering to multidimensional diagnostic testing in an educational setting.* Paper presented at the annual meeting of the National Council on Measurement in Education, Denver, CO.

Lane, S., Raymond, M., Haladyna, R., & Downing, S. (2016). Test development process. In S. Lane, M. Raymond, & T. Haladyna (Eds.), *Handbook of test development* (2nd ed., pp. 3–18). New York, NY: Routledge.

Leighton, J. P., & Gierl, M. J. (2007). Defining and evaluating models of cognition used in educational measurement to make inferences about examinees' thinking processes. *Educational Measurement: Issues and Practice, 26*, 3–16.

Luecht, R. M. (2013). An introduction to assessment engineering for automatic item generation. In M. Gierl & T. Haladyna (Eds.), *Automatic item generation: Theory and practice* (pp. 59–101). New York, NY: Routledge.

Mattern, K., & Hanson, M. (2015). ACT holistic framework of education and work readiness. In W. Camara, Camara, R. O'Connor, K. Mattern, & M. Hanson (Eds.), *Beyond academics: A holistic framework for enhancing education and workplace success.* (pp. 1–9). Iowa City, IA: ACT.

Mislevy, R. J., Steinberg, L. S., & Almond, R. G. (2003). On the structure of educational assessments. *Measurement: Interdisciplinary Research and Perspectives, 1,* 3–67.

Michelucci, P., & Dickinson, J. (2016). The power of crowds. *Science, 351,* 32–33.

O'Connor, R., Gambrell, J., & Pulvermacher, R. (2015). Cross-cutting capabilities. In W. Camara, Camara, R. O'Connor, K. Mattern, & M. Hanson (Eds.), *Beyond academics: A holistic framework for enhancing education and workplace success.* (pp. 19–24). Iowa City, IA: ACT.

Pan, Y. (2016). Heading toward artificial intelligence 2.0. *Engineering, 2,* 409–413.

Perie, M., & Huff, K. (2016). Determining content and cognitive demands for achievement tests. In S. Lane, M. Raymond, & T. Haladyna (Eds.), *Handbook of test development* (2nd ed., pp. 119–143). New York, NY: Routledge.

Rudner, L. (2010). Implementing the graduate management admission test computerized adaptive test. In W. van der Linden & C. Glas (Eds.), *Elements of adaptive testing* (p. 151–165), New York, NY: Springer.

Russell, S. J., & Norvig, P. (2010). *Artificial intelligence: A modern approach* (3rd ed.). Upper Saddle River, NJ: Prentice Hall.

Schmeiser, C. B., & Welch, C. J. (2006). Test development. In R. L. Brennan (Ed.), *Educational measurement* (4th ed., pp. 307–353). Westport, CT: National Council on Measurement in Education and American Council on Education.

Shermis, M., Burstein, J., Brew, C., Higgins, D., & Zechner, K. (2016). Recent innovations in machine scoring of student- and test taker-written and spoken responses. In S. Lane, M. Raymond, & T. Haladyna (Eds.), *Handbook of test development* (2nd ed., pp. 335–254). New York, NY: Routledge.

Singley, M. K., & Bennett, R. E. (2002). Item generation and beyond: Applications of schema theory to mathematics assessment. In S. H. Irvine & P. C. Kyllonen (Eds.), *Item generation for test development* (pp. 361–384). Mahwah, NJ: Erlbaum.

van der Kleij, F. M., Vermeulen, J. A., Schildkamp, K., & Eggen, T. J. (2015). Integrating data-based decision making: Assessment for learning and diagnostic testing in formative assessment. *Assessment in Education: Principles, Policy & Practice, 22*(3), 324–343.

van der Kleij, F. M., Eggen, T. J., Timmers, C. F., & Veldkamp, B. P. (2012). Effects of feedback in a computer-based assessment for learning. *Computers & Education, 58,* 263–272.

Wilson, M. (2005). *Constructing measures: An item response modelling approach.* Mahwah, NJ: Erlbaum.

Zheng, N., Liu, Z., Ren, P., Ma, Y., Chen, S., Yu, S.,... Wang, F. (2017). Hybrid-augmented intelligence: Collaboration and cognition. *Frontiers of Information Technology & Electronic Engineering, 18,* 153–179.

CHAPTER 2

RECONCEPTUALIZING ITEMS

From Clones and Automatic Item Generation to Task Model Families[1]

Richard Luecht
University of North Carolina at Greensboro

Matthew Burke
American Board of Internal Medicine

ABSTRACT

From a traditional assessment perspective, test items are *unique* entities that have static statistical characteristics in a population and conditions of use that seldom if ever change. That perspective is being challenged by modern principled assessment design and automatic item generation methods that reconceptualize items as instantiated units within larger *task-* and *item-model families* created from either tightly controlled, template driven item writing or computer algorithms that employ item-cloning templates or item shells/models. We present the genesis of these new developments with implications for the generalizability of scores and decisions. Two important evaluative criteria—substantive isomorphism and statistical isomorphism—are also introduced as a means of judging the quality of these task-model families. The serious need for ongoing, strong quality control mechanisms is also discussed.

Application of Artificial Intelligence to Assessment, pages 25–49
Copyright © 2020 by Information Age Publishing
All rights of reproduction in any form reserved.

Large-scale testing operations in education and the professions are increasingly facing enormous demands for high-quality test items to support more frequent testing. This is especially true for computer-based testing (CBT) and computerized adaptive testing (CAT), and especially where the limited capacity of secure test centers often requires extending test administration windows to weeks or even months. These types of scenarios introduce three inevitable challenges: (a) meeting item production demands, (b) managing incremental item-writing costs, and (c) item calibration under sparse sampling conditions. A hopefully provocative premise is offered that neither our current test development practices nor our application of increasingly more sophisticated psychometric models to the response data can fully meet all three challenges. The seemingly insurmountable challenge may stem from our characterization of test items as unique entities created under restricted conditions of measurement that limit their generalizability. An alternative, integrated test design and scale maintenance strategy is suggested that involves reconceptualizing items as members of a *task-model family*[2] from the onset. The following sections describe the above challenges in more depth.

Item Production Demands, Costs, and Analysis Challenges

Item writing (production) is a basic supply problem. How can we generate sufficient numbers of high-quality items to meet our demands? Higher stakes exams must generate sufficient numbers of test forms to mitigate cheating and item exposure risks, where highly popular items in terms of their content and/or psychometric properties need to be replaced and/or rotated out of active use more frequently (Way, Steffen, & Anderson, 2002). CBT and CAT further exacerbate the demands because of the limited workstation/seat capacities of secure testing sites.[3] Holding large-scale CBT administrations on a single day is usually infeasible because of these capacity restrictions and must instead be offered within one or more testing windows that may extend to days, weeks, or even months.

This huge demand for items has led to procedures for efficiently mass-producing items. Proposed solutions have ranged from human-intensive efforts such as holding special item-writing events with teams of item writers working together or open-ended solicitation of items from the field,[4] to using computer-generated items assembled by a computer algorithm—that is, automatic item generation (AIG).

AIG begins with selecting or designing one or more *parent* items represented as a common template, item shell, or item model (Bormuth, 1970; Haladyna & Shindoll, 1989; Hively, Patterson, & Page, 1968; Osburn, 1968).

An item-generative mechanism is then used to produce multiple children or *sibling* items (Bejar, 2002, 2010; Bejar & Yocum, 1991; Enright & Shee-han, 2002; Irvine, 2002; LaDuca, 1994; LaDuca, Staples, Templeton, & Holzman et al., 1986; Meisner, Luecht, & Reckase, 1993). These are also sometimes synonymously referred to as *clones*. The most common generative mechanism is to use a computer algorithm called a *generator* or *engine* to exhaustively create the children items by replacing surface features or specific content placeholders in the template with variables from a database source (Bejar, 2002; Embretson, 1999, 2016; Embretson & Kingston, 2018; Gierl & Haladyna, 2012; Gierl & Lai, 2012; Gierl, Lai, & Turner, 2012; Gorin & Embretson, 2012; Meisner et al., 1993). To date, AIG applications have largely been limited to item models for multiple-choice items.

The transition from a subject-matter expert perspective on item design to a more automated, production-oriented manufacturing engineering view of item and test design and development was succinctly stated by Dras-gow, Luecht, and Bennett (2006):

> The demand for large numbers of items is challenging to satisfy because the traditional approach to test development uses the item as the fundamental unit of currency. That is, each item is individually hand-crafted—written, re-viewed, revised, edited, entered into a computer, and calibrated—as if no other like it had ever been created before. (p. 473)

The second challenge is cost reduction. If item writing and test production costs are fixed—by some estimates ranging from $500 to $2,000 per multiple-choice test item—the increased supply chain will correspondingly drive up testing costs that, in turn, get passed onto the test taker or testing agency (Luecht, 2005). For example, if our item production demands grow from 300 to 1,500 items per year, there will be a five-fold increase in test development costs that needs to be absorbed or passed onto test takers. Now suppose that each item, on average, costs $1,000 when all item writing, editing, item banking, and pilot testing expenses are properly included in the calculations. Without effective ways to significantly reduce costs, our annual item production expense would likewise increase from $300,000 to $1.5 million. The potential cost reduction for item writing is often cited as a primary reason to consider AIG (Gierl & Haladyna, 2012; Gierl, Lai, & Turner, 2012).

The third challenge is a subtle, technical challenge involving item re-sponse theory (IRT) calibration and scale-linking practices.[5] For most types of testing, items are *calibrated* to determine their statistical characteristics such as item difficulty relative to the underlying score scale. IRT calibra-tions require substantial quantities of scored item response data from a finite data source—the eligible test takers in the target population. An ex-ample may help illustrate this point.

Suppose that we are able to successfully generate a sizeable item bank of 4,000 items using AIG. Even if we have 50,000 examinees on which to pilot test the items, on average, we would only obtain 12.5 observations per item—a number that would be wholly insufficient for stable item calibration and banking purposes. The bottom line is that there can be serious psychometric scale maintenance issues as an indirect result of successfully addressing the item production/supply issue.

The issue is further complicated when considering various choices of IRT models, estimation techniques, and equating/linking sampling designs. Let's look at the modeling choices in particular. The one-parameter (1PL or Rasch) logistic model can be expressed by the relatively simple mathematical function,

$$\text{prob}(u_i = 1 | \theta; b_i) = P_i(\theta) = \left[1 + \exp(b_i - \theta)\right]^{-1} \qquad (2.1)$$

where u_i is a dichotomous scored item response ($u_i = 1$ if correct or $u_i = 0$ otherwise), θ is the underlying score scale, and b_i is an item difficulty parameter. Descriptively speaking, the 1PL model characterizes the probability of a correct response to a dichotomously scored item as a function of the examinee's proficiency, θ, and the item difficulty, b_i. Conservative estimates suggest a need for minimum samples of 150 to 1,000 examinees per item to stably estimate the item difficulty parameters.[6]

In contrast, the more complex the three-parameter logistic (3PL) IRT model characterizes the same item response probability by:

$$\text{prob}(u_i = 1 | \theta; a_i, b_i, c) = P_i(\theta) = c_i + (1 - c_i)\left\{1 + \exp\left[-a_i(\theta - b_i)\right]\right\}^{-1} \qquad (2.2)$$

with θ again representing the underlying proficiency score scale and b_i denoting the item difficulty. In addition, the model includes a "discrimination" parameter, a_i, that functions as both a type of scoring weight as well as an indicator of the sensitivity of the item to the changes in the underlying proficiency scores, and a "lower asymptote" parameter, c_i, that adjusts for noise in the response function at the lower end of the proficiency scale—sometimes called the "pseudo-guessing" parameter. Here, practical estimates of minimum sample sizes per item range from 1,000 to 2,000 test takers. In general, a minimum random sample of $N = 500$ has been suggested for any IRT model (Hambleton & Jones, 1993).

The estimation techniques used, the quality of the test forms over all, and sampling design choices also come into play. For example, shorter tests tend to result in less reliable score estimates than longer tests and the ensuing error estimates can be shown to indirectly impact the item calibrations.

Sampling designs also matter. In general, non-random samples or sampling classrooms, schools, or districts usually results in both the standard errors of estimate and the required sample sizes to be underestimated (see, e.g., Cochran, 1977—also see Footnote #6). Related to the issue of sampling design is that of *connectivity*. Successful calibration of the item statistics requires reasonably strong data connections between the items and examinees (e.g., the same examinees taking different items and different examinees taking the same items—see Kolen & Brennan, 2014; Searle, 1987 for general discussions).

Unfortunately, any attempts to significantly increase item production—through AIG or other means—implies that sample sizes and connectivity will suffer because fewer examinees per item will be available for pilot testing and ultimately calibrating the items. If the empirical connections become weak enough, they break. A thorough technical discussion of the statistical estimation and sampling design/connectivity issues is beyond the scope of this discussion. However, it seems suffice to say that current IRT calibration methods can be severely *stressed* when a large collection of items is administered under highly sparse sampling design conditions.[7]

Our point is that, regardless of IRT model choice, accurate and stable statistical estimation of the item parameters' properties requires large sample sizes—certainly more than 12.5 test takers per item. The calibration process is "data hungry" and that hunger tends to grow when more complex IRT models are used. Even large census samples of test takers may eventually be exhausted. And when estimation fails, the entire calibration and scale-maintenance architecture is at risk.

The combination of these three factors (mass item production, incremental item production costs, and data-hungry psychometric procedures) presents a somber dilemma. Mass item production solves the supply problem and reduces costs; however, it introduces a serious [new] statistical calibration problem. Our premise is that the real problem lies in conceptualizing items as unique entities. Conversely, we suggest that the solution is to instead reconceptualize items as *exchangeable* units—that is, members of a *task model family*. Of course, that assertion assumes that we also need to design the items that same way—as exchangeable units.

The Restricted Generalizability of Unique Items

Why are items treated as unique *entities* with exclusive statistical and content properties? One reason is simple semantics. We declare items to be unique entities and assume that they are just that. However, consider a multi-part problem that requires the test taker to complete each part in sequence, and where some of the earlier responses are used in subsequent parts. Is the entire problem one item or multiple items in a "set"? Semantics. Another reason is that items are seen as the fundamental units of analysis because they are typically *designed* to be unique. That is, each item is hand-crafted by an item writer to fulfill one or more content categories, goes through a prescribed set of editorial and review procedures, ideally undergoes sufficient empirical pilot testing where its statistical character-istics such as item difficulty and discrimination are initially estimates, and ultimately is included as an operational (scored) item on one or more test forms (Schmeiser & Welch, 2006). Once an item navigates this rather in-tense and expensive developmental gauntlet, we assume that we can ascribe substantial inferential power to it—at least when combined with the other items on the form—if we do not modify anything about the item.

Figure 2.1 shows these *conditions of measurement.* The statistical item oper-ating characteristics of a single item are depicted by the rounded rectangle in the center of the figure. The rectangles denote fixed-effect design condi-tions that may influence the item characteristics. The ellipses imply the ran-dom components (random assignment/sampling and occasions of use). The point of Figure 2.1 is to highlight the large number of fixed effects/constraints incorporated into the item design, test-form assembly process, and test administration.

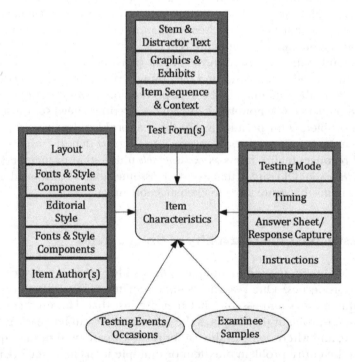

Figure 2.1 Conditions of measurement for a single item.

The "no modifications" policy inherent at most testing organizations would certainly preclude alterations to the item text, images, or distractors (if selected response). For example, even changing a comma or word is considered serious enough to suggest that the item be treated as a new item (Haladyna, 2004). The policy could further extend to (a) changes to the rubric/answer keys; (b) the presentation and sequencing of the item on the test form; (c) test timing, test mode, and other test administrative factors; and (d) the target or reference group used for obtaining the statistical properties. In short, standardizing and holding constant the *conditions of measurement* helps theoretically justify the inferences that we make from performance on the item to the knowledge and skills measured by the test. The policy seems logical but also needs to be recognized as highly impractical in the modern realm of testing.

Consider the example of generalizing the use of an item for both a paper-and-pencil test (PPT) and a computer-based test (CBT). Is it one item or two items? The plethora of studies that purport to compare PPT and CBT sometimes fail to recognize that there are more conditions of measurement in play than those rather vague modal descriptors. What about different computer operating systems and browsers for displaying the items? What about administering the item on a desktop computer, a laptop, and a notebook computer? Is the computerized version of the item really multiple mode-specific items? The point is that it becomes infeasible to completely isolate and standardize ALL the potentially relevant (and influential) conditions of measurement. Furthermore, even if we could standardize everything, the estimated statistical item characteristics and generalizability of our inferences would likewise be *limited* to those specific conditions of measurement.[8]

Should we treat mode as a random or a fixed effect? Arguably, we already naively make these types of concessions to random sampling errors for many types of minor standardization violations such as the conditions of the testing facilities, the actions/demeanor of proctors, the time of day, and so forth. More serious, uncontrolled factors that matter may include differential opportunity to learn, quality of available preparation and other potential factors that could be directly detrimental to examinee performance. By assuming that any of those factors do not matter we are in effect relegating them to the category of uncontrolled nuisance factors.

From experimental design and sampling theory perspectives, a nuisance (i.e., uncontrolled) condition can be treated as a random factor if we adopt a sampling design that randomly assigns the conditions to subjects (e.g., Kirk, 2013). Consider a measurement-specific example. The issue of position effects for "anchor items" presents somewhat of a dilemma for test score equating (Brennan, 1992a; Kolen & Brennan, 2014). If the anchor items appear in fixed positions—effectively holding constant that condition—we assume that the estimated statistical properties of those items or scores on the "anchor test" can be exploited to equate the scores of two or more nonequivalent groups of examinees taking different test forms. The usual advice to keep the item position (context) intact for equating is certainly solid advice when only a limited number of test form "scrambles" are allowed per test administration due to test booklet printing or other logistic factors.

But, what if we instead randomize the item positions,[9] other context effects, or mode of administration through random assignment to test forms and examinees? The resulting item parameter estimates would acquire some small amount of additional error variance—like random versus fixed effects for the expected mean squares for analysis of variance. However, the positive trade-off for that additional error variance is increased generalizability over the nuisance factors. Specific to the issue of anchor items for test equating, this would suggest randomly assigning items to as many positions as feasible, in which case the estimated item parameters (for IRT) would theoretically have larger standard errors of estimate,[10] but the parameter estimates should generalize over those types of conditions.

If the conditions of measurement cannot be randomized or otherwise minimized as influential effects, our fallback position could be to calibrate or otherwise estimate the relevant statistical parameters or functions within conditions—effectively treating an item as two or more different items, specific to the conditions of measurement. This is the approach currently being used by large testing organizations that use differential item functioning or similar statistical procedures for detecting differences in the operating characteristics of items used on both PPTs and CBTs. The question is, can this same rationale be extended to item hierarchies called task-model families? The remainder of this chapter argues that, not only IS it possible, but that the concept of task-model families is essential for the evolution of the measurement field.

Item Difficulty As a Statistical Control

Current content and cognitive schemes often fail to account for the estimated difficulty of test items. That is, the statistical associations between coded item content or cognitive levels like Bloom's taxonomy (Anderson & Krathwohl, 2001; Bloom, Engelhart, Furst, Hill & Krathwohl, 1956), or Webb's depth of knowledge (Webb, 2005), and item difficulty are modest, at best. That seems troubling in that content ought not be invariant to difficulty.

For example, consider the two items shown in Figure 2.2 and Figure 2.3. These items are from the 2017 eighth grade National Assessment of Educational Progress (U.S. DOE, IES/NCES, 2018). Both questions were written to the same content (algebra involving procedural knowledge at a

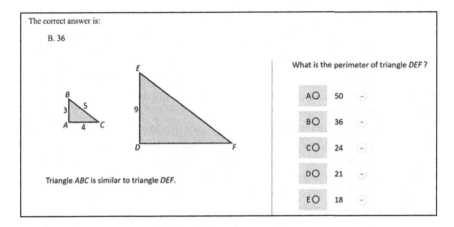

Figure 2.2 An "easy" NAEP eighth grade geometry question.

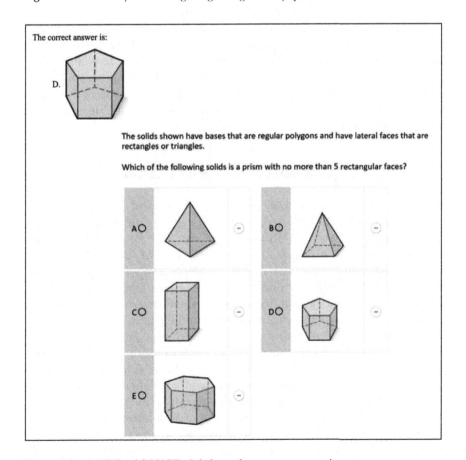

Figure 2.3 A "difficult" NAEP eighth grade geometry question.

moderate level of complexity). However, the geometry problem displayed in Figure 2.2 is substantively easier (proportion correct or $p = .62$) than the problem presented in Figure 2.3 ($p = .35$). Why? From a content perspective, these two items might be considered exchangeable. They clearly are not exchangeable in terms of their statistical properties; yet, those statistics are estimated only long after item-design decisions were made that apparently led to this item-difficulty differential.

A thorough cognitive analysis of these items is outside of the scope of this chapter. Nonetheless, we might note that the easier item uses a common right triangle and the most complicated geometric concept is "perimeter." In contrast, the more difficult item (Figure 2.3) uses terms like "polygon," "surface," "lateral," and "prism." It also requires conceptualizing—possibly mentally rotating—a three-dimensional solid shape projected onto a two-dimensional plane. (We might even note that the solids are depicted as being semitransparent to show the hidden surfaces of each object—a subtle graphical distortion of a literal interpretation of "solid.")

The disconnect between the content blueprint categories used in designing the items and the empirically estimated item difficulty remains a fundamental challenge in test development. Can we hope to control item difficulty *by design*. Traditional approaches to coding content and even broad cognitive levels are clearly ineffective. A different design strategy seems needed; a strategy that looks beyond the individual item to designing classes of items.

TASK-MODEL FAMILIES BY DESIGN

The term *task model* is generally associated with evidence-centered design (ECD) to conceptualize the tasks that elicit evidence in support of proficiency claims (Mislevy, 2006; Mislevy & Haertel, 2007; Mislevy & Riconscente, 2006; Mislevy, Steinberg, & Almond, 2002). Luecht (2012, 2013) elaborated the definition of a "task model" to imply a *structured* specification of the cognitive complexity undergirding an entire family of items. This type of cognitive specification indicates all salient design features that determine the apparent difficulty of the items in the family. The specification is far more detailed than typical content blueprint specifications, cognitive schema such as Bloom's taxonomy (Anderson & Krathwohl, 2001; Bloom et al., 1956) or depth-of-knowledge (Webb, 1997, 2005), as well as being more concrete than most assessment standards and performance-level descriptors. Included are the item content, a prescription of the types and levels of skills needed to perform the tasks, assumptions about prior knowledge, the declarative complexity/information density of any materials (text, graphics, etc.), tools, resources or scaffolding provided, and applicable contexts.

Two key principles under the AE-based conceptualization of task models are: (a) complexity-ordering principles and (b) location of the task model family within a task model map (TMM). *Complexity-ordering principles* account for all the salient cognitive features that are likely to affect the difficulty of items within each task-model family. Examples include depth of content knowledge required, essential prior knowledge requirements assumed, prerequisite or general skills that come into play, specific skills, actions or procedural requirements to complete items within this task-based class, scaffolding or resources available, use of relevant tools or auxiliary information, coherence of the information and instruction for completing the task problem, overall information density (depth), extent of information provided (breadth), clarify/acuity of the information versus obscurity, presentation style of the problem, and the complexity of contextual information. These features are then combined and manipulated to define an entire class of tasks that involve the same content, require the same or highly similar procedures or levels of skill, are presented using the same relative complexity of information, and have the same level of scaffolding and resource/tool access.

The location principle can be best articulated as a point of average difficulty of a task-model family of items on the underlying proficiency scale. In this case, "average" does not imply a mean item difficulty. It implies the expected difficulty of the task-model family within an examinee population (cf. Horst, 1933). Lower proficiency examinees might perceive the items from a task-model family to be very difficult. In contrast, higher proficiency examinees might find the same class of items to be relatively easy. This rather subtle point about task-model location is actually fully consistent with most classical test theory and IRT conceptualizations of item difficulty. For example, under IRT, an expected (dichotomous) item response score can be expressed as the following integral (summation) over an examinee population with a distributional proficiency score density, $g(\theta)$:

$$E(u_i) = \int P_i(\theta)g(\theta)\, d\theta. \tag{2.3}$$

Furthermore, this same expression holds whether we are referring to the 1PL IRT model (Equation 2.1) or the 3PL model (Equation 2.2). The design-based importance of the location is that it provides a concrete target difficulty (complexity) for generating an entire family of items. The location also provides an important quality control (QC) mechanism for empirically evaluating the quality of the task-model family.

Figure 2.4 shows a task-model map (TMM) and zooms into a single task-model family of items. The TMM provides the distribution of content along the proficiency scale—like an IRT test information function, but with each circle denoting an entire family of items. (Ideally, this type of TMM

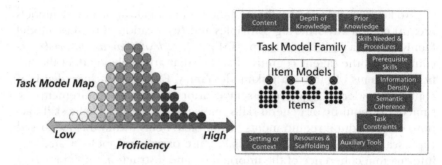

Figure 2.4 A task-model map and task-model family of items.

actually replaces the more traditional content blueprint with a far more detailed set of form assembly specifications that simultaneously incorporates content, cognitive complexity and the measurement precision.) The highlighted task model is located toward the upper regions of the scale, implying that that class of items would tend to be rather difficult for most examinees—at least relative to other task models. As shown in more detail (see inset), that single task model is represented by one or more item models (i.e., templates, associated data structures, and scoring components). In turn, each item model has multiple items that might be generated by AIG or a principled, highly regulated item writing process. The location of each task model is not happen-stance. The level of complexity is intentionally designed as part of the task model and associated item models. Ultimately, all items affiliated with a task model should be exchangeable units in the same manner that manufacturers produce interchangeable parts and assemblies.

One of the core principles for designing and building viable task-model families is *isomorphism* (Bejar, 2002). Isomorphism is generically defined as having similar form or shape. In an assessment context, isomorphism is about two items providing the same measurement information about a test taker and supporting the same claim(s) about candidate proficiency. More specifically, the isomorphic items within a given task-model family must be *completely exchangeable* in terms of three key criteria: (a) content, (b) the nature and level of challenge/cognitive task requirements, and (c) statistical characteristics of the individual items.

Items that belong to functional task-model families need to be exchangeable both by design as well as in terms of their statistical properties. That is, the items are viewed as random instantiations from a task-model family. Although there may be some benefit in considering the individual items as members of a hierarchy, with estimated hyperparameters at the task-model or item-model levels aiding in the quality of the individual item parameter estimates, the operational utility of needing to estimate the unique statistical properties for each item is counter to the isomorphism goal of creating fully exchangeable test content (within families). But, as noted above, the goal of practical isomorphism requires highly similar content of all items with the family, equivalent cognitive task requirements, scaffolding and challenges; and acceptably indistinguishable statistical characteristics of all items within each task-model family. For convenience, content and the cognitive task requirements can be combined into a broader requirement for *substantive isomorphism*. That is, items in a task-model family may not have the exact same look-and-feel—that is, the items are not necessarily clones of a common parent. In fact, the notion of a task model makes the provision for multiple item models to avoid overly restricting the task-model family to a single parent item or model. However, it is essential that the inferences from successful completion of the task requirements be substantively comparable for any two item models or for pairs of items drawn from a task-model family.

Substantive Isomorphism

Substantive isomorphism implies that the items within a family are comparable in terms of the content complexity and cognitive task requirements specified by the task model. Each task model is a design specification. As depicted in Figure 2.4, the item models provide mechanisms for generating items that each meet the design specifications of the task model. This implies that every item in each task-model family must: (a) involve highly similar content; (b) be at the same depth of knowledge; (c) comprise the same constellation of problem skills and/or procedural steps; (d) require the same prior knowledge; (e) encompass the same level of semantic coherence (i.e., integration of the task components); (f) reflect similar magnitudes of information density of the problems (data density, text, and/or graphical complexity); (g) include the same task constraints or conditions; (h) demonstrate comparable instantiations of the settings or contexts; and (i) involve the same available problem-solving resources and scaffolding, and auxiliary tools.

The item models subsequently developed from the task models may be highly detailed guidelines and constraints that are used by human item writers, or they may be formal AIG-based templates that can be used, along with variabilized content from a database, as inputs to an automatic item generator (software). Regardless, the starting point for substantive isomorphism is the task model. Strong task models can enhance the potential for isomorphic items with each family. Conversely, experience and empirical research have suggested that weak task models lead to highly variable item families.

Statistical Isomorphism

Statistical isomorphism can be interpreted in different ways. Here, it implies that a common set of parameter estimates per task-model can be used for scoring purposes. This is a decidedly pragmatic, operational definition. It does not necessarily mean that the item operating characteristics are perfectly coincident. Rather, the implication is that any item-level variation or covariation among the parameter estimates within task families are ignorable for all practical scoring and decision-making purposes—that is, it ought to be a matter of indifference to a test taker which items across task-model families comprise his or her test form.

If the goal is to obtain a set of stable set of item parameters on a common scale that can be used for classification or scoring, then the question becomes, *how should we obtain those parameters?* Using what Sinharay and Johnson (2012) termed the *identical siblings model* (ISM) we might simply constrain the item parameter estimates to be equal for each task-model family. For example, a constrained two-parameter logistic model (C2PL; Embretson, 1999) can be expressed as

$$\text{prob}(u_{i:f} = 1 | \theta; b_f) = P_f(\theta) = \left[1 + \exp\left[-a_f(\theta - b_f)\right]\right]^{-1} \quad (2.4)$$

where $u_{i:f}$ is an observed binary item score for an item in task-model family f, a_f is a task-model family discrimination parameter, and b_f is a family-level item difficulty. This approach can provide relatively stable item parameter estimates since all of the item responses per family are used (e.g., see empirical results reported by Shu, Burke, & Luecht, 2010). The downside is that it ignores variability within the task-model families[11] (Glas & van der Linden, 2003).

We can alternatively use Embretson's (1999) generalization of the linear logistic test model (LLTM; Fischer, 1973) to predict the family-level item parameters as linear combinations of design-focused covariates, q_{kf}, for $k = 1, \ldots, K$ complexity-based design attributes going into the design of each task model. Referring to the C2PL (Equation 2.4), a_f is a task-model family discrimination parameter expressed as a linear combination of the design-focused covariates

$$a_f = \tau_1 q_{f1} + \tau_2 q_{f2} + \cdots + \tau_K q_{fK} = \sum_{k=1}^{K} \tau_k q_{fk}, \quad (2.5)$$

with characteristic weights, τ_k. The family-level item difficulty can be similarly expressed as

$$b_f = \eta_1 q_{f1} + \eta_2 q_{f2} + \cdots + \eta_K q_{fK} = \sum_{k=1}^{K} \eta_k q_{fk} \quad (2.6)$$

with a different set of coefficient weights, η_k, that are related to item difficulty.

The weights, τ_k and η_k can be empirically determined predictions (i.e., estimated effects of the design-based covariates making up each task model, q_{kf}), or could in principle be specified by the task designers. A slight simplification of the generalized LLTM for task-model families would set the discrimination parameter inversely proportional the estimated residuals of items within each family. That is,

$$a_f = \left\{ \sum_{i=1}^{I:f} \left[p_{i:f} - \int P_f(\theta)\phi(\theta)\,d\theta \right]^2 \right\}^{-1} \qquad (2.7)$$

where $p_{i:f}$ denotes an empirical item mean (p-value for dichotomously scored items) and $\phi(\theta)$ is the probability density function for θ within the target population. The logic of using a family-level weight to be the reciprocal of the residual variance is to "reward" task model families that are working well and "penalize" those that are not—at least insofar as the effect of the item parameters on scoring/decision-making.

More complex hierarchical IRT models have been proposed (e.g., Geerlings, van der Linden, & Glas, 2011; Glas & van der Linden, 2003; Glas, van der Linden & Geerlings, 2010; Johnson & Sinharay, 2005). In most cases, these models introduce a family-level covariance matrix to account for potential dependencies among the parameters of models like the 3PL (Equation 2.2) and polytomous models like the generalized partial credit model (GPCM; Muraki, 1992). Empirical investigations have demonstrated that the added complexity of these models, while improving [family-wise] item fit, does not substantially improve scoring accuracy (Glas & van der Linden, 2003; Sinharay & Johnson, 2008).

A thorough comparative discussion of the relative merits of various modeling approaches is outside of the bounds of this chapter. In general, a parsimonious solution like the identical siblings model may be a good place to start for several reasons. First, the ISM allows all available data from each task-model family to be included in the calibration. This ensures that stable item parameter estimates can be obtained using commercial off-the-shelf IRT calibration software. The only minor complication involves the data management needed to reliably collapse the response data across items within families. Second, the ISM avoids the complications of explaining the nuances of complicated calibration and scoring procedures to end users. Finally, starting with the ISM simplifies quality control, as discussed in the next subsection.

Parameter Estimation and Scoring

As noted above, the ISM strategy simplifies item parameter estimation by collapsing the response data for the entire family. A single (common) set of

IRT structural parameters is therefore estimated for each task-model family. A somewhat more complex procedure involves estimating the joint multivariate posterior distribution of the item parameters (Glas & van der Linden, 2003; Sinharay & Johnson, 2005). This more complex approach has the advantage of not necessarily relying on point estimates of the item parameters as well as allowing for covariances between the parameters (i.e., a non-orthogonal parameter space). However, the multivariate strategy is not supported by current commercial software. The choices of estimators under the ISM strategy include maximum likelihood estimation (MLE), marginal maximum likelihood estimation (MML), and Markov chain Monte Carlo (MCMC) estimation. The multivariate strategy has been primarily implemented using MCMC estimation using a multivariate normal distribution (Glas & van der Linden, 2003).

Scoring is relatively straightforward under both approaches. If family-level parameter estimates are used, we can employ IRT maximum likelihood estimation (MLE) or Bayesian estimation (mean or modal). For example, Lord (1980) demonstrated a generalized form of the first derivatives of the likelihood that can be readily adapted for task model families as

$$\frac{\partial Ln(L)}{\partial \theta} = \sum_{i \in f=1}^{F} \frac{u_{i:f} - P_f(\theta)}{P_f(\theta)\left[1 - P_f(\theta)\right]} \frac{\partial P_f(\theta)}{\partial \theta}. \tag{2.8}$$

Setting Equation 2.8 to zero and numerically solving for θ using the Newton-Raphson algorithm provides the MLE score.

Following Sinharay & Johnson (2012), the multivariate procedure requires estimating the posterior distribution proportional to

$$p(\theta) \prod_{f=1}^{F} \int_{\eta_f} P_f(\theta, \eta_f) N_3(\eta_f | \mu_{i:f}, \Sigma_{i:f}) p(\mu_{i:f}, \Sigma_{i:f} | \mathbf{U}) d\eta_f \mu_{i:f} d\Sigma_{i:f} \tag{2.9}$$

where η_f denotes the IRT model item parameters, $\mu_{i:f}$ and $\Sigma_{i:f}$ are the mean vector and covariance matrix for the task-model family that includes item i, and $p(\mu_{i:f}, \Sigma_{i:f} | \mathbf{U})$ is the posterior distribution of the family parameters given the observed response data, $\mathbf{U}$.

Quality Control for Task-Model Families

Both substantive and statistical isomorphism require strong quality control (QC) mechanisms and continual monitoring. From an engineering perspective, QC has three purposes: (a) checking adherence to the design, (b) detecting root causes and flaws in procedures or outcomes, and (c) suggesting design modifications for future versions. An example of checking adherence to a design would be to produce a detailed drawing of a bookcase, build it, and then check the correspondence between what you built and the original design. If you made any design modifications during the building process, you would of course want to note those in the drawing as intentional changes. If you wanted to build additional bookcases, the modified design could ensure that each matches the original and all match the same design. In the context of assessment, adherence to a design implies that there IS a formal design—the task model—and a collection of item models and associated items that represent what we built.

Detecting root causes implies that something went wrong. For example, most testing organizations use item analyses and key validation procedures to flag potentially mis-keyed items or to signal other subtle flaws. In the short term, these types of issues might be corrected by changing an answer key or dropping an item from scoring. In the longer term, they should signal modifications in the quality control of data management procedures—especially changes and modifications to stored item data—as well as potential issues with the task models or item models, subtle changes in the construct being assessed over time (e.g., integration of more technology in a testing program to enhance the construct). We might also expect some task model families to get easier as time passes due to factors such as opportunities to learn.

Design modifications are inevitable if we value improvement. Task-model design is no different. Each version of a task model should represent a substantive improvement over the prior version. Systematic QC issues should almost always signal the potential need for design changes. There are obviously many tedious implications of making any types of changes to an operational item, an item model or a task model. However, open-ended systems architectures and standardized, high-integrity software procedures can and should be developed to accommodate reasonable change and ensure that the modifications are properly propagated across the test development, data management, test administration and processing systems.

Evaluating the substantive isomorphism of the items involves more than just checking content codes and surface-level features. Subject-matter experts (SMEs) should judge all of the items from a model to be providing the same information about candidates. As illustrated earlier in Figure 2.4, every item in the family needs to be evaluated in terms of content, depth-of-knowledge, needed skills/procedural steps, prior knowledge requirements, semantic coherence, information density of the problems, task constraints or conditions, comparability of the settings or contexts, available problem-solving resources, scaffolding, and auxiliary tools. Some of the evaluation process can certainly be automated by using psycho-linguistic and semantic analysis of text, measures of readability, and even visual recognition mechanisms with neural nets to gauge the complexity of any images used. Small groups of SMEs can also evaluate the alignment, task model by task model, between the individual items and the design. These SMEs can further help articulate complexity features like "coherence" that are not easily obtained by automated text analyses or natural language processors (e.g., see Kirsch & Mosenthal, 1990). Usability analyses with test subjects drawn from the target population verbally documenting their progress through multiple items from the same task model can also help confirm the specifications of key information and the types of skills and procedures indicated in a task model. Thoroughness and detailed documentation are key aspects of this evaluative process. If there are important and necessary design changes, those need to either be tabled for a future version of the task model(s) or incorporated into the current design and then propagated to all of the current items in the family.

Statistical isomorphism is akin to checking that the dimensions of the bookcase(s) that we built correspond within acceptable tolerances to the design dimensions. If we make the bookcase too narrow, it might leave unwanted gaps on either side. If we make it too wide, it may not fit in the available space. There are three options for evaluating statistical isomorphism within families: (a) deviations for a fixed set of task-model family characteristics; (b) deviations of estimated characteristics from an expected value of those characteristics; and (c) conditional impact (i.e., person fit across families).

Given an IRT model of choice,[12] the expected response function (ERF) for a task-model family can be written as

$$\text{ERF}(\theta; \xi) = \pi_f = \sum_{c=1}^{C} U_c P_{fc}(\theta). \tag{2.10}$$

Given the observed (scored) item responses for any item within a family, $u_{i,f}$, there are two types of residuals. The first is the deviation between the ERF and the scored item responses,

$$\varepsilon_u = u_{i:f} - \pi_f. \tag{2.11}$$

The second residual is the deviation between the ERF for a task-model family and the ERFs for the individual items within families:

$$\varepsilon_\pi = \pi_{i:f} - \pi_f \tag{2.12}$$

Both the expected response functions and the above residuals can be highly informative. For example, Sinharay, Johnson, and Williamson (2003) demonstrated how the item-level and family-wise ERFs could be graphically compared.

We can also focus on the deviations, themselves. That is, we can evaluate the residuals in terms of conditional or unconditional means, variances, and covariances. Unconditional aggregations of the residuals can be useful for general flagging purposes relative to empirically based thresholds, tolerances, or expected values. For example, many IRT-based item fit statistics compare the sum of squared residuals to an expected variance (Lord, 1980; Wright & Masters, 1982). Conditional statistics can further identify item-model or item design flaws relative to a proficiency level or for one or more examinee or mode-based grouping variables—much like differential item functioning (DIF) analyses.

Impact, the third option for evaluating statistical isomorphism, is defined here as the pragmatically differential effect of using a particular scoring mechanism on the scores or outcome decisions for one or more population subgroups. In the context of IRT, this is usually viewed as "person fit," aggregated relative to some grouping variable—including the option for conditioning the groups on score intervals or proficiency levels along the scale. Person fit can be addressed using response residuals (e.g., Equations 2.11 & 2.12 re-expressed relative to the examinees) or using conditional likelihood ratios. A detailed description of person fit is not possible here (see, e.g., Emons, Sijtsma, & Meijer, 2005; Meijer & Sijtsma, 2001). Suffice to state, detectable person-fit issues usually signal some type of differential interaction between the items and the examinees in the focal and referential groups. From a design-focused perspective, these types of results would trigger a re-evaluation of the task models and/or item models to ideally remove the cause of the interaction.

More generally, these types of residual-based fit statistics can also be used to explore validity-related issues for demographic, ethnic, or racial subgroups. For example, graphical displays or statistics demonstrating patterns of larger-than-expected residuals could signal issues with a second language, opportunity to learn/prior knowledge issues, and so forth. The point is to develop in-depth, yet flexible, data management and associated fit-related analytical and graphical procedures that can flag potential issues before they occur or, in the case of challenges for external advocates, provide appropriate investigative mechanisms. It is further essential to establish empirically based baseline statistics to effectively and efficiently detect "aberrance."

When differentials are uncovered, a two-step procedure is needed. First, in the short term, we might drop items from scoring as a policy decision or simply calibrate the individuals items within particular subset of task families that appear have non-trivial variance in the expected response functions for individual items or task-model misfit. As alluded to above, however, the important second step would be to implement a design modification either to the cognitive specifications or constraints embodied in the task model, or to the constraints/guidelines for the item models under a particular task model.

CONCLUSIONS

There seems to be little debate that the increasing demands for items and test materials is outpacing the production capacity of traditional item writing and test development practices. Some see AIG as a panacea that can meet and or even exceed those demands. However, the potential mass production capabilities of AIG cannot overcome the ratio of examinees to items when it comes to pretesting and statistically estimating the item characteristics of large numbers of items and test forms.

We suggest that there is a fundamental problem when items are designed to be unique, stand-alone entities. Items are usually not exchangeable in terms of content—a point easily demonstrated by considering two items of differential difficulty that belong to the same content category. Nor are items necessarily exchangeable when they are developed from a common item shell or template that merely creates permutations of variabilized content.

Items need to be designed to be exchangeable units from the onset. The concept of a task model family was introduced to denote a class of items designed from a common set of task specifications that include the same content, level of cognitive complexity, constellation of skills or procedures, and that may use comparable tools, resources and scaffolding. Item models—ranging from strict item-writing guidelines provided to item writers with constraints and other explicit controls—are next developed for each task model. In turn, the item models are used to generate the sibling items for each family.

Finally, the task-model development process must include strong quality control procedures that ensure substantive and statistical isomorphism. Substantive isomorphism refers primarily to ensuring that every item exhibits identical, or at least highly similar qualitative properties that are completely aligned with the task model specifications. Statistical isomorphism implies gathering ongoing quantitative evidence that every item in the family is performing similar enough to justify treating the items as completely exchangeable for purposes of test scoring.

NOTES

1. Paper presented October 2017 at MARCES 2017, College Park MD. Manuscript submitted January 2019.
2. A clarification of terminology is important from the onset. The terms *task-model family* and *item-model family* are both used in this discussion; however, they NOT exchangeable as used here.
3. Note that "bring-your-own-device" (BYOD) test administrations and remote testing over the internet with online proctoring are being explored by a

number of CBT vendors and testing organizations as solutions to some (not all) types of cheating.

4. This approach has been labeled "item harvesting." Subject-matter experts are contacted and asked to generate and submit test items in specified content areas. The items are then reviewed and edited, with acceptable items then moved into the pilot-testing pipeline.

5. Statistical linking of test scores can be carried out without IRT using equating (e.g., Kolen & Brennan, 2014). However, CAT and other CBT test designs such as linear-on-the-fly testing necessitate items calibrated to a common item bank scale.

6. These *N*-count estimates also presuppose that the scores or score distributions of the examinees taking each item are well-estimated and provide sufficient person information relative to each item's *location* on the scale, b_i. From the perspective of sampling theory, the sample size can be analytically determined if we are willing to pre-specify a maximally acceptable standard error (see Cochran, 1977; Jaeger, 1984).

7. Adaptive sampling can somewhat help with respect to the effective sample size issue but does not solve the sparse connectivity issue—at least not without strong assumptions such as random equivalence of the groups taking different items.

8. Interestingly, we all-too-often ignore the inherent inference limitations of excessive standardization. Holding constant those factors as "fixed effects" restricts rather than supports generalization. For example, how often do we turn to well-worn, convenient (but vague) assumptions such as "domain sampling" to generalize test scores to student learning, cognitive growth, teacher effectiveness, and a myriad array of other speculations, when in fact, the conditions of measurement are restricted to taking a timed, standardized multiple-choice test tangentially related to the content and style of instruction. Standardization equally penalizes everybody, but in doing so, may limit of "universe of generalization" (a subtle reference to an important concept introduced by G-theory; Cronbach, Rajaratnam, & Nanda, 1972; Brennan, 1992b, 2001).

9. This only holds if there are sufficient numbers of scrambled test forms to assume that items can theoretically be assigned to any position. Item sets are obvious exceptions.

10. In a classical test equating context, the standard errors of the equating functions could likewise be larger if properly computed to reflect all relevant conditions of measurement.

11. From an engineering perspective, excessive variability in the statistical operating characteristics of items within families is considered to be symptomatic of fundamental task-model or item-model design flaws. That outcome suggests the need to modify or constrain the task design features to significantly reduce the variance.

12. The subscripts $c = 1, \ldots, C$ denote score categories for generalization to most polytomous models. For dichotomously scored (binary) items, the ERF simplifies to $P_f(\theta)$.

REFERENCES

Anderson, L. W., & Krathwohl, D. R. (Eds). (2001). *A taxonomy for learning, teaching, and assessing. A revision of Bloom's taxonomy of educational objectives.* New York, NY: Longman.

Bejar, I. I. (2002). Generative testing: from conception to implementation. In S. H. Irvine & P. C. Kyllonen (Eds.), *Item generation for test development* (pp. 199–217). Mahwah, NJ: Erlbaum.

Bejar, I. I. (2010). Recent prospects and developments in item generation. In S. E. Embretson (Ed.), *Measuring psychological constructs with model-based approaches* (pp. 1–8). Washington, DC: American Psychological Association.

Bejar, I. I., & Yocom, P. (1991). A generative approach to the modeling of isomorphic hidden-figure items. *Applied Psychological Measurement, 15,* 129–137.

Bloom, B. S., Engelhart, M. D., Furst, E. J., Hill, W. H., & Krathwohl, D. R. (1956). Taxonomy of educational objectives: The classification of educational goals. Handbook I, Cognitive Domain. New York, NY: David McKay.

Bormuth, J. R. (1970). *On a theory of achievement test items.* Chicago, IL: University of Chicago Press.

Brennan, R. L. (1992a). The context of context effects. *Applied Measurement in Education, 5,* 225–264.

Brennan, R. L. (1992b). Generalizability theory. *Educational Measurement: Issues and Practice, 11,* 27–34.

Brennan, R. L. (2001). *Generalizability theory.* New York, NY: Springer.

Cochran, W. (1977). *Sampling techniques* (3rd ed.). New York, NY: Wiley.

Cronbach, L. J., Gleser, G. C., Nanda, H., & Rajatnam, N. (1972). *The dependability of behavioral measurements: Theory of generalizability for scores and profiles.* New York, NY: Wiley.

Drasgow, F., Luecht, R., & Bennett, R. (2006). Technology and testing. In R. L. Brennan (Ed.) *Educational measurement* (4th ed., pp. 471–516). Washington, DC: American Council on Education.

Embretson, S. E. (1999). Generating items during testing: Psychometric issues and models. *Psychometrika, 64,* 407–433.

Embretson, S. E. (2016). Understanding examinees' responses to items: Implications for measurement. *Educational Measurement: Issues and Practice, 35*(3), 6–22.

Embretson, S. E., & Kingston, N. M. (2018). Automatic item generation: A more efficient process for developing mathematics achievement items? *Journal of Educational Measurement, 55*(1), 112–131.

Emons, W. H. M., Sijtsma, K., & Meijer, R. R. (2005). Global, local and graphical person-fit analysis using person response functions. *Psychological Methods, 10,* 101–119.

Enright, M. K., & Sheehan, K. M. (2002). Modeling the difficulty of quantitative reasoning items: Implication for item generation. In S. Irvine & P. Kyllonen (Eds.), *Item generation for test development* (pp. 129–157). Mahwah, NJ: Erlbaum.

Fischer, G. H. (1973). The linear logistic test model as an instrument in educational research. *Acta Psychologica, 37,* 359–374.

Geerlings, H., van der Linden, W. J., & Glas, C. A. W. (2011). Modeling rule-based item generation. *Psychometrika, 76,* 337–359.

Gierl, M. J., & Haladyna, T. M. (Eds.). (2012). *Automatic item generation: Theory and practice*. New York, NY: Routledge.

Gierl, M. J., & Lai, H. (2012). Using weak and strong theory to create item models for automatic item generation: Some practical guidelines with examples. In M. J. Gierl & T. M. Haladyna (Eds.), *Automatic item generation: Theory and practice* (pp. 47–63). New York, NY: Routledge.

Gierl, M. J., Lai, H., & Turner, S. R. (2012). Using automatic item generation to create multiple-choice test items. *Medical Education, 46*, 757–765.

Glas, C. A. W., & van der Linden, W. J. (2003). Computerized adaptive testing with item cloning. *Applied Psychological Measurement, 27*, 247–261.

Glas, C. A. W., van der Linden, W. J., & Geerlings, H. (2010). Estimation of the parameters in an item-cloning model for adaptive testing. In W. J. van der Linden & C. A. W. Glas (Eds.), *Elements of adaptive testing* (pp. 289–314). New York, NY: Springer.

Gorin, J. S., & Embretson, S. E. (2012). Using cognitive psychology to generate items and predict item characteristics. In M. J. Gierl & T. M. Haladyna (Eds.), *Automatic item generation: Theory and practice* (pp. 136–156). New York, NY: Routledge.

Haladyna, T. M. (2004). *Developing and validating multiple-choice items* (3rd ed.). Mahwah, NJ: Erlbaum.

Haladyna, T. M., & Shindoll, R. R. (1989). Item shells: A method of writing effective multiple-choice items. *Evaluation and the Health Professions, 12*, 97–104.

Hambleton, R. K., & Jones, R. W. (1993). Comparison of classical test theory and item response theory and their applications to test development. *Educational Measurement: Issues and Practice, 12*(3), 38–47.

Hively, W., Patterson, H. L., & Page, S. H. (1968). A "universe-defined" system of arithmetic achievement tests. *Journal of Educational Measurement, 5*, 275–290.

Horst, P. (1933). The difficulty of a multiple choice test item. *Journal of Educational Psychology, 24*, 229–232.

Irvine, S. (2002). The foundations of item generation for mass testing. In S. Irvine & P. Kyllonen (Eds.), *Item generation for test development* (pp. 3–34). Mahwah, NJ: Erlbaum.

Jaeger, R. M. (1984). *Sampling in education and the social sciences*. New York, NY: Longman.

Johnson, M. S., & Sinharay, S. (2005). Calibration of polytomous item families using Bayesian hierarchical modeling. *Applied Psychological Measurement, 29*, 369–400.

Kirk, R. E. (2013). *Experimental design: Procedures for the behavioral sciences* (4th ed.). Thousand Oaks, CA: SAGE.

Kirsch, I. S., & Mosenthal, P. B. (1990). Exploring document literacy: Variables underlying the performance of young adults. *Reading Research Quarterly, 25*, 5–30.

Kolen, M. J., & Brennen, R. L. (2014). *Test equating, scaling, and linking: Methods and practices* (3rd ed.). New York, NY: Springer.

LaDuca, A. (1994). Validation of a professional licensure examination: Professions theory, test design, and construct validity. *Evaluation in the Health Professions, 17*, 178–197.

LaDuca, A., Staples, W. I., Templeton, B., & Holzman, G. B. (1986). Item modelling procedures for constructing content equivalent multiple-choice questions. *Medical Education, 20,* 53–56.

Lord, F. M. (1980). *Applications of item response theory to practical testing problems.* Mahwah, NJ: Erlbaum.

Luecht, R. M. (2005). Some useful cost-benefit criteria for evaluating computer-based test delivery models and systems. *Journal of Applied Testing Technology, 7*(2). Retrieved from www.testpublishers.org/journal.htm

Luecht, R. (2012). An introduction to assessment engineering for automatic item generation. In M. J. Gierl & T. M. Haladyna (Eds.), *Automatic item generation* (pp. 59–76). New York, NY: Routledge.

Luecht, R. M. (2013). Assessment engineering task model maps, task models and templates as a new way to develop and implement test specifications. *Journal of Applied Testing Technology, 14.* Retrieved from https://www.testpublishers.org/jatt-volume-14

Meijer, R. R., & Sijtsma, K. (2001). Methodology review: Evaluating person-fit. *Applied Psychological Measurement, 25,* 107–135.

Meisner, R., Luecht, R. M., & Reckase, M. R. (1993). *Statistical characteristics of items generated by computer algorithms* (ACT Research Report Series RR-93-9). Iowa City, IA: ACT.

Mislevy, R. J. (2006). Cognitive psychology and educational assessment. In R. L. Brennan (Ed.), *Educational measurement* (4th ed., pp. 257–306). Washington, DC: American Council on Education.

Mislevy, R. J., & Haertel, G. (2007). Implications of evidence-centered design for educational testing. *Educational Measurement: Issues and Practice, 25,* 6–20.

Mislevy, R. J., & Riconscente, M. M. (2006). Evidence-centered assessment design. In S.M. Downing & T. M. Haladyna (Eds.), *Handbook of test development* (pp. 61–90). Mahwah, NJ: Erlbaum.

Mislevy, R. J., Steinberg, L. S., & Almond, R. G. (2003). Focus article: On the structure of educational assessments. *Measurement: Interdisciplinary Research and Perspectives, 1*(1), 3–66.

Muraki, E. (1992). A generalized partial credit model: Application of an EM algorithm. *Applied Psychological Measurement, 16,* 159–176.

Osborn, H. G. (1968). Item sampling for achievement testing. *Educational and Psychological Measurement, 28,* 95–104.

Schmeiser, C. B., & Welch, C. J. (2006). Test development. In R.L. Brennan (Ed.), *Educational measurement* (4th ed.; pp. 307–353). Washington, DC: American Council on Education.

Searle, S. R. (1987). *Linear models for unbalanced data.* New York, NY: Wiley.

Shu, Z., Burke, M., & Luecht, R. M. (2010, April). *Some quality control results of using a hierarchical bayesian calibration system for assessment engineering task models, templates, and items.* Paper presented at the Annual Meeting of the National Council on Measurement in Education, Denver, CO.

Sinharay, S., & Johnson, M. S. (2008). Use of item models in a large-scale admissions test: A case study. *International Journal of Testing, 8,* 208–236.

Sinharay, S., & Johnson, M. S. (2012). Statistical modeling of automatically generated items. In M. J. Gierl & T. M. Haladyna (Eds.), *Automatic item generation* (pp. 183–195). New York, NY: Routledge.

Sinharay, S., Johnson, M. S., & Williamson, D. M. (2003). Calibrating item families and summarizing the results using family expected response functions. *Journal of Educational and Behavioral Statistics, 28*, 295–313.

U.S. Department of Education, Institute of Education Sciences, National Center for Education Statistics. (2018). *NAEP questions tool.* Retrieved from https://nces.ed.gov/NationsReportCard/nqt/ (*Source:* 2017 NAEP 8th Grade Examination).

Way, W. D., Steffen, M., & Anderson, G. S. (2002). Developing, maintaining, and renewing item inventory to support CBT. In C. N. Mills, M. T. Potenza, J. J. Fremer, & W. C. Ward (Eds.), *Computer-based testing: Building the foundation for future assessments* (pp. 143–164). Mahwah, NJ: Erlbaum.

Webb, N. (1997). *Research monograph no. 6: Criteria for alignment of expectations and assessments on mathematics and science education.* Washington, DC: CCSSO.

Webb, N. (2005, November). *Depth-of-knowledge levels for four content areas.* Presentation to the Florida Education Research Association, 50th Annual Meeting, Miami, Florida.

Wright, B. D., & Masters, G. N. (1982). *Rating scale analysis.* Chicago, IL: MESA Press.

CHAPTER 3

ARTIFICIAL INTELLIGENCE FOR SCORING ORAL READING FLUENCY

Jared Bernstein
Stanford University

Jian Cheng
Analytic Measures Inc.

Jennifer Balogh
Intelliphonics

Ryan Downey
Analytic Measures Inc.

ABSTRACT

We describe assessments in which machine learning has been applied to develop automatic scoring services for constructed responses; specifically to score students' spontaneous spoken responses. We review a few current large-scale examples and then describe recent work with automatic scoring of an oral reading fluency (ORF) instrument that runs on mobile devices. We re-

Application of Artificial Intelligence to Assessment, pages 51–76
Copyright © 2020 by Information Age Publishing

port data that verified the accuracy of the ORF scores and summarize student engagement and teacher responses to the ORF instrument.

ARTIFICIAL INTELLIGENCE AND MACHINE LEARNING

Artificial intelligence (AI) has promised to improve decision-making and to relieve the burden of tedious human tasks. In education, teachers face a tradeoff between offering more instruction time and devoting more time to evaluating student skills (to inform the instruction). In the United States, where measured outcomes (e.g., "adequate yearly progress" for the *Every Student Succeeds Act* of 2015) may determine school funding and teacher pay, the need to quantify students' performance has resulted in an environment where some teachers feel they spend too much time testing (cf. Common Core, 2011), leaving less time for instruction.

First, we differentiate *machine learning* (ML) from AI. Then, we consider how machine scoring relates to educational testing. Note that both ML and AI are relatively recent terms, so their meanings may change over the next decades. Briefly put:

AI refers to an automated activity that recently needed biological systems to be accomplished;

ML is the engineering field that develops technology to build AI systems.

ML refers to algorithmic processes that operate on data sets to produce algorithms that cluster, classify, or identify patterns in new (unseen) data sets. Typically, an algorithm infers a function (or a model) that assigns labels to new data from an analysis of labeled training data. For example, thousands of transcribed voice recordings are analyzed by an ML procedure, which produces an algorithm that transcribes new voice recordings.

Linear regression from one independent variable to predict a dependent variable is an ML method that has been in use for 200 years and that will be familiar to many readers. Newer ML algorithms implement many more complex statistical models and methods, including more familiar techniques such as logistic regression and decision trees, and others such as Bayesian models including hidden Markov models (HMM) which are commonly used in sequential pattern recognition. New statistical models are appearing continuously; recent ones include support vector machines (SVMs) and deep neural networks (DNN) used for classification, and many other models and methods that are emerging every year. These techniques can be combined and applied to data to support classification or predicting continuous variables (e.g., expected time to task completion).

Artificial Intelligence is an ability of automated systems to perform tasks that *until recently* required human or other biological information processing, often including sensory perception, decision, and sometimes, verbal and/ or mechanical response. With the wide adoption of any new ML technologies, the AI label seems to fade. What was AI 10 years ago, is now accepted without question. Currently, in 2020, systems that effectively search within vast bodies of text are commonplace, but 10 years ago, effective search required "AI" to produce accurate results. This year, autonomous vehicles seem magical, and they are now seen as AI systems, but 10 years from now, they may seem to be just computer-based systems that rely on well-understood computational methods. The usage of these terms is fluid and may crystalize in unforeseen ways. Machine learning has already had an impact on assessment and there are more applications underway.

ASSESSMENT

Assessment is the evaluation of a test taker's ability, skills, or knowledge. It has several elements. The process of assessment (see Figure 3.1) involves identifying the test taker (security, proctoring) and presenting content (items, test forms) to the test taker (administrative platform). This platform also collects test taker responses (e.g., selections, completions, written or spoken performances, or other behavior samples), and the responses are scored and reported. Finally, the results of an assessment are consumed by the score user, often a teacher or administrator, to satisfy a decision demand (e.g., refine curriculum, apply an instructional intervention, pass/ fail, rank for acceptance).

AI Impact on Assessment

The *purpose* of an assessment depends on the decisions that are made based on test results. In education, assessments often quantify some aspect of a learner's state, with the goal of enabling test score users to make

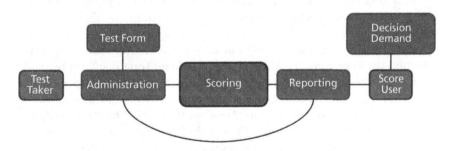

Figure 3.1 Select components in assessment.

warranted decisions about the learner or about the efficacy of an instructional approach. Examples of educational decisions include:

- Has the test-taker mastered the content of a particular lesson? (curriculum mastery)
- Does the test-taker exhibit reading skills adequate for success? (placement, screening)
- Has the test-taker reached skill levels needed to succeed in college? (admission, achievement)
- Do the test-takers meet curriculum goals? (program evaluation, accountability)

To ensure that a test score reflects an evaluation of the performance that is needed to inform a particular decision, test tasks should elicit behavior that resembles the test-taker's actions in the target situation. For example, a test that intends to evaluate a candidate's conversational skills should include tasks that themselves resemble conversations, or should require the candidate to produce spontaneous speech. With the advent of optical mark recognition technology in the 1930s, machines were able to score items as correct or incorrect, which dramatically increased scoring efficiency and testing volume. However, this technology also shifted the focus of testing to receptive skills like listening and reading, or to more discrete subskills such as vocabulary, because those skills are easier to test by selection and score by optical mark recognition.

American K–12 students are increasingly asked to demonstrate proficiency in academic skills using constructed-response tasks. As students mature, they are expected to move beyond merely demonstrating knowledge of academic facts and are expected to be able to apply knowledge in productive ways. This trend is driven by the spirit of the Common Core State Standards (CCSS), which acknowledges that, to be successful in college or in a career, students must synthesize and produce complex material, rather than just select the correct answer from among a given set (CCSO & NGA, 2012).

Some new assessments that align with CCSS use "technology-enhanced items" (TEIs), with response types that include "drag and drop," "multiple select," or "hot spots." These digitally enabled response types can be somewhat more constructive, informative, or authentic than traditional selection-response item types. However, such items usually still produce dichotomous scores and do not enable students to demonstrate productive control of integrative, complex skills such as an ability to "propel conversations by posing and responding to questions that relate the current discussion to broader themes or larger ideas; actively incorporate others into the discussion; and clarify, verify, or challenge ideas and conclusions" (CCSS. ELA-Literacy.SL.9-10.1.c).

Practicality also informs test design. Because constructed-response items have traditionally required human scoring, the operational burden of human scoring (often double scoring) has resulted in a testing culture in which large scale assessments design the vast majority of test tasks for multiple-choice responding.

Given the need to demonstrate academic progress for some 55 million K–12 students in the United States, some states have invested in automated scoring technology to evaluate productive skills (e.g., speaking) in tests such as the Arizona English Language Learner Assessment (AZELLA; see Cheng, Zhao, D'Antilio, Chen & Bernstein, 2014) or the Texas English Language Proficiency Assessment System (TELPAS). Figure 3.2 schematizes a typical tradeoff in costs associated with human scoring versus machine scoring constructed response items and performance-based items in a hypothetical test.

As shown in Figure 3.2, automated scoring involves higher up-front costs. After one develops test tasks that elicit constructed responses that can be scored reliably by human raters, one still has to run training procedures that generate accurate algorithmic scoring models for the constructed-response items. However, with time, the cumulative cost of the automatically scored testing should be much less.

Automatic scoring is also more practical because scores generally come back immediately. In a formative, classroom-based context, a teacher needs to know what areas of strength and weakness a student has, or whether the instructional material has been effective; the sooner the teacher has this information, the sooner appropriate intervention can be introduced. (Traditional formative classroom assessment was a simple poll, such as: "Raise your hand if you think it's answer A.")

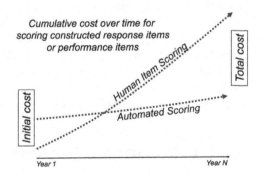

Figure 3.2 Cumulative cost over time; higher initial cost for automated scoring combined with lower recurring costs; lower development cost for human scored tests with higher recurring costs.

Rapid turnaround of scores for higher stakes assessment means the candidate can more quickly decide whether to retake the test. For example, candidates taking certain high-stakes tests may experience a delay of days or weeks before their scores are released, largely due to the need for human scoring of the written and spoken portions. Recent tests, such as the Pearson Test of English-Academic, can guarantee that scores are returned within 3–5 days because speaking and writing are machine scored.

If ML procedures are applied to well-designed training data, computer scoring can reduce bias and help ensure fairness and reliability. Test tasks may need to be reworked to increase human rater agreement, and a larger, more diverse sample of candidates may be required. Most important, to establish reliable training targets, it often helps to train with scores from three or four human raters, rather than just one or two raters. To the extent that a digital system is trained properly, automatic scoring should produce accurate and consistent scores over time, and across location and candidate characteristics.

Thus, an automated scoring system that evaluates performances in constructed-response tasks may serve secondarily to expand the test developer's toolkit, increasing the range of performance types that can be scored affordably, immediately, and consistently. Automatic scoring systems need to produce scores that are consistent with, or that improve on, the scoring expected from trained human judges. Beyond simply replicating the scores that a human would produce, AI can expand the range of information used in an assessment.

Artificial intelligence has also changed educational practice and assessment demands. Grammar checkers and spell checkers use ML and natural language processing (NLP) techniques to identify ungrammatical constructions and flag unconventional word choices; some make stylistic recommendations that better capture what the writer (is predicted to have) intended. As spelling- and grammar-checking improves toward very high accuracy, these correction functions are being included in some testing platforms, as it may seem less important to assess accurate spelling and grammar conventions, because prescribed orthography and grammar are normally tracked and corrected in text processing interfaces. By analogy, when starting a gasoline engine, we no longer need to know how to retard the spark and choke the carburetor, and so these skills are not part of current driving exams.

Artificial Intelligence in Assessment of Language

Advances in ML permit the reliable scoring of new kinds of tasks, including performance-based tasks, which previously could only be scored by trained expert human judges. In recent decades, natural language processing (NLP) techniques have made it possible for computers to generate scores for some aspects of written essays such that the scores agree well with scores from trained human graders (cf. Foltz, this volume). Note, however, that ML methods have had more success scoring more global qualities of student essays, for example, general content coverage and coherence, while some superficial, and seemingly easier, tasks like correcting grammar and usage are not yet accurate enough to be very helpful to either student writers or teachers. Automated scoring of writing has been applied in several commercial applications such as TurnItIn.com's plagiarism checker and Pearson's *WriteToLearn*. Van Moere and Downey (2016) provide an approachable description of the automated scoring technology underlying such applications.

Machine learning supports the automated assessment of speaking skills, as well. For example, automated speech recognition (ASR) converts an acoustic signal into a stream of feature vectors (about 100 vectors per second) that are then decoded to find the most likely word sequence that the ASR system is trained to hear. Limited applications of ASR have been included in language teaching systems since their introduction in 1995, by Syracuse Language Systems. Since then, Rosetta Stone, Duolingo, Babbel, and others have applied ASR in ways that are sometimes useful to learners. Several products also present visual representations of a learner's speech for comparison to visual displays of model native speech. Bernstein and Franco (1996) and Young (1996) provide relatively accessible descriptions of how speech recognition systems work. Both papers are a bit out of date, but at a first level of understanding, they are still accurate.

Automatic spoken response scoring may focus on the content of the speech, which includes its turn structure, pragmatic force, linguistic form, and lexical content. Scoring might also focus on qualities of the speech itself such as its fluency and pronunciation, or it may combine content and quality aspects into a more general estimate of speaking ability. Figure 3.3 shows the elements in a system that elicits and scores spoken responses from a student.

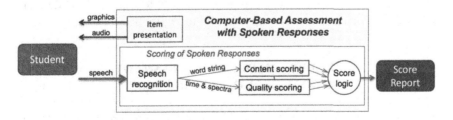

Figure 3.3 A system for presenting and scoring spoken-response test items.

Current computer scoring systems estimate speaking ability by combining measures of linguistic and lexical structures with measures of fluency and pronunciation, returning scores with high consistency and accuracy. How is it done?

When a digital recording of speech is made, the acoustic signal is transduced into an electronic signal and then converted into a digital signal. The samples in this digital wave file are grouped into small sets of adjacent samples, called *frames*, which extend over 10 or 25 milliseconds of signal. ASR technology extracts timing and frequency information from these samples and applies acoustic models, language models, and a dictionary (with expected pronunciations) to decode the speech based on the digital information. When the test-taker's words are recognized and aligned in time with the signal, the words-in-time are evaluated with reference to statistical models that represent various levels of performance to estimate which level a given performance belongs to. Bernstein (2012) describes the application of these technologies for spoken language tutoring and testing, and attempts to explain their limits. A fuller discussion of validity in automated assessment of spoken language can be found in Bernstein, Van Moere, and Cheng (2010).

Training and Validation

To have confidence in automatic scores, one has to ensure that machine learning produces accurate and consistent results. Large training data sets are required to ensure adequate representation of the variability expected in the target performances when the models are optimized. In addition, validation testing ensures that the scoring models appropriately evaluate unseen data. When using ML to support the assessment of human language, one usually needs to demonstrate that machine-derived scores are comparable to those assigned by trained human judges. This step is accomplished using a new sample of responses, previously unseen by the system during optimization. When available data is limited, an efficient way to predict the machine-human agreement for future (unseen) data sets is by partitioning all available data into 5 or 10 subsets and performing a cross-validation (see Hastie, Tibshirani, & Friedman, 2009; Chapter 7). However, if data is plentiful, then, at a high level, the steps required to train and validate an automated scoring system are schematized in Figure 3.4.

EXAMPLE IN DETAIL: ASSESSMENT OF ORAL READING FLUENCY (ORF)

To illustrate how ML is applied to build AI into an assessment, we describe the development and evaluation of an automated reading test. It performs

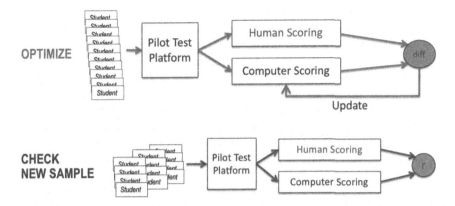

Figure 3.4 Optimizing the scoring system and confirming its accuracy on a new sample.

tasks that until recently required the attention and actions of a trained reading teacher. The first part of this chapter described how ML can enable automated scoring of spoken responses to complex linguistic tasks. In this section, we describe the development of one ORF test, Moby.Read®, that evaluates reading skill in young students.

Oral Reading Fluency

The National Reading Panel (2000) defined oral reading *fluency* as a reader's ability to "read a text quickly, accurately, and with proper expression." *Accurate rate* is the number of words read correctly per minute (WCPM). Note that WCPM can be obtained by collecting reading performances with durations shorter or longer than one minute. For example, a student correctly reading 55 words in 30 seconds has a reading rate of 110 words correct per minute. *Accuracy* of reading is an important measure because it reflects a student's skills in recognizing common words and in decoding letter sequences in unfamiliar words. A student who reads quickly but makes errors will receive a different accuracy score from a student who reads more slowly but with high accuracy, and these two patterns carry different information about the reader's comprehension of text and application of text-embedded information in real-life situations. Finally, *expression* takes into account appropriate pacing, pausing, syllable- and word-level stress and pitch, and other aspects of speech which differentiate a monotonous, non-expressive reading from a reading that embodies text meaning and/or structure (Schwanenflugel & Benjamin, 2012; Schwanenflugel, Hamilton, Kuhn, Weisenbaker, & Stahl, 2004).

All three components of ORF (rate, accuracy, and expression) have been shown to correlate with reading comprehension (Daane, Campbell, Grigg, Goodman, & Oranje, 2005; Fuchs, Fuchs, Hosp, & Jenkins, 2001). Students who read aloud with high accuracy also tend to score high on measures of reading comprehension.

Oral reading fluency has been used for decades as a reliable reflection of early reading ability (e.g., Shinn, Good, Knutson, Tilly, & Collins, 1992), as well as an indicator of a student's general academic level (Hasbrouck & Tindal, 2006), particularly in Grades K–6, when core reading skills develop. Available standardized ORF measures are popular because they are relatively reliable and brief. These include *aimswebPlus* (Pearson, 2018a), *Dynamic Indicators of Basic Early Literacy Skills* (Dynamic Measurement Group, 2018), and *EasyCBM* (Houghton Mifflin Harcourt, 2018), among others. Typically, students are asked to read three separate passages, reading as much of the passage as they can in 1 minute, to establish a reliable baseline or benchmark. For monitoring progress during an instructional intervention program, a single 1-minute reading is often accepted as sufficient. A teacher times the reading while following along with the student, annotating another copy of the passage for errors (e.g., word omissions, substitutions, transpositions). Once the readings are finished, the teacher tallies up the errors and records accuracy and reading rate. To enhance score stability, the median score across the three passages may be selected as the final record for each trait. A judgment of reading expression is sometimes a part of the official record.

A complete profile of the reader also includes a measure of comprehension (e.g., Deeney, 2010). For example, the CCSS (CCSSO, 2010) include reading comprehension in its foundational skills in the English language arts standards, which state that students should be able to:

- "Read with sufficient *accuracy* and fluency to support *comprehension*" (CCSS.ELA-LITERACY.RF.2.4).
- "Read grade-level text orally with *accuracy*, appropriate *rate*, and *expression* on successive readings" (CCSS.ELA-LITERACY.RF.X.4.B).

Despite their widespread use, there are drawbacks to traditional ORF measures. To score ORF performances, administrators have to learn annotation conventions to properly categorize reading errors and learn what to do when unusual performances are observed (e.g., when a student skips an entire line of the text, or when a student gets stuck on an unfamiliar word). Because a teacher follows along and annotates the reading in real time, oral reading performances are administered one-on-one, taking the teacher away from the rest of the class for 20 to 30 minutes per assessment. Teachers often skip rating the read-alouds for expression because reporting expression scores is not required, and many teachers are unsure of their skill in making such a judgment when they have concentrated on reporting rate and accuracy (Schwanenflugel & Benjamin, 2012).

Development of Moby.Read

The Moby.Read assessment was developed to provide teachers with an easy way to get accurate ORF measures for children in Grades 1 through 5. The Moby.Read assessment measures four components of reading skill (comprehension, accuracy, reading rate, and expression) on leveled text for children in Grades 1–5. In addition, the Moby.Read app also reports an overall Moby.Read level that integrates these separate components into a reader-level estimate. The Moby.Read test was developed to be taken on touchscreen-enabled devices to facilitate ease of interaction for the youngest students and to enable on-device speech recognition technology to provide scores and feedback immediately, that is, without the need for a teacher to follow along annotating and tallying errors.

Test Structure

The Moby.Read test has several sections (see Figure 3.5). First, students watch an *instruction video* explaining the test and showing a student taking the test and providing spoken responses. The video introduces the test sections and provides a model for students, reminding them to read for meaning. At the end of the video, the student reads a *word list* out loud, and then

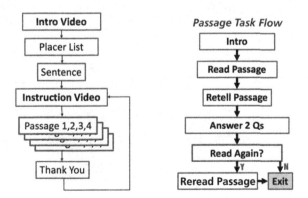

Figure 3.5 Left: Overall task flow during a Moby.Read session. Right: Per-Passage task flow.

reads a *sentence* out loud. These responses can be used to help estimate the student's reading level.

The passage-reading section starts with a video that shows an example of a student reading a passage out loud, retelling the passage, and then answering comprehension questions. Beginning with an initial unscored practice passage, the test flow consists of three test blocks, which proceed as follows: Students read a passage on the screen out loud; then students retell the passage aloud in their own words from memory; finally, students answer two comprehension questions about the passage (see Figure 3.6). In all cases, the response is spoken out loud by the student. Students who wish to read the passage again may select that option, hear a fluent reading of the passage with synchronized text highlighting. If they do not wish to reread a passage, they tap the screen to advance to the next passage.

Moby.Read passages are written to conform with the two broad text types described in the CCSS: (a) literature such as stories and (b) informational texts that cover topics such as history, art, social studies, science, and technology (CCSSO & NGA, 2012). For appropriate domain sampling, each form of the Moby.Read test includes both narrative stories and informational texts that provide facts and background knowledge on selected topics. Passages are leveled using the method prescribed by the CCSS (as described in the test development section). Passages contain 40–145 words,

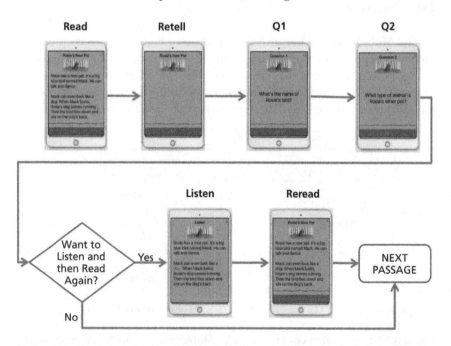

Figure 3.6 Test block flow for Moby.Read.

designed to provide enough spoken material for reliable scoring while being short enough to allow for efficient testing and completion in a reasonable time by the typical student given the grade level (Hasbrouck & Tindal, 2006). For empirical leveling, 376 students participated in studies piloting a total of 82 passages. Based on student performance in these studies, passages that were too hard or too easy compared to the passage's assigned Common Core level were assigned either one grade higher or lower, or were removed from the item pool.

The decision to include a passage *retelling* task is twofold. First, retelling a story requires that the reader understood the content of the passage. The extent to which the retelling captures key elements of the reading is a reflection of the reader's comprehension. Further, retelling is an established strategy for encouraging deeper processing of text (Morrow, 1985; Wilson, Gambrel, & Pfeiffer, 1985).

Comprehension questions elicit responses that might be a single word, a short phrase, or a sentence. Passage questions range in their cognitive processing requirements, from literal questions about facts in the text to questions that require the intersection of facts and/or inference. Most Moby. Read comprehension questions are direct and literal.

Speech Recognition System

Before applying the algorithms that produce specific oral reading scores, the child's recorded reading is analyzed by Moby.Read's ASR system. The acoustic model used for the ASR system was a Deep Neural Network-Hidden Markov Model (DNN-HMM; Zhang, Trmal, Povey, & Khudanpur, 2014) with four hidden layers. Language models for reading responses were rule-based and are specific to each reading passage. Language models for retelling responses and comprehension questions are also item-specific. Given that the language models are item specific and that correct readings are generally more likely than incorrect readings, the ASR system gives the reader the benefit of the doubt and will usually accept that a child has said a word correctly, even if the child's speech is accented. The Moby.Read ASR engine is based on Kaldi (Povey et al., 2011), and has been optimized for children's speech and to run in an iOS device. Jurafsky and Martin's book (2009) is a reliable textbook introduction to speech and language processing that covers most of the underlying ML methods discussed below. At this writing, a .pdf version of the forthcoming 3rd edition is available at https://web.stanford.edu/~jurafsky/slp3/ and can be downloaded from there.

Time-aligned response strings generated from the ASR system are scored with respect to the read text. For example, timing information at syllable, word, and phrase level, along with inter-word silences, are used in expression scoring.

Models for Automatic Scoring

Automated scoring models were trained on reading performances by 383 students in Grades 2 through 6 in California ($n = 261$) and New Jersey ($n = 122$). The data-collection tests were automatically administered on an iPad with children wearing headsets with inline microphones. The tests advanced as appropriate based on the system's detection of the student's speech or screen touches. Typically, a human proctor monitored several students in concurrent sessions, with students sitting more than 1 meter apart.

Accuracy

Accuracy quantifies the percentage of words the reader decoded and spoke correctly. For accuracy scoring, the response string produced by the ASR system is aligned to the passage text to determine the first word attempted by the reader and the last word attempted. The alignment in combination with the language model allow an algorithm to be developed that calculates the number of words the student read correctly. Self-corrections are correct, but omissions, substitutions, and radical mispronunciations are not counted as correct. The accuracy score is reported as a percentage of words read correctly over the number of words attempted.

Accurate Reading Rate

For each scored passage, the words read correctly between the first word attempted and last word attempted are tallied. This tally is then divided by the time between the onset of the first word attempted and the offset of the last word attempted. Accurate reading rate uses WCPM as its unit, with the median rate over three passage texts reported to users.

Comprehension

Comprehension is the degree to which a reader can identify or present the major and minor concepts, themes, and/or facts contained in a passage. Moby.Read comprehension scores are reported to score users on a 0.0–8.0 scale, with higher values representing greater comprehension. Comprehension scores are derived from scores of the *retellings* and scores on *comprehension questions* combined across passages. The reported comprehension score gives equal weight to the retellings and to the answers to comprehension questions, averaged across the three passages.

The scoring algorithm for *retelling* measures the semantic similarity between the passage text and the retelling response using trained networks and

TABLE 3.1	Rubric for Rating Responses to Passage Retellings
Rating	Description
0	**Not rated.** Silent, irrelevant, or unintelligible.
1	**Minimal.**
2	**Limited.** Some concept sequences; missing major concepts and main narrative arc.
3	**Partial.** Several concept sequences and related parts of the main narrative.
4	**Adequate.** Enough major and minor concepts suggest main narrative logic.
5	**Good.** Major & minor concepts convey main narrative path and causal logic.
6	**Complete.** All major & many minor concepts support close narrative fidelity.

natural language processing. Specifically, Moby.Read uses Google's *word2vec* word vectors that were trained on about 100 billion words. The scoring model holds 300-dimensional vectors for 3 million words and phrases.

We collected human retelling judgments to validate the scoring model. Human judges rated retell responses on a 7-point scale shown in Table 3.1. Ratings from at least two different human raters were collected to each retell passage and each comprehension question. For comprehension questions, the human ratings provided models of answer quality spread over the scale range.

The retelling measured how semantically similar the words and sequences were between each passage and the student's retelling of that passage. These measures were combined over the three passages and then mapped onto a 0–4 scale as the retelling component of the comprehension score. For comprehension questions, similar techniques were used. The question component of the comprehension score was also mapped onto a 0–4 scale. Then, the mapped scores from retelling and from the comprehension questions were combined into an overall comprehension score.

Expression

Expression is the degree to which a student can clearly express the meaning and structures of the text through appropriate rhythm, phrasing, intonation, and emphasis. Expressive readings enhance the understanding and enjoyment of the text by a listener (Schwanenflugel & Benjamin, 2012). Scoring models for expression were based on human ratings. Raters were presented with rubrics and given training sets of responses so that they could practice rating actual student readings. Ratings were then compared with master ratings agreed upon by several assessment professionals with PhDs and at least 15 years of experience creating reading assessments. Discrepancies with the master ratings were reviewed and more training responses were presented to the rater until the rater was reliably assigning ratings consistent with the masters.

TABLE 3.2	Rubric for Expression
Rating	Description
0	Insufficient sample for rating.
1	Word-by-word rendition with no reflection of word, phrase or sentence meaning.
2	Some local word grouping; little sentential phrasing.
3	Exhibits some text-inappropriate phrasing; sentence- and passage-level meaning is partially conveyed.
4	Prosody generally reflects meaning, but phrasing or intonation is sometimes inconsistent with the text.
5	Read for a listener; intonation, phrasing, and emphasis nicely express the meaning of the passage.

The data used to train the automatic scoring models had at least two human ratings of expression for each passage reading. Human raters used a 6-point scale to rate passage readings, as shown in Table 3.2.

Human judgments were then used to train a neural network with the goal of predicting how a human rater would rate the expression of the passage reading. The features used in the neural network were produced from the ASR system and included the pattern of phonetic segment durations and the log likelihoods of inter-word silence durations. The output values from the neural network were then mapped to a 5-level expression scale that ranges from 0 to 4.

VALIDATION

Machine scoring was validated in studies that compared the automated scores with human ratings. In addition, usability was measured through follow-up questions to evaluate ease of use and engagement of Moby.Read. We found that for several machine scores the correlation between the machine scores and the human ratings was better than our average human–human correlations. This is possible because the average human scores are generally much more reliable than individual human scores.

Study 1: Participants, Procedures, and Data Preparation

Participants

Participants in the study were 99 school-aged children from four different elementary schools: one public and one parochial school in New Jersey, and two public elementary schools in California. The female to male ratio was 47:52. Ages ranged from 7 to 10 with an average age of 8. Students were enrolled in second grade (29%), third grade (40%), and fourth grade (31%). With regard to ethnic background (using classifications set forth by the U.S. Census), 51 of the students were European American, 19 were African American, 4 were Asian American, and 25 were identified as Hispanic or Latino.

Procedure

Two facilitators assisted with test administration: one in New Jersey and one in California. Both facilitators were assessment professionals. The experimental sessions with student-participants were conducted during the normal course of a school day at the participant's elementary school. In preparation for the experimental sessions, the facilitators set up two or three chairs about eight feet apart in a quiet area of the room or just outside the classroom. The Moby.Read assessment was delivered on an iPad Mini. Before the assessment, each student was fitted with a set of GearHead headphones with an inline microphone (the microphone was incorporated into the headset wire). Facilitators were present to help with technical problems, but they did not help students take the Moby.Read assessment. If a student asked a question during the assessment, the facilitator encouraged the student to keep trying with the app.

For all graded items, responses were transcribed, readings were human-rated for expressiveness, and retells and comprehension questions were human-rated for comprehension. Following the administration, students were presented a brief usability survey.

Analysis

Five participants were screened out because their test responses were silent or completely unintelligible. This left 94 participants whose results are presented in these analyses.

Accurate Reading Rate

For accurate reading rate, two analyses were performed. The first was a comparison of accurate reading rate generated by the Moby.Read automated system versus scores generated from human transcriptions. For single passages, the correlation between these two scores was high, at $r = 0.96$.

Each recording of a passage reading was analyzed independently by two human raters. The human raters had PhDs and at least 10 years of experience in reading assessment. Each rater listened to recorded student reading, marked errors, and measured the length of time during which the student read. Raters computed the WCPM for the passage by dividing the number of words read correctly over the duration of time of the reading (in seconds) times 60 (to place the units in minutes). Inter-rater reliability in this task was 0.99. Averages of the human-computed WCPM values were computed and the median score for each 3-passage session was derived for each participant. These median human scores were then correlated with the median machine-generated WCPM score. The resulting correlation coefficient was 0.99, confirming that the median scores produced by the Moby.Read app are comparable to median value of scores produced by human raters. Figure 3.7 presents a scatterplot of machine versus human scores at the session level. This comparison of median WCPM between the two methods suggests that scoring based on automatic speech processing and alignment with text has a high degree of accuracy.

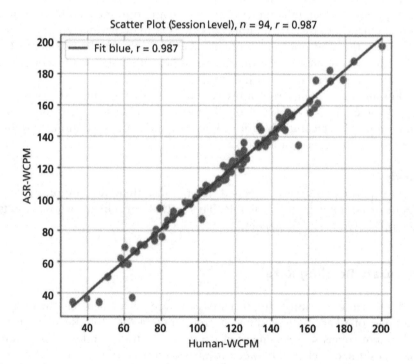

Figure 3.7 Accurate Reading Rate (WCPM) scores from human judges vs. machine (ASR).

Comprehension

We validated the comprehension scores from passage retelling. Machine-generated comprehension scores on retellings were compared with human ratings of retellings. Average machine scores were generated for each participant and were correlated with average human ratings. The human–machine correlation coefficient was 0.92. This correlation was better than that of the average human–human inter-rater correlation of 0.88. A scatterplot of the scores is presented in Figure 3.8.

Expression

To verify expressiveness scores, Moby.Read scores were compared to an average of three human ratings of expressiveness. For the three pairs of human raters, the average inter-rater correlation at the response level was 0.74. The correlation coefficient of machine-generated expressiveness scores and average human ratings of expressiveness was 0.88 (0.94 at the

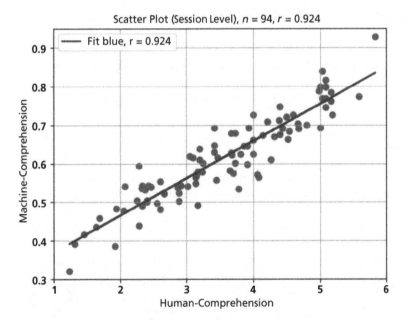

Figure 3.8 Plot of Comprehension scores from human raters and from machine models.

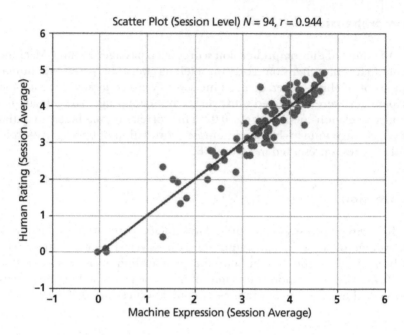

Figure 3.9 Plot of Expression scores from human judges vs. machines.

session level; see Figure 3.9), a statistically significant improvement. These correlations indicate that the machine scores were more reliable in producing consistent expressiveness scores than human raters.

Usability

Usability was evaluated on the iPad device at the end of the Moby.Read assessment. Students were presented the image shown in Figure 3.10 and

Figure 3.10 Four point rubric displayed on screen to students.

asked to tap the screen image that best represented their experience with the app.

Two students failed to respond to any items. Among the remaining 97 who responded, 48 selected *Easy. I always knew what to do*; 42 selected *I knew what to do most of the time*; and 7 selected *Not sure*. No students selected *totally confused*. These results show that 97 of 99 (or 98%) students knew what to do most or all of the time, suggesting self-administration is viable for the majority of students.

Study 2: Concurrent Validity

A second study compared the scoring derived from Moby.Read with that of the Dynamic Indicators of Basic Early Literacy Skills (DIBELS) NEXT assessment (Dynamic Measurement Group, 2018), a widely used human-administered and scored ORF assessment.

Participants

Twenty students from an elementary school in California participated. Nine were female and 11 were male. Seven were in second grade, six were in third grade, and seven were in fourth grade. Students were given a $15 gift card to a local toy store as remuneration for their participation.

Procedure

Students were administered both a Moby.Read assessment and a DIBELS NEXT assessment. For half the participants, Moby.Read was administered first, and for the other half DIBELS was administered first. Sessions were held at a private residence with the child's guardian close by, but not interfering with the session. The administrator was an assessment professional with experience using the DIBELS framework.

For the Moby.Read portion, each child was fitted with a GearHead microphone headset and the Moby.Read test was self-administered and automatically scored by the Moby.Read system. Students were administered a form appropriate for their grade. Moby.Read was delivered on an iPad Mini.

For the DIBELS assessment, students were administered the fall benchmark test form, which consisted of three grade-level passages of about 250 words in length. The administrator followed the administration and scoring procedures described in the test's official documentation (Good et al., 2011). Students were given a passage and asked to read it out loud using the instruction prompts from the DIBELS assessment manual. The administrator started a timer when the student started reading the first word of the passage. As the student read the passage, the administrator marked reading errors on a scoring sheet. After one minute, the timer beeped and the student's place in the passage was marked on the scoring sheet (none of the students finished the passage). Then the student was asked to tell the administrator about the story. Responses were timed for 1 minute and marked on a comprehension scoring sheet which tracked the number of words spoken in the student's response.

At the conclusion of the session, the administrator pointed out that the student had done both a test on the iPad ("Moby.Read") and on paper ("teacher administered") and asked which the students preferred, and why. Consistent with standard practice, after the session, the administrator used the scoring sheets to calculate errors and WCPM.

Concurrent Results

Moby.Read accurate reading rate scores from 20 participants were compared to scores from the ORF task of DIBELS NEXT. The correlation between the two scores was 0.88. Published studies investigating DIBELS report a test-retest reliability of 0.82 and an inter-rater reliability of 0.85 (Goffreda & DiPerna, 2010). The reliability of an instrument limits the strength of the correlation between that instrument and others measuring the same construct. So, the correlation with Moby.Read is at the ceiling of what would be expected given the reliability of DIBELS.

When asked which experience they preferred, 18 out of 20 students (90%) said they preferred "Moby.Read," and 2 students said they preferred "both"; no students preferred the teacher administration. Useful qualitative information was provided by the students when asked why they preferred the Moby.Read administration. The feedback can be clustered as shown in Table 3.3.

TABLE 3.3	Examples of Student Responses When Asked Why They Preferred the Automated Assessment to the Human Administered Test
Theme	**Student Feedback**
Technology	• "I like the screens" • "There's this Siri thing"
Questions	• "It asks questions, so you're reading for purpose" • "You get to answer questions"
Re-read option	• "I can read the stories again" • "You could read it again"
Administration	• "The iPad tells you what to do" • "It tells you about the story before you read it"
Privacy	• "It's more private" (i.e., no teachers are watching and judging)
User interface	• "You have more time so you can finish the story" • "More pictures and stuff"

These qualitative data provide support for an assertion that this tablet-enabled assessment that allows students to self-administer ORF can produce an engaging experience for students.

DISCUSSION OF MOBY.READ

Several forms of evidence support the validity and utility of the Moby.Read instrument. As a voice-interactive digital app, students found the assessment engaging and easy to use. The Moby.Read test structure and instruction format have been developed iteratively through user studies and feedback. The pilot studies demonstrate that the Moby.Read test experience was sufficiently self-explanatory for 98% of students to successfully self-administer the tests without teacher intervention. Further, 90% of students indicated they enjoyed using the Moby.Read application more than traditional ORF as administered by a teacher.

The Moby.Read app also includes ready tools for teachers to monitor student progress over time and to share recordings of a student's performance with parents or with a reading specialist. Two of the teacher's displays are shown in Figure 3.11.

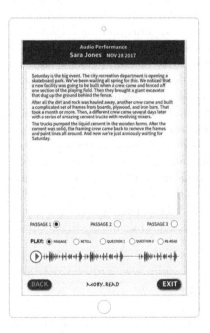 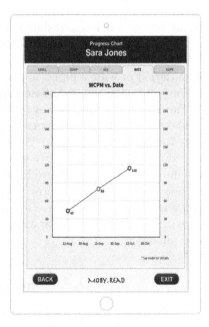

Figure 3.11 Two displays for teachers. Left supports playing responses; right tracks progress.

In summary, a Moby.Read assessment measures the three components of ORF—accuracy, accurate rate, and expression—while providing a concurrent measure of reading comprehension that helps locate a student's reading level. Student data indicates that these scores are comparable to scores produced by human raters. In some cases, such as for comprehension and expression, the scores produced by Moby.Read are closer to average human ratings than scores from individual human raters are to each other. Empirical data also provide evidence of construct validity with a high correlation between Moby.Read scores and fluency scores from other standardized reading assessments. Finally, the content in the Moby.Read passages samples a broad range of texts appropriate for students in Grades 1 through 5. In sum, evidence supports the use of Moby.Read scores as a reliable measure of ORF and indicator of reader level.

CONCLUSION

For assessing spoken language proficiency and oral reading, advances in ML have brought computers the ability to present spoken items and score spoken responses in ways that match or exceed the accuracy of single human scorers. As the technology advances and more individuals acquire skill in ML, the costs of creating such systems is diminishing. Recognizing the trend, school districts and state departments of education are increasingly evaluating automated scoring as an option (e.g., Arizona Department of Education, 2013; Texas Education Agency, 2018). Evanini, Hauck, and Hakuta (2017) provide a practical list of considerations for schools or organizations intending to use AI-based approaches in assessing language.

Fundamentally, the studies reported here demonstrate that thoughtful application of ML to assessment enables improved score reliability (compared to human judgments). AI scoring can also promote the use of preferred assessment methods (e.g., comprehension measured from passage retelling) that previously have been too time-consuming, expensive, or unreliable for general use. Newer assessments that use AI scoring can provide rich and timely information to teachers, reading specialists, and administrators, in ways that relieve their assessment burden while improving accuracy and reliability.

REFERENCES

Arizona Department of Education. (2018). Assessment: Azella. Retrieved from https://www.azed.gov/assessment/azella/

Bernstein, J. (2012). Computer scoring of spoken responses. In C. A. Chapelle (Ed.), *The encyclopedia of applied linguistics.* https://doi.org/10.1002/9781405198431.wbeal1044

Bernstein, J., & Franco, H. (1996). Speech recognition by computer. In N. Lass (Ed.), *Principles of experimental phonetics* (pp. 408–434). St. Louis, MO: Mosby.

Bernstein, J., Van Moere, A., & Cheng, J. (2010). Validating automated speaking tests. *Language Testing, 27*(3), 355–377.

Cheng, J., Zhao D'Antilio, Y., Chen, X., & Bernstein, J. (2014, June). Automatic spoken assessment of young English language learners. Proceedings Ninth Workshop on Innovative Use of NLP for Building Educational Applications, Baltimore, MD.

Common Core. (2011). *Learning less: Public school teachers describe a narrowing curriculum.* Retrieved from https://www.americansforthearts.org/sites/default/files/cc-learning-less-mar12.pdf

Council of Chief State School Officers & National Governors Association. (2012). *Supplemental information for Appendix A of the Common Core State Standards for English language arts and literacy: New research on text complexity.* Retrieved from http://www.corestandards.org/assets/E0813_Appendix_A_New_Research_on_Text_Complexity.pdf

Daane, M., Campbell, J., Grigg, W., Goodman, M., & Oranje, A. (2005). *Fourth-grade students reading aloud: NAEP 2002 special Ssudy of rral reading* (NCES 2006-469). U.S. Department of Education. Institute of Education Sciences, National Center for Education Statistics. Washington, DC: Government Printing Office.

Deeney, T. A. (2010). One-minute fluency measures: Mixed messages in assessment and instruction. *The Reading Teacher, 63*(6), 440–450.

Dynamic Measurement Group. (2018). *DIBELS.* Retrieved from https://dibels.org/dibels.html

Evanini, K., Hauck, M. C., & Hakuta, K. (2017). Approaches to automated scoring of speaking for K–12 English language proficiency assessments. *ETS Research Report Series, 2017*, 1–11. https://doi.org/10.1002/ets2.12147

Fuchs, L. S., Fuchs, D., Hosp, M. K., & Jenkins, J. R. (2001). Oral reading fluency as an indicator of reading competence: A theoretical, empirical, and historical analysis. *Scientific Studies of Reading, 5*, 239–256.

Goffreda, C. T., & DiPerna, J. C. (2010). An empirical review of psychometric evidence for the Dynamic Indicators of Basic Early Literacy Skills. *School Psychology Review, 39*(3), 463.

Good, R. H., Kaminski, R. A., Cummings, K., Dufour-Martel, C., Peterson, K., Powell-Smith, K., & Wallin, J. (2011). *DIBELS next assessment manual.* Eugene, OR: Dynamic Measurement Group.

Hastie, T., Tibshirani, R., & Friedman, J. (2009). *The elements of statistical learning: Data mining, inference, and prediction* (2nd ed.) New York, NY: Springer.

Hasbrouck, J., & Tindal, G. A. (2006). Oral reading fluency norms: A valuable assessment tool for reading teachers. *The Reading Teacher, 59*, 636–644.

Houghton Mifflin Harcourt. (2018). *EasyCBM.* Retrieved from https://www.easyCBM.com

Morrow, L. M. (1985). Retelling stories: A strategy for improving young children's comprehension, concept of story structure, and oral language complexity. *The Elementary School Journal, 85*(5), 647–661.

National Reading Panel (U.S.), & National Institute of Child Health and Human Development (U.S.). (2000). *Report of the National Reading Panel: Teaching children to read: An evidence-based assessment of the scientific research literature on reading and its implications for reading instruction: Reports of the subgroups.* Washington, DC: National Institute of Child Health and Human Development, National Institutes of Health.

Pearson. (2018a). *aimswebPlus.* Retrieved from https://www.aimswebplus.com/

Povey, D., Ghoshal, A., Boulianne, G., Burget, L., Glembek, O., Goel, N.,...Vesely, K. (2011). The KALDI speech recognition toolkit. In *Proceedings of IEEE 2011 workshop on automatic speech recognition and understanding.* Big Island, HI: IEEE Signal Processing Society.

Schwanenflugel, P. J., & Benjamin, R. G. (2012). Reading expressiveness: The neglected aspect of reading fluency. In T. Rasinski, C. Blachowicz, & K. Lems (Eds.), *Fluency instruction, second edition: Research-based best practices* (pp. 35–54). New York, NY: Guilford.

Schwanenflugel, P. J., Hamilton, A. M., Kuhn, M. R., Wisenbaker, J., & Stahl, S. A. (2004). Becoming a fluent reader: Reading skill and prosodic features in the oral reading of young readers. *Journal of Educational Psychology, 96,* 119–129.

Shinn, M. R., Good, R. H., Knutson, N., Tilly, W. D., & Collins, V. C. (1992). Curriculum-based measurement of oral reading fluency: A confirmatory analysis of its relation to reading. *School Psychology Review, 21,* 459–479.

Texas Education Agency. (2020). *TTELPAS resources.* Retrieved from https://tea.texas.gov/student-testing-and-accountability/testing/texas-english-language-proficiency-assessment-system-4

Van Moere, A., & Downey, R. (2016). Technology and artificial intelligence in language assessment. In D. Tsagari & J. Banerjee (Eds.), *Handbook of second language assessment* (pp. 341–358). Boston, MA: Walter de Gruyter.

Wilson, R. M., Gambrell, L. B., & Pfeiffer, W. R. (1985). The effects of retelling upon reading comprehension and recall of text information. *The Journal of Educational Research, 78*(4), 216–220.

Young, S. (1996). Large vocabulary continuous speech recognition. *IEEE Signal Processing Magazine, 13*(5), 45–57.

Zhang, X., Trmal, J., Povey, D., & Khudanpur, S. (2014). Improving deep neural network acoustic models using generalized maxout networks. Retrieved from https://www.danielpovey.com/files/2014_icassp_dnn.pdf

CHAPTER 4

NATURAL LANGUAGE PROCESSING AND THE LITERACY CHALLENGE

Jill Burstein
Educational Testing Service

ABSTRACT

Natural language processing (NLP) affords real-time generation of linguistic information that can be used to build tools and provide meaningful analytics to support reading and writing skills development. Specifically, NLP technology can be used to (a) *build* capabilities to support formative assessment and instruction of reading and writing for a diverse population of learners, and (b) *provide educational analytics* for various stakeholders, including students, instructors, parents, administrators, and policy makers. This chapter will discuss the history of NLP for educational applications, provide a literacy-based motivation for NLP technology development, and describe two NLP-based technology use cases of AWE-based reading and writing applications that broaden access to literacy solutions.

Application of Artificial Intelligence to Assessment, pages 77–100
Copyright © 2020 by Information Age Publishing

NATURAL LANGUAGE PROCESSING
AND THE LITERACY CHALLENGE

The Literacy Challenge

Low literacy is a social challenge that affects citizens on a global level. This challenge has implications for critical and practical aspects of social participation, such as employability, and self-esteem and self-confidence (EU High Level Group, 2012). In terms of the global impact of the literacy issue, the Organisation for Economic Co-operation and Development (OECD) reports that, on average, about 20% of students in OECD countries do not attain the baseline level of proficiency in reading (PISA, 2016). In the United States, we find literacy challenges in K–12 and postsecondary levels. The National Center for Education Statistics (NCES) reports that average National Assessment for Educational Progress (NAEP) reading assessment scores are marginally proficient for 12th graders in the United States (NCES, 2016a). Contributing to the U.S. literacy challenge is the large number of English language learners (ELL) enrolled in U.S. K–12 schools. In 2014–2015 it was reported that 4.8 million ELLs were enrolled in K–12, and about 9.6% were participating in ELL programs.[1,2] It is reported that ELL students in cities made up an average of 14.2% of total public school enrollment, and in suburban areas ELL students made up an average of 8.9% of public school enrollment (NCES, 2016a). In postsecondary contexts, it is reported that in Fall 2017, approximately 20.4 million students were expected to be enrolled in 2- and 4-year institutions and is expected to rise over the next several years.[3] Millions of these enrolled students reportedly lack the prerequisite skills to succeed (NCES, 2016b).

Further, it is reported that more than 50% of students entering 2-year colleges, and nearly 20% of students enrolled in 4-year post-secondary institutions are placed in math, reading and writing developmental courses (Complete College America, 2012). Nearly 40% of 2-year college students do not complete their developmental courses, and in 4-year institutions, one-third or fewer of students placed in remediation graduate in 6 years; a number of reasons for low course and college completion rates are noted, including lack of preparation in reading and writing (Complete College America, 2012).

Natural Language Processing and Social Challenges

Natural language processing (NLP) research has been applied to a number of social challenges. In addition to education which is the focus of this chapter, examples of NLP applications to social challenges include, abusive language in social media (Nobata, Tetreault, Thomas, Mehdad, & Chang, 2016), racial profiling (Voigt et al., 2017), biomedical information (Cohen & Demner-Fushman, 2014), clinical psychology and mental health (Mowery et al., 2017), and human trafficking (Wang, Philpot, Hovy, & Latonero, 2012). In the education domain, there has been considerable NLP text and speech research for education. Much of this work focuses on automated evaluation of writing (text) and spoken language in assessment and instruction (Crossley & MacNamara, 2016). This chapter discusses text-based technologies.

The past two decades of automated writing evaluation (AWE) is aligned with the growth of an emerging field coined as "writing analytics."[4] Writing analytics embraces the bodies of work in corpus linguistics and computational linguistics research that have been conducted for many years. Writing analytics is intended to leverage corpus linguistics, computational linguistics, and writing research to provide meaningful information for a variety of stakeholders and support for diverse learners. Beyond the discussion of text-based work which is the focus of this chapter, there is a rapidly growing area of speech-based education technologies that support reading literacy (see Mostow, 2016; and Beigman Klebanov, Loukina, Sabatini, & O'Reilly, 2017, for examples of a reading support systems).

This chapter will discuss how NLP capabilities can support writing and reading literacy solutions for a diverse population of learners by providing 24/7 accessibility through digital means. The availability of these technologies afford more flexibility to learners for whom daytime, face-to-face traditional settings may not be possible due to work schedules, family responsibilities, and other life circumstances. The remainder of the chapter reviews the trajectory of NLP technology relevant to literacy—specifically writing and reading. The chapter will discuss examples of NLP solutions for reading and writing literacy. While literacy affects K–12 through adult learners in academic and workforce contexts, focus of this chapter is on K–12 and postsecondary academic settings.

BACKGROUND: EARLY TEXT-BASED TECHNOLOGY TO SUPPORT LITERACY

Brief History

Automated Writing Evaluation
Automated writing evaluation (AWE) began in the 1960s with Project Essay Grade (PEG; Page, 1966). This early system used as its primary feature predictor, a length measure, that is, the *fourth root of the length of the essay* (where length was measured as word count). PEG has evolved into one of the leading commercial AWE engines (Shermis, Burstein, Elliot, Miel, &

Foltz, 2015). Writer's Workbench (WWB) was a Unix-based editing tool. This application was developed in the early 1980s that was designed to help students edit their writing, and provided automated feedback mostly related to writing mechanics and grammar (MacDonald, Frase, Gingrich, & Keenan, 1982). The application also provided information about topic sentences which was the first attempt to address discourse. Pearson's Intelligent Essay Assessor (IEA; Landauer, Foltz, & Laham, 1998; Landauer, Laham, & Foltz, 2003) and Educational Testing Service's (ETS) e-rater® (Burstein et al., 1998; Attali & Burstein, 2006), both developed in the mid-1990s, are now among the leading commercial AWE engines. IEA uses latent semantic analysis as a primary method to predict holistic writing scores; e-rater uses a variety of linguistic features that map to major writing sub constructs, including English conventions (Burstein, Tetreault, & Madnani, 2013), discourse structure (Burstein, Marcu, & Knight, 2003), discourse coherence (Somasundaran, Burstein, & Chodorow, 2014), argumentation (Beigman Klebanov et al., 2016), and source relevance (Beigman Klebanov, Madnani, Burstein, & Somasundaran, 2014). Picking up where WWB left off, Pearson's Write-to-Learn™ and ETS's Criterion® online essay evaluation service (Burstein, Chodorow, & Leacock, 2004) provided immediate automated feedback for student essay writing. Of course, since the development of the early AWE feedback systems, including WWB, Write-to-Learn, and Criterion, a number of commercially-deployed systems are now available that support learner writing. Examples include Grammarly® and the Turnitin® Revision Assistant and Feedback Studio.

Readability

Research in the area of analyzing text complexity investigates linguistic properties of text that render a text relatively more or less accessible. Research in this area often feeds into applications offering readability measures—specifically, measures that predict the grade level of a text.

Foundational research in this area examined the effect of morphological and syntactic text properties. Flesch (1948) reported that text features such as syllable counts of words and sentence length were predictors of text difficulty. This early research led to the Flesch-Kincaid readability measure, which is a common baseline readability measure, and often incorporated into other products, such as Microsoft Word. Research in this area has continued (Chall & Dale, 1995; MacGinitie & Tretiak, 1969; Stenner, 1996). The Lexile® readability measure continues to be a measure widely used by large textbook publishers and testing companies for identifying relationships between text complexity and grade levels for reading materials (such as textbooks). There has been continued interest in the NLP community in the area of text complexity and readability (Collins-Thompson & Callan, 2004; Deane, Sheehan, Sabatini, Futagi, & Kostin, 2006; Elhadad

& Sutaria, 2007; Miltsakaki, 2009; Napolitano, Sheehan, & Mundkowsky, 2015; Schwarm & Ostendorf, 2005), and text quality in terms of discourse coherence in well-formed texts (Barzilay & Lapata, 2005; Barzilay & Lapata, 2008; Graesser, McNamara, & Kulikowich, 2011; McNamara, Graesser, Louwerse, & Cai, 2004; Pitler & Nenkova, 2008).

EMERGING TEXT-BASED TECHNOLOGY TO SUPPORT LITERACY

NLP-based technology that provides literacy support continues to develop rapidly. As mentioned earlier in the chapter, there are several text-based, AWE applications that provide support for writers and readability measures to support curriculum development and instruction. This section discusses two novel technology solutions: (a) the Language Muse® Activity Palette for reading, and (b) the Writing Mentor™ app for writing.

The Language Muse Activity Palette[5]

The Language Muse Activity Palette (LM) is a web-based application designed to support teachers of English learners (ELs). The application uses NLP to automatically generate language-based activities to build instructional materials that support learners' reading comprehension and language skills.

Motivation
Educational standards adopted by most U.S. states (CCSSO, 2010) explicitly emphasize the need for students to read progressively more complex texts in subject areas to prepare for college and careers. Classroom texts may contain academic language and structures unfamiliar to ELs, for example, figurative language and complex sentences. With limited English language skills, learners could be disadvantaged further if complexity of texts increases without scaffolding to help them with the language demands (Coleman & Goldenberg, 2012). The Language Muse Activity Palette engine (LM) was developed to provide curriculum development support for teachers of ELs. LM is an NLP-based open-access, web-based tool that automatically generates language-based activities intended to support reading comprehension and language skills development for struggling readers. Teachers can use LM to automatically generate customizable activities which can be administered as traditional paper-and-pencil or online assignments to their students. The activities are generated using NLP algorithms and lexical resources; activities are designed to help ELs with multiple aspects of

language learning needed to support content comprehension: vocabulary, syntactic structures, and discourse structure. LM is related to NLP work on automatic question generation (Brown, Frishkoff, & Eskenazi, 2005; Heilman & Smith, 2010; Mitkov & Ha, 2003). It can generate over 20 activity types for a single classroom text, cover a significantly larger set of language constructs, and offer teachers much more customizability than earlier, related systems. In addition, many activities are automatically scored. Using automated scoring and teacher-provided feedback, LM generates information about students' language proficiency that can be used by teachers and students. Current study findings will be discussed. These show promise and feasibility with regard to addressing ELs' content comprehension and language learning needs and teachers' user experience.

Application

NLP methods and lexical resources are used to generate linguistic features from an input text (Madnani, Burstein, Sabatini, Biggers, & Andreyev, 2016). The features categories include: (a) lexical entities (for example, cognates and multi-word expressions); (b) syntactic structure; and (c) discourse relations. Lexical entities are identified using lexical resources (e.g., antonyms) and more sophisticated NLP methods (e.g., synonym detection) as follows. Lexical resources are used for activities related to these language elements: (a) academic words (Coxhead, 2000); and (b) antonyms (Fellbaum, 1998), cognates (Burstein et al., 2012), and homonyms (Burstein et al. 2004). Additional NLP-driven methods to identify lexical entities are as follows. Synonym detection is used to generate synonym activities using a thresholded combination of WordNet, a distributional thesaurus (Lin, 1998), and SMT-based paraphrases (Bannard & Callison-Burch, 2005). Multiword expression activities are generated using a rank-ratio based collocation detection algorithm trained on the Google Web1T n-gram corpus (Futagi, Deane, Chodorow, & Tetreault, 2008). Syntactic structures are identified as follows. Regular expressions based on constituency parsers generate phrasal and sentential structure information for activities related to contractions, complex verb and noun phrases, relative clauses, and multi-clause sentences. A morphological analyzer and word-form database are used to generate activities related to derivational and inflectional word forms (Madnani et al., 2016). Discourse relations related to cause–effect, compare–contrast, and evidence draw from an adapted rule-based, discourse analyzer (Burstein et al., 1998). For passage-level summary activity scaffolding, key (main topic) words, a heuristic measures word repetition across paragraphs.

Teachers upload a classroom text into LM. The engine automatically generates over 20 activities using the linguistic features identified in the text. Teachers then use available activities to create an "activity palette"—a set text-specific activities—to support a particular learning objective, such as "practice with derivational word forms." Assignments can be printed and administered in traditional paper-and-pencil for, or assigned and completed online by students. Multiple choice, and cloze activities are automatically scored. Teachers can otherwise manually provide scores and personalized feedback. All scores and feedback (analytics) are viewable by teachers and students.

Instructional Intervention

At the time that this chapter was being written, a randomized-control instructional invention was still underway (Burstein et al., 2017a). The intervention was designed to assess the feasibility and promise of LM in an authentic classroom setting—specifically: (a) "Can teachers use the tool effectively?"; and (b) "Does integration of LM-generated activities into classroom instruction help to improve reading comprehension and language skills of English learners?" A brief description of the intervention is described to provide the reader with context.

Participants

Twenty-six English-as-second-language (ESL) teachers participated in the study: 13 treatment and 13 control teachers from across 24 schools (13 middle schools, 1 elementary/middle school, 1 middle/high school, and 9 high schools). Approximately 360 students participated across the school sites.

Methods

Teacher Training and Instructional Intervention

Treatment teachers received a 2-day training to learn how to use the tool. Over an approximate duration of 8–10 weeks following the training, these teachers used the tool to create and administer LM-generated activities to their students—all of whom are ELs. The LM activities were administered as part of instruction, either via paper-and-pencil by printing out the activities, or through online administration for which students can complete the activity using a computer, tablet, or smartphone.

Data Collection Instruments

Pre-posttests. The treatment and control teachers administered the RISE reading components assessment to their students (Sabatini, Bruce,

Steinberg, & Weeks, 2015). This assessment is a battery that measures basic reading skills such as decoding, word recognition, vocabulary, and fluency. Outcomes will be used to measure change before and after the intervention.

Professional Experiences Survey.   A survey of teachers' demographics and educational background, student population, typical instructional strategies, and digital skills.

Observation Protocol.   A protocol used to collect qualitative data about teaching practices related to reading, comprehension, ELs, and assessment.

Perception Survey.   A post-intervention measure of treatment teachers' instructional choices and an overall evaluation of the LM intervention adapted from the System Usability Survey (SUS; Brooke, 1996). A post-intervention measure of control teachers' instructional choices, and a survey of their interest future LM use.

Web usage logs.   Tool use, feature access, and timestamps are captured for all users from login to exit. These data allow the identification of frequent feature use and user preferences.

Preliminary Findings: Teacher Experience

The study's data collection to date allows us to report on the teacher user experience as it pertains to the treatment teacher perceptions of tool utility.[6] Arguably, a positive teacher experience is more likely to help with classroom adoption of the technology into the classroom. Figure 4.1 illustrates average response rankings from the 13 treatment teachers who had responded to the perception survey at the time that this chapter was written. In Figure 4.1, light grey bars indicate rankings for positive statements (e.g., *I think I would use the Palette[7] frequently*) and dark grey bars indicate rankings for negative statements (e.g., *I found the Palette unnecessarily complex*). As we would hope, the green bars have an upward trend and are at or over 3 (agree), and orange bars a downwards trend and most are below 3. However, the average response to the negative statement: *The Palette is not intuitive* was 3.00 (agree). This suggests that interface changes or additional training resources may be needed to increase interface intuitiveness. The average response of 3.23 to the statement: *I think I would like to use the Palette frequently* suggests that teachers had a largely positive experience and would continue to use the tool after the study.

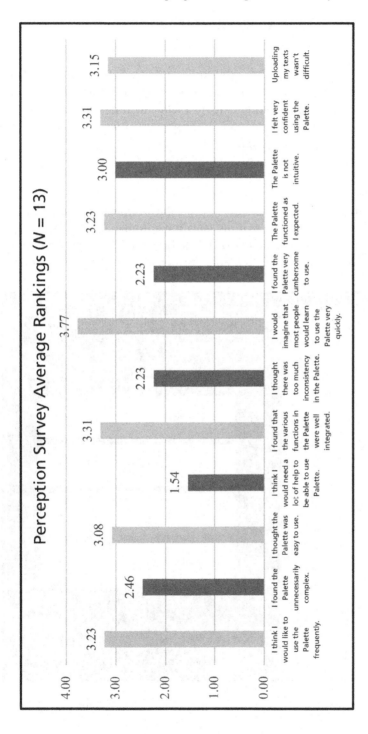

Figure 4.1 Treatment teacher perception survey responses about the Language Muse Activity Palette (*N* = 13). 1 = *strongly disagree;* 2 = *disagree;* 3 = *agree;* 4 = *strongly agree.*

The Writing Mentor® Application[8]— A Google Docs Add-On

The Writing Mentor (WM) application (Figure 4.2) is a Google Docs add-on[9] designed to provide instructional writing support. The app is intended to help struggling writers with academic writing, especially those in postsecondary settings. To that end, the app focuses on four key writing sub constructs expected in academic writing—specifically, credibility of claims, topic development, coherence, and editing.

Motivation

Automated writing evaluation systems have typically supported the measurement of pertinent writing skills for automated scoring of large-volume, high-stakes assessments (Attali & Burstein, 2006) and online instruction (Burstein et al., 2004; Foltz, Streeter, Lochbaum, & Landauer,

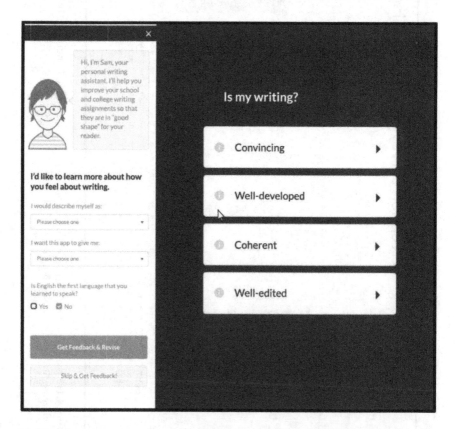

Figure 4.2   Screenshot taken from the Writing Mentor app landing page.[10]

2013; Roscoe, Varner, Weston, Crossaley, & McNamara, 2014). AWE has been used primarily for on-demand essay writing on standardized assessments. However, real-time, NLP-based AWE affords the ability to generate linguistic analyses for a range of writing genres in postsecondary education, such as, on-demand essay writing tasks, argumentative essays from the social sciences, and lab reports in STEM courses (Burstein, Beigman Klebanov, Elliot, & Molloy, 2016b). Burstein, McCafferey, Beigman Klebanov, & Ling (2017b) conducted an exploratory secondary data analysis that examined relationships between NLP-derived linguistic features extracted from on-demand writing samples from college students, and broader success indicators (such as the SAT and ACT composite and subject scores). Findings from Burstein et al. (2017b) suggested that writing can provide meaningful information about student knowledge related to broader outcomes (college success indicators and learning outcomes measures). This also suggests that AWE may have greater potential for educational analytics beyond prevalent uses for writing assessment and instruction. AWE analyses can be used to generate feedback (to provide students with meaningful information to support their writing) and educational analytics (to inform various stakeholders, including students, instructors, parents, administrators, and policy makers).

The Writing Mentor (WM) application targets struggling writers and EL populations enrolled in 2- and 4-year colleges. The app is intended to provide one-stop-shopping for writers who are looking for some writing help. Other apps that provide access to individual users, such as Grammarly, typically focus on English conventions. Applications, such as ETS' Criterion and Turnitin's Revision Assistant, provide feedback above and beyond English conventions, but are not consumer-based, and require institutional subscriptions. A main motivation of the Writing Mentor app was to conduct research; therefore, the application collects user event logs that can be used to better understand the types of feedback that users seek and how writing feedback promotes document revision. The app contains an optional entry survey that asks users how confident they are as writers, and if English is the first language they learned to speak. Responses to that survey allow us to examine how self-reported writing self-efficacy and English language proficiency may be related to feedback preferences. The app also includes a user perception survey of the application which can help us to understand user likes and dislikes of the tool.

Application

The Writing Mentor app can be installed from the Google Docs Add-on store, and is freely accessible in the current beta version. The app provides users with actionable feedback related to the writing being convincing (e.g., claims and sources), well-developed (topic development), coherent (e.g., flow of ideas), and well-edited (e.g., English conventions). The fuller set of features is shown in Table 4.1. Features selected for use in the WM were informed by previous research with university faculty (Burstein, Elliott, & Molloy, 2016a; Burstein et al., 2016b), literature related to ELs' language development that informed the Language Muse Activity Palette (Madnani et al., 2016) as well as collaboration with writing research

Table 4.1. Feature types, subconstructs, and related NLP features and lexical resources experts and practitioners. Feedback leverages ETS' NLP capabilities and lexical resources, and provides synonyms for unfamiliar words that users may encounter while reading external sources. Feedback is presented by a friendly, non-binary[11] persona named "Sam" (a gender-neutral name). The app also includes a brief, optional 3-question entry survey that asks users to let us know about (a) self-reported confidence about writing, (b) why they are using the app, and (c) English language status (i.e., was English the first language they learned to speak). The app also includes an exit perception survey which is an 11-question survey adapted from the System Usability Survey (SUS; Brooke, 1996). In addition to feedback, the app provides a report illustrating the different feedback types that the user viewed.

The report can be saved as a PDF file that can be shared with their instructor. The report can give the instructor a sense of how their students are engaging with the tool, and what aspects of writing they are working on. The Writing Mentor app's flexible architecture supports the ability to add or modify features easily, and it is designed to capture user log data for research purposes.

Writing Mentor Use

WM was first released in November 2017. By early January 2018 approximately 1,000 user event logs had been captured through the app.[12] Events for these "users-in-the-wild" include information such as, total time spent, which app features were used, and how much time a user has spent with different features. Users may also opt to respond to the entry and exit surveys (described earlier). User responses to these surveys may be used to try to understand users' experiences with the app. Since all personally identifiable information must be removed from the event logs for research, we do not know who these users-in-the-wild are, or the purpose of the tool. Potential tool use scenarios may include the following. Users may have come to the tool in good faith to work on their writing. However, some users, such as writing instructors, may be using the tool just to test its instructional utility. Writing instructors who have been interested in using the tool for students have informed us of their use in this capacity. Others may be using the tool for the purpose of identifying tool idiosyncrasies (Winerip, 2012). The latter has been a common scenario over the years with regard to evaluations of AWE systems.

TABLE 4.1   Feature Types, Subconstructs, and Related NLP Features and Lexical Resources

Feature Name	*Writing Mentor* Subconstruct	NLP-Based Feature/Resource Description
Claims	Convincing	Arguing expressions from a discourse cue and argument expression lexicon that contains sets of discourse cue terms and relations (e.g., contrast, parallel, summary), and arguing expressions, classified by *stance* (i.e., for/against), and *hedge* and *booster* status. This is an extension of the *cluelex* from Burstein et al. (1998).
Sources	Convincing	Rule-based scripts detect in-text formal citations consistent with MLA, APA, and Chicago style citation formats.
Topic Development	Well-Developed	Detection of main topics and their related word sets (Beigman Klebanov et al., 2013; Burstein et al., 2016b).
Flow of Ideas	Coherent	Leverages terms in a document generated from Topic Development (above) main topics and their related word sets (Beigman Klebanov et al., 2013; Burstein et al., 2016b).
Transition Terms	Coherent	Discourse cue and argument expression lexicon that contains sets of discourse cue terms and relations (e.g., contrast, parallel, summary), and arguing expressions, classified by *stance* (i.e., for/against), and *hedge* and *booster* status. This is an extension of the *cluelex* from Burstein et al. (1998).
Long Sentences	Coherent	Sentences identified with a syntactic parser that contain 1 independent clause and > = 1 one dependent clause.
Title & Section Headers	Coherent	Rule-based scripts detect titles and section headers.
Pronoun Use	Coherent	Pronouns identified from a syntactic parser.
Errors in Grammar, Usage, & Mechanics	Well-Edited	Nine automatically detected *grammar* error feature types, 12 automatically detected *mechanics* error feature types, and 10 automatically detected *word usage* error feature types (Attali & Burstein, 2006).
Claim Verbs	Well-Edited	Verbs from a discourse cue and argument expression lexicon that contains sets of discourse cue terms and relations (e.g., contrast, parallel, summary), and arguing expressions, classified by *stance* (i.e., for/against), and *hedge* and *booster* status. This is an extension of the *cluelex* from Burstein et al. (1998).
Word Choice	Well-Edited	Rule-based script that detects words and expressions related to a set of 13 "unnecessary" words and terms, such as *very, literally, a total of.*
Contractions	Well-Edited	*Contractions* are identified from a syntactic parser.

This section provides a snapshot of information derived from the event logs from users-in-the-wild approximately 8 weeks after the release of the app. This is the kind of information that may help to inform continued app development.

Who Is Using the Writing Mentor app?

At the time that this chapter was written, 862 users had responded to the entry survey out of the 974 users-in-the-wild who installed and tried out the tool. Figure 4.3 shows the percentages of users who self-reported at the different levels of writing self-efficacy—specifically, if they believed they were very confident (7%), pretty confident (55%), or not very confident (38%) writers. In addition, the majority of users (84%) responded that English was the first language that they learned to speak.

User Perceptions

The exit perception survey mentioned earlier is adapted from the SUS survey (Brooke, 1996), and contains 11 questions.[13] Ten of the eleven survey questions were statements; the 11th question was open-ended. The user could select one (*) to five stars, (*****) and half-stars could be selected as well. For example, if a user selected a half-star on the first star, that response would be associated with a 0.5 (i.e., low score indicating a lower impression), and if the user selected a four and a half stars, that response would

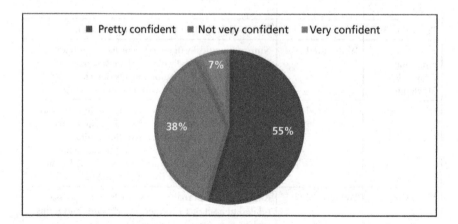

Figure 4.3 Self-reported writing self-efficacy. Percentage or users who reported being pretty confident, very confident, or not very confident writers. $N = 862$ users.

be associated with a 4.5 (i.e., higher score indicating a higher impression). A question that may be most indicative of how much a user enjoyed or believed that they benefited from using the tool would be their response to this statement: "I think that I would use the Writing Mentor frequently."

Given the scope of this chapter, we therefore decided to show results for this statement. For 85 users who responded to the exit survey, results in Table 4.2 show that on a scale of 0.5 through 5 at half-point intervals. A mean of 3.85, a median of 4.5, and a mode of 5.0 suggests a favorable outcome toward the user experience and continued tool use. Consistent with this, for these 85 users, Table 4.3 shows that some users are returning to use the system multiple times to work on one or more documents (i.e., Google Docs).

In this section, we provide a snapshot of relationships between self-efficacy, English language status, and tool engagement. We use the responses to the entry survey, and the event log data to illustrate tool use based on self-efficacy and English language status.

The event logs provide information about how users interact with the Writing Mentor app. To generate the information in Figure 4.4, we computed, for each user, the single feature which that user preferred (i.e., used most frequently) across all documents and all sessions (i.e., each time the user entered and used the app). Figure 4.4 shows for each self-efficacy and English language status category, the features used most frequently by users from each category. The frequency is represented by a proportion. For each self-efficacy category (very confident, not very confident, and pretty confident), we computed a sum across all users from that category, and then averaged across the total number of users in a self-efficacy category.

Figure 4.4 suggests that across users there is a variety of preferred feature types. Notably, however, across self-efficacy categories, the most preferred feature appears to be the *grammar errors* feature, followed by the *claims* feature, and then the *topic development* feature. The data also suggest that for *not very*

TABLE 4.2   Descriptive Statistics Based on 85 User Responses to the Exit Survey Statement: "I Think That I Would Use the Writing Mentor Frequently"

Mean	Std. Dev.	Median	Mode	Minimum	Maximum
3.85	1.29	4.5	5	0.5	5

TABLE 4.3   Descriptive Statistics Based on 85 User Responses to the Exit Survey, Showing Frequency (Number of Times) With Which Users Returned to Use the System

Mean	Std. Dev.	Median	Mode	Maximum
3.01	2.55	2	1	16

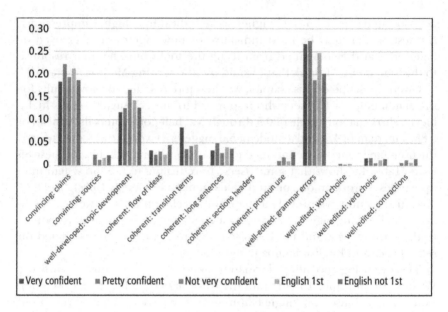

Figure 4.4 Most frequently used features based on self-reported self-efficacy and English language status from the entry survey. Not very confident ($n = 326$), very confident ($n = 60$), pretty confident ($n = 469$). "English 1st" indicates the user responded that English was the first language they learned to speak ($n = 721$); "English not 1st" indicates that the user responded that English was not the first language they learned to speak ($n = 134$). The Writing Mentor subconstruct class precedes a ":" which is followed by the name of the specific feature in a subconstruct class. For instance, "convincing: claims" indicates that the feature "claims" is the in the "convincing" class. The *y*-axis illustrates a proportion of users. This figure is generated from 864 users who responded to the entry survey.

confident writers, there is a relatively similar distribution of preference across these three feature types. For *pretty confident* writers and *very confident* writers, grammar errors is clearly the most preferred. Very confident writers also seem to have a slightly higher preference for a fourth feature, *transition terms*. The *English 1st* users have a pattern similar to the pretty confident users. The *English not 1st* users, similar to all other users, prefer grammar errors, claims and topic development, though grammar errors and claims are more closely tied for the top two. There is also a slight bump in *flow of ideas* for these users as well.

User Suggestions

The exit perception survey contained an open-ended statement: "I wish that Writing Mentor had . . ." User could fill in a dialog box with suggestions.

Example suggestions are quoted from users are shown in Table 4.4. Suggestions are categorized by type: interface, usability, feature enhancements, and new features.

TABLE 4.4 Use Suggestions in Response to the Exit Survey Question: "I Wish That Writing Mentor Had..."

Interface	Usability	Feature Enhancements	New Features
A better proportioned interface. The add-on scales a bit oddly on my monitor. I had to use sliders to position the interface properly.	I loved the writing mentor I thought it worked well I just wish I had more experience in writing to actually use the advice better.	A better understanding of run-ons. There were lines in my writing that I don't believe to be run-ons.	More active walkthroughs to help make changes instead of just highlighting problems.
A clear word count and easy high contrast text.	Easier navigation: full screen instead of a smaller window/frame, and function/menu tabs across the top, as in a word processing program rather than on the right side.	Recommended words to use for the sentences as a correction.	More interactive comments.
A little larger screen area.		More suggestions for pronouns.	Could write my paper for me.
A slightly easier-to-follow flow. The "Done" button generally brings you back to the next session, except under "Review Topic Development."		Correction of citations.	Shown me examples.
Simple animations for the avatar. The suggestions/tips are straightforward text. It would help if the avatar has simple animations.		Spelling helping.	I wish it had personalized comments and feedback.
		More humor.	A way to check for a conclusion.

DISCUSSION

A global literacy challenge is fairly well documented. On an international level, PISA and OECD reports show substantial proportions of low literacy as discussed earlier in this chapter. Consistent with this, the National Center for Education Statistics reports low literacy in K–12 through postsecondary education. There is also evidence that many students entering postsecondary contexts lack the skills necessary to successfully complete their postsecondary education.

Natural language processing solutions as support for the literacy challenge now has a substantial body of knowledge that spans across reading and writing. As was discussed earlier in this chapter, NLP solutions for writing instruction and assessment have a relatively long history and a substantial body of work that is now commercially available. This chapter discussed a number of technology solutions that address reading and writing, and focused on two more recent solutions. The Language Muse Activity Palette is a web-based application that uses NLP to automatically generate language-based activities intended to support reading comprehension and language skills development. Teachers can customize these activities for ELs and other struggling readers. The activities can be incorporated into classroom assignments and delivered and completed online. Writing Mentor is a Google Docs application designed to provide writing instruction to struggling writers. These are just two examples of how NLP technology can create literacy solutions that are globally accessible 24/7. As NLP researchers continue to consider solutions to help to address literacy, they should carefully consider the needs of different populations of learners, and scalability of these solutions to ensure that they are accessible to a broad range of learners.

AUTHOR NOTE

Research presented in this chapter was supported by ETS, and the Institute of Education Science, U.S. Department of Education, Award Numbers R305A140472. Any opinions, findings, conclusions, or recommendations are those of the authors and do not necessarily reflect the views of the IES or ETS. I would like to acknowledge and thank my ETS colleagues who made significant contributions to research and applications discussed in this chapter: John Sabatini, Dan McCaffrey, Nitin Madnani, Beata Beigman Klebanov, Diane Napolitano, Maxwell Schwartz, Kietha Biggers, and Kelsey Drier. I would also like to thank Norbert Elliot, Dolores Perin, and Mya Poe for their expert advice on the Writing Mentor application research.

NOTES

1. https://www2.ed.gov/datastory/el-characteristics/index.html
2. https://ncela.ed.gov/files/fast_facts/05-19-2017/ProfilesOfELs_FastFacts.pdf
3. https://nces.ed.gov/programs/digest/d16/tables/dt16_105.20.asp?current=yes
4. See the *Journal of Writing Analytics*: https://journals.colostate.edu/analytics
5. See https://languagemuse.org/
6. The pre-post reading assessment data analysis were still underway at the time this chapter was written.
7. Note that during the intervention, the research team and teachers referred to the tool as "the Palette."
8. https://mentormywriting.org
9. The app was in beta at the time that this chapter was written.
10. https://mentormywriting.org
11. *Non-binary* in this context indicates that the gender of the character is not exclusively masculine or feminine.
12. An additional approximately 113 users had participated in an Amazon Mechanical Turk (AMT) study conducted as a way to collect more formal evaluation of the tool. These users are excluded from this analysis, and we report only on the non-AMT users in the wild.
13. The full set of questions are as follows:
    1. I think that I would like to use the Writing Mentor frequently.
    2. I found the Writing Mentor to be unnecessarily complex.
    3. I thought the Writing Mentor was easy to navigate.
    4. I needed to learn a lot of things before I could get going with the Writing Mentor.
    5. I found the various functions in the Writing Mentor were well-integrated.
    6. I thought there was too much inconsistency in the Writing Mentor.
    7. I would imagine that most people would learn to use an application like this one very quickly.
    8. I found the Writing Mentor very cumbersome to follow.
    9. I felt very confident navigating the Writing Mentor.
    10. I would need to learn a lot about Writing Mentor before I would recommend it to others.
    11. I wish Writing Mentor had . . .

REFERENCES

Attali, Y., & Burstein, J. (2006). Automated essay scoring with e-rater v.2.0. *Journal of Technology, Learning, and Assessment, 4*(3). Retrieved from the ERIC database. (EJ843852)

Bannard, C., & Callison-Burch, C. (2005, June). Paraphrasing with bilingual parallel corpora. In *Proceedings of the 43rd Annual Meeting on Association for Computational Linguistics* (pp. 597–604). Association for Computational Linguistics.

Barzilay, R., & Lapata, M. (2005). Modeling local coherence: An entity-based approach. In K. Knight, H. T. Ng, & K. Oflazer (Eds.), *Proceedings of the 43rd annual meeting of the ACL* (pp. 141–148). Ann Arbor, MI: Association for Computational Linguistics.

Barzilay, R., & Lapata, M. (2008). Modeling local coherence: An entity-based approach. *Computational Linguistics, 34*(1), 1–34.

Beigman Klebanov, B., Loukina, A., Sabatini, J., & O'Reilly, T. (2017). Continuous fluency tracking and the challenges of varying text complexity. In J. Tetreault, J. Burstein, C. Leacock, & H. Yannakoudakis (Eds.), *Proceedings of the 12th workshop for innovative use of NLP for building educational applications* (BEA12; pp. 101–108).

Beigman Klebanov, B., Madnani, N., Burstein, J., & Somasundaran, S. (2014, June). Content importance models for scoring writing from sources. In *Proceedings of the Annual Meeting of the Association of Computational Linguistics*, Baltimore, MD.

Beigman Klebanov, B., Stab, C., Burstein, J., Song, Y., Gyawali, B., & Gurevych, I. (2016) Argumentation: Content, structure, and relationship with essay quality, In *Proceedings of the 3rd workshop on argument mining* (pp. 70–75), ACL 2016, Berlin, Germany.

Brooke, J. (1996). SUS: A quick and dirty usability scale. In P. W. Jordan, B. Thomas, B. A. Weerdmeester, & I. L. McClelland (Eds.), *Usability evaluation in industry* (pp. 189–194). London, England: Taylor and Francis.

Brown, J. C., Frishkoff, G. A., & Eskenazi, M. (2005). *Automatic question generation for vocabulary assessment.* Retrieved from http://sealang.net/archives/sla/hlt05 -jonbrown.pdf

Burstein, J., Beigman Klebanov, B., Elliot, N., & Molloy, H. (2016b, September). A left turn: Automated feedback & activity generation for student writers. In *Proceedings of the 3rd language teaching, language & technology workshop*, San Francisco, CA.

Burstein, J., Chodorow, M., & Leacock, C. (2004). Automated essay evaluation: The criterion online service. *AI Magazine,. 25*(3), 27–36.

Burstein, J., Elliott, N., & Molloy, H. (2016a). Informing automated writing evaluation using the lens of genre: Two studies. *CALICO Journal, 33*(1). Retrieved from ERIC database. (EJ1143728)

Burstein, J., Kukich, K., Wolff, S., Lu, C., Chodorow, M., Braden-Harder, L., & Harris, M. D. (1998, August). Automated scoring using a hybrid feature identification technique. In *Proceedings of the 36th annual meeting of the association for computational linguistics and 17th international conference on computational linguistics* (Vol. 1; pp. 206–210). Stroudsburg, PA: Association for Computational Linguistics.

Burstein, J., Madnani, N., Sabatini, J., McCaffrey, D., Biggers, K., & Dreier, K. (2017a). Generating language activities in real-time for English learners using language muse. In *Proceedings of the fourth (2017) ACM conference on learning@ scale* (pp. 213–215). New York, NY: ACM.

Burstein, J., Marcu, D., & Knight, K., (2003). Finding the WRITE Stuff: Automatic Identification of Discourse Structure in Student Essays. *IEEE Intelligent Systems: Special Issue on Advances in Natural Language Processing, 18*(1), 32–39.

Burstein, J., McCaffrey, D., Beigman Klebanov, B., & Ling, G. (2017b). Exploring Relationships between writing and broader outcomes with automated writing evaluation. In *Proceeding of the 12th workshop on innovative use of NLP for building educational applications* (EMNLP 2017). Copenhagen, Denmark.

Burstein, J., Shore, J., Sabatini, J., Moulder, B., Holtzman, S., & Pedersen, T. (2012). *The Language Muse system: Linguistically focused instructional authoring ETS RR-12-21.* Princeton, NJ: ETS.

Burstein, J., Tetreault, J., & Madnani, N. (2013). The E-rater® automated essay scoring system. In M. D. Shermis & J. Burstein (Eds.), *Handbook for automated essay scoring* (pp. 55–67). New York, NY: Routledge.

Chall, J. S., & Dale, E. (1995). *Readability revisited: The new Dale-Chall readability formula.* Cambridge, MA: Brookline Books.

Cohen, K. B., & Demner-Fushman, D. (2014). *Biomedical natural language processing* (Vol. 11). Amsterdam, Netherlands: John Benjamins.

Coleman, R., & Goldenberg, C. (2012, February). The Common Core challenge: English language learners. *Principal Leadership, 12*(5), 46–51.

Collins-Thompson, K., & Callan, J. (2004). *A language modeling approach to predicting reading difficulty.* Retrieved from https://www.cs.cmu.edu/~callan/Papers/hlt04-kct.pdf

Complete College America. (2012). *Remediation: Higher education's bridge to nowhere.* Retrieved from https://www.insidehighered.com/sites/default/server_files/files/CCA%20Remediation%20ES%20FINAL.pdf

Council of Chief State School Officers. (2010). *Common Core state standards for English language arts & literacy in history/social studies, science, and technical subjects: Appendix A: Research supporting key elements of the standards.* Washington, DC: Common Core. Retrieved from http://www.corestandards.org/assets/Appendix_A.pdf

Coxhead, A. (2000). A new academic word list. *TESOL Quarterly, 34*(2), 213–238.

Crossley, S. A., & McNamara, D. S. (Eds.). (2016). *Adaptive educational technologies for literacy instruction.* New York, NY: Routledge.

Deane, P., Sheehan, K. M., Sabatini, J., Futagi, Y., & Kostin, I. 2006. Differences in text structure and its implications for assessment of struggling readers. *Scientific Studies of Reading, 10*(3), 257–275.

Elhadad, N., & Sutaria, K. (2007). Mining a lexicon of technical terms and lay equivalents. In *Proceedings of the 45th annual meeting of the association of computational linguistics* (pp. 49–56). Prague, Czech Republic. Retrieved from https://www.aclweb.org/anthology/W07-1007.pdf

EU High Level Group of Experts on Literacy. (2012). *Final report.* Retrieved from https://op.europa.eu/en/publication-detail/-/publication/96d782cc-7cad-4389-869a-bbc8e15e5aeb/language-en

Fellbaum, C. (1998). *WordNet: An electronic lexical database.* Cambridge, MA: MIT Press.

Flesch, R. (1948). A new readability yardstick. *Journal of Applied Psychology, 32,* 221–233.

Foltz, P. W., Streeter, L. A., Lochbaum, K. E., & Landauer, T. K (2013). Implementation and applications of the Intelligent Essay Assessor. In M. Shermis & J.

Burstein (Eds.), *Handbook of automated essay evaluation* (pp. 68–88). New York, NY: Routledge.

Futagi, Y., Deane, P., Chodorow, M., & Tetreault, J. (2008). A computational approach to detecting collocation errors in the writing of non-native speakers of English. *Computer Assisted Language Learning, 21*(4), 353–367.

Graesser, A. C., McNamara, D. S., & Kulikowich, J. (2011). Coh-Metrix: Providing multilevel analyses of text characteristics. *Educational Researcher, 40,* 223–234.

Heilman, M., & Smith, N. A. (2010). *Good question! Statistical ranking for question generation.* Retrieved from https://www.aclweb.org/anthology/N10-1086.pdf

Landauer, T. K., Foltz, P. W., & Laham, D. (1998). Introduction to latent semantic analysis. *Discourse Processes, 25*(2/3), 259–284.

Landauer, T. K., Laham, D., & Foltz, P. W. (2003). Automated scoring and annotation of essays with the Intelligent Essay Assessor. In M. D. Shermis & J. Burstein (Eds.), *Automated essay scoring: A cross-disciplinary perspective* (pp. 87–112). Mahwah, NJ: Erlbaum.

Lin, D. (1998, July). An information-theoretic definition of similarity. In *ICML, 98*(1998), 296–304.

MacDonald, N., Frase, L., Gingrich, P., & Keenan, S. (1982). The writer's workbench: Computer aids for text analysis. *IEEE Transactions on Communications, 30*(1), 105–110.

MacGinitie, W. H., & Tretiak, R. (1969). Measures of sentence complexity as predictors of the difficulty of reading materials. In *Proceedings of the 77th annual convention of the American Psychological Association.* Retrieved from ERIC database. (ED038254)

Madnani, N., Burstein, J., Sabatini, J., Biggers, K., & Andreyev, S. (2016). Language muse: Automated linguistic activity generation for English language learners. In *Proceedings of ACL-2016 System Demonstrations* (pp. 79–84). https://doi.org/10.18653/v1/P16-4014

McNamara, D. S., Graesser, A. C., & Louwerse, M. M. (2012). Sources of text difficulty: Across the ages and genres. In J. P. Sabatini & E. Albro (Eds.), *Assessing reading in the 21st century: Aligning and applying advances in the reading and measurement sciences.* Lanham, MD: R&L Education.

Miltsakaki, E. (2009). Matching readers' preferences and reading skills with appropriate web texts. In *Proceedings of the European Association for Computational Linguistics.* Retrieved from http://delivery.acm.org/10.1145/1610000/1609062/p49-miltsakaki.pdf?ip=73.75.228.200&id=1609062&acc=OPEN&key=4D4702B0C3E38B35%2E4D4702B0C3E38B35%2E4D4702B0C3E38B35%2E6D218144511F3437&__acm__=1574411633_1807f4be2e68d4d235995670c78d6c78

Mitkov R., & Ha, L. A. (2003). Computer-aided generation of multiple-choice tests. In *Proceedings of the Workshop on Building Educational Applications.* Retrieved from https://www.aclweb.org/anthology/W03-0203.pdf

Mostow, J. (2016). Project LISTEN's reading tutor. In S. A. Crossley & D. S. McNamara (Eds.), *Adaptive educational technologies for literacy instruction* (pp. 263–267). New York, NY: Routledge.

Mowery, D., Smith, H., Cheney, T., Stoddard, G., Coppersmith, G., Bryan, C., & Conway, M. (2017). Understanding depressive symptoms and psychosocial stressors on Twitter: A corpus-based study. *Journal of medical Internet research, 19*(2).

Napolitano, D., Sheehan, K., & Mundkowsky, R. (2015). Online readability and text complexity analysis with TextEvaluator. In *Proceedings of the 2015 Conference of the North American Chapter of the Association for Computational Linguistics: Demonstrations* (pp. 96–100). https://doi.org/10.3115/v1/N15-3020

National Center for Education Statistics. (2016a). *Status and trends in the education of racial and ethnic Groups* (NCES 2016-007). Retrieved from https://nces.ed.gov/pubs2016/2016007.pdf

National Center for Education Statistics. (2016b). *Remedial coursetaking at U.S. public 2- and 4-Year Institutions: Scope, experience, and outcomes* (NCES 2016-405). Retrieved from https://nces.ed.gov/pubs2016/2016405.pdf

Nobata, C., Tetreault, J., Thomas, A., Mehdad, Y., & Chang, Y. (2016), Abusive language detection in online user comments In *Proceedings of the 25th international world wide web conference.* Retrieved from http://www.yichang-cs.com/yahoo/WWW16_Abusivedetection.pdf

Page, E. B. (1966). The imminence of…grading essays by computer. *The Phi Delta Kappan, 47*(5), 238–243.

Pitler, E., & Nenkova, A. (2008). Revisiting readability: A unified framework for predicting text quality. In *Proceedings of Conference on Empirical Methods in Natural Language Processing.* Retrieved from https://www.aclweb.org/anthology/D08-1020.pdf

Programme for International Student Assessment. (2016). *PISA 2015 results in focus.* Retrieved from https://www.oecd.org/pisa/pisa-2015-results-in-focus.pdf

Roscoe, R., Varner, L., Weston, J., Crossley, S., & McNamara, D. (2014). The writing pal intelligent tutoring system: Usability testing and development. *Computers and Composition, 34*, 39–59.

Sabatini, J., Bruce, K., Steinberg, J., & Weeks, J. (2015). *SARA reading components tests, RISE forms: Technical adequacy and test Design* (2nd ed.; Technical Report ETS-RR-15-32). Retrieved from https://files.eric.ed.gov/fulltext/EJ1109935.pdf

Schwarm, S., & Ostendorf, M. (2005). Reading level assessment using support vector machines and statistical language models. In *Proceedings of the Annual Meeting of the Association of Computational Lingusitics* (pp. 523–530). https://doi.org/10.3115/1219840.1219905

Shermis, M., Burstein, J., Elliot, N., Miel, S., & Foltz, P. (2015). Automated writing evaluation: An expanding body of knowledge. In C. A. McArthur, S. Graham, & J. Fitzgerald (Eds.), *Handbook of writing research* (2nd ed.; pp. 395–409). New York, NY: Guilford.

Somasundaran, S., Burstein, J., & Chodorow, M. (2014). *Lexical chaining for measuring discourse coherence quality in test-taker essays.* Dublin, Ireland: COLING.

Stenner, A. J. (1996). *Measuring reading comprehension with the Lexile Framework.* Durham, NC: MetaMetrics.

Voigt, R., Camp, N. P., Prabhakaran, V., Hamilton, W. L., Hetey, R. C., Griffiths, C. M.,…Eberhardt, J. L. (2017). Language from police body camera footage shows racial disparities in officer respect. *Proceedings of the National Academy of Sciences, 114*(25), 6521–6526.

Wang, H., A., Philpot, E. H. Hovy, & Latonero, M. (2012). Data mining and integration to combat child trafficking. In *Proceedings of the 13th International Conference on Digital Government Research.* College Park, MD.

Winerip, M. (2012, April 22). Facing a robo-grader? Just keep obfuscating mellifluously. *New York Times,* p. A11. Retrieved from http://www.nytimes.com/2012/04/23/education/robo-readers-used-to-grade-test-essays.html

CHAPTER 5

PRACTICAL CONSIDERATIONS FOR USING AI MODELS IN AUTOMATED SCORING OF WRITING

Peter W. Foltz
Pearson and University of Colorado

Artificial Intelligence (AI) is becoming more readily available in all electronic devices and is quickly being integrated into daily life. Virtual assistants, such as Siri and Alexa seem to "understand" communication, are able to find relevant information, and respond in natural language. Data of all online interactions are being logged, mined to provide intelligent placements of advertisements, personalized news, and linking to articles and people with relevant expertise. Indeed, it is estimated that AI technology will contribute up to 15 trillion dollars to the global economy by 2030 (PwC, 2018).

This growth in AI is due primarily to three interacting factors. The first is the availability of data. As more information is produced and consumed online, data is stored about what people are doing (logs, locations, interactions, who they communicate with) as well as information about the world

Application of Artificial Intelligence to Assessment, pages 101–113
Copyright © 2020 by Information Age Publishing

(e.g., newspapers, textbooks, training material, articles, chats). Second, new machine learning algorithms have been developed that are able to process more data and extract better features that can characterize what humans are doing, what humans know, and what information they may want to know. Finally, more powerful parallelizable computational methods have been developed that work remotely in the cloud (e.g., AWS, Google Cloud), allowing efficient processing of interactions and data with real-time feedback. Together these factors allow AI-based systems to provide a form of ubiquitous computing where data can be collected processed and served to people to be integrated into devices.

Concomitant with this growth of overall use of AI is the increased use of AI in educational practice. This is evidenced by growth in research through journals, conferences, and societies such as *AI in Education, Journal of the Learning Sciences, Learning at Scale,* and the *International AIED Society,* among others. It is also evidenced through the availability of greater amounts of commercial educational software incorporating intelligent tutoring systems, automated scoring of writing and speaking, adaptive learning platforms, and educational chatbots. The approaches range from use in summative assessment, tracking students through courses, as well as formative feedback. Use of AI in education is not new, indeed, early systems in the late 1960s and early 1970s showed the promise of personalized assessment and student pathways customized to a student's knowledge deficiencies (Carbonnel, 1970). However, because computers with sufficient power could not be easily deployed in the classroom, the dream had not yet been realized. Now with the ubiquity of devices, data, algorithms, and processing, we are at a potential inflection point where applications with embedded automated educational assessment can be readily available.

There is much anticipation of the potential benefits of AI for improving personalization, relieving rote work, and allowing more efficient learning. At the same time, there is also a fear of AI from the general public and the media. These fears encompass fear of change, fear of AI taking jobs, and fear that it may do harm in unanticipated ways (Friend, 2018). These fears are partially justified. We want to understand how new technology will affect society, our work, and our education. We want technology to provide accurate characterization of student abilities and effective feedback. We want to ensure that AI does not differentially affect subgroups. At the same time, we don't want to just throw out innovation that could have potential benefit to mankind over the fears or lack of understanding of the technological innovations.

For educational use of AI, we see similar fears. Automated scoring of writing has been dubbed robo-graders by the popular press (Smith, 2018) and educators have warned that their use will cause all students to write like robots, will miss the geniuses in the classrooms, or can be easily tricked

(Perelman, 2018). However many studies show the benefit of their use for efficient, accurate scoring of writing (Foltz, Streeter, Lochbaum, & Landauer, 2013; Shermis & Burstein, 2013; Shermis & Hamner, 2012), gain in writing skills (Franzke. Kintsch, Caccamise, Johnson, & Dooley, 2005; Foltz & Rosenstein, 2015), and growth in content knowledge. From the perspective as an implementer of AI for assessment, it is not good enough to just show that AI can be effective in educational settings. Implementers must also show that they apply best practices, and can document that AI-based educational approaches do not cause differential harm to users. In this way, the field can allay the fears of the general public and the media as well show that they treat the approaches as serious science.

The goals of this chapter are to focus on a few of the best practices for AI in assessment. There are many best practices, ranging from effective assessment design for AI-based systems to valid psychometric evaluation of AI results to creation of effective algorithms. For the present chapters, we focus on two practices related to effective use of AI methods in assessment. These practices are:

1. Understanding the assumptions that go into the modeling.
2. Keeping humans in the loop.

The chapter further focuses on one area of AI-based assessment, automated scoring of writing, because this area is now widely used in educational practice and has a deep literature ranging from the computational side to the implementation side and to the educational implications. While focused on writing assessment, the issues and approaches that will be raised nevertheless remain relevant to other AI-based approaches to education, including tutoring and adaptive systems. The goal is to illustrate some cases from the area and how best practices can be applied to mitigate some of the issues to make these systems more effective.

AI-BASED SCORING OF WRITING

Before we discuss the best practices, it is important to understand the underlying approach of automated scoring of writing. Conceptually, the task of automated scoring is simple: convert a written student performance into scores or feedback. But, digging deeper, this conversion means that a computer must be able to process aspects of language, detect which features are relevant to scoring the student performance, and then scale those features to scores or feedback. Automated analyses have been applied to understanding aspects of writing since the 1960s. Content analysis (e.g., Gerbner, Holsti, Krippendorff, Paisley, & Stone, 1969; Krippendorff & Bock, 2009) was designed to allow analysis of textual data in order to make replicable, valid inferences about the content. However, the methods focused primarily on counts of key terms used in the texts. Page (1967) pioneered techniques to convert the language features of student writing into scores that correlated highly with teacher ratings of the essays. With the advent of increasingly sophisticated natural language processing and machine learning techniques over the past 50 years, automated essay scoring (AES) has now become a widely used set of approaches that can provide scores and feedback instantly. AES has become more accepted with multiple systems available for implementing the scoring of writing (e.g., Shermis & Burstein, 2013; see also Bunch, Vaughn, & Miel, 2016; Williamson et al., 2010; Wilson & Andrada, 2013, 2016). Research of AES systems have shown that they can be as accurate as human scorers (e.g., Burstein, Chodorow, & Leacock, 2004; Landauer, Laham, & Foltz, 2001; Shermis & Hamner, 2012; Williamson, Xi, & Breyer, 2010), can score on multiple traits of writing (e.g., Foltz et al., 2013), can be used for feedback on content (Beigman-Klebanov, Madnani, Burstein, & Sumasundaran, 2014; Foltz, Gilliam, & Kendall, 2000), and can score short responses (e.g., Higgins et al., 2014; Thurlow, Herman, & Foltz, 2010). AES is now being used operationally in a number of high-stakes assessments (e.g., GED, and various state K–12 assessments), placement tests (e.g., Pearson Test of English, ACCUPLACER), and for writing practice (e.g., Criterion, WriteToLearn). AES is therefore becoming more widely accepted as part of educational and assessment practice.

Building a Scoring Model

Underlying these scoring methods is an assumption that the system is able to consistently convert the student's performance (e.g., essay) into scores or feedback that are accurate, reliable, and align to the constructs relevant to the assessment. This approach is typically called a "scoring model." A scoring model is built by first obtaining a sample of student responses that represent the full range of student responses and scores. Typically the set of essays should represent a normal distribution, while ensuring that there are sufficient (e.g., at least a minimum of 10–20) examples at each score point. During training of the system, the responses should be 100% double-scored by human scorers and also receive resolution scores for non-adjacent agreement. By having scores from multiple human scorers, a system can be trained on something closer to the true score (e.g., the average of multiple human raters) rather than the scores of an individual rater. The goal is to have as much and as accurate information as possible about the range of possible responses and how those responses should be evaluated. Generally, essay sets that are not as accurately scored by human raters will result in less accurate automated scoring models (e.g., Foltz, Rosenstein, Lochbaum. & Davis, 2012).

Using the sample of responses, the system is then trained to associate the extracted features in each essay to scores that are assigned by human scorers. Machine learning-based approaches are typically used to determine the optimal set of features and the weights for each of the features to best model the scores for each essay. From these comparisons, a prompt and trait-specific scoring model can be derived to predict the scores that the same scorers would assign to any new responses. Based on this scoring model, new essays can be immediately scored by analysis of the features weighted according to the scoring model. The number of responses typically required to train the scoring engine varies depending on the type of prompt and expected use of the response. For general formative and content-based scoring, 200–300 essays are required to train the scoring engine. For an essay prompt in a high stakes assessment, a sample of about 500–1,000 student responses is typically preferred, while for a short-answer prompt 1,000 responses are recommended for best performance (see Foltz et al., 2013). These numbers allow for using part of the data to train the scoring engine while holding out the other part for testing and validation.

EVALUATION OF SCORING PERFORMANCE

AI-based prediction of scores should not be deployed unless it is tested and validated to determine if the performance matches a variety of criteria that can assure that the system will perform effectively across cases of its intended use. In scoring writing, a scoring engine's performance is typically evaluated by how well the scores match human scoring, but a better criterion should be how well the scores align with the constructs of interest (e.g., Williamson et al., 2012). Common benchmarks of performance compute the reliability of the scoring engine by examining the agreement of a scoring engine's predicted scores to human scorers, as compared to the agreement between human scorers. Metrics for computing the reliability include correlation, kappa, weighted kappa, and exact and adjacent agreement. Using "true scores" (e.g., the average of multiple scorers or the consensus score) for the comparison can provide more accurate measures of an engine's accuracy. However, human agreement is seldom sufficient as a means to evaluate performance (e.g., Rupp, 2018). Performance can be compared against external variables that provide a measure of the validity of the scoring, including comparison of engine scores with scores from concurrent administrations of tests with a similar construct, agreement with scores from subsequent tests, predicting student age or grade level, agreement to scorers with different levels of skill, and tests of scoring across different population subgroups.

UNDERSTANDING THE UNDERLYING ASSUMPTIONS OF MODELING

Construct Relevance

Building any machine learning model requires a number of assumptions that the combination of features provides an effective model of human performance. Just accurately predicting human scores is not enough. One key assumption is that the features being used are relevant to the constructs of interest. Building a scoring model can be considered to be similar to Evidence Centered Design (ECD; e.g., Mislevy, Behrens, Dicerbo, & Levy, 2012). In ECD, an evidence model defines the writing constructs of interest. Human scorers who score the essays assess this construct representation through using a scoring rubric as they evaluate the essays. By performing computational modeling on construct relevant features, the model provides an explicit linkage between the features being scored and the constructs. In this manner, automated scoring models can support validity arguments for how combined scoring features represent the constructs of interest.

However, features may appear to be effective measures of writing quality and may be loosely tied to the construct, yet may not be appropriate features to use in modeling. For example, a count of the number of words in an essay is often a good predictor the quality (e.g., Chodorow & Burstein, 2004; Page, 1967). There are sensible reasons why length serves as a proxy for attributes of the quality of a response, such as adequate content coverage requires a sufficient length to cover the topic and students without much knowledge on a topic or with low language ability typically can not generate sufficient words during a timed essay test. However, it doesn't provide a true measure of writing quality. Figure 5.1 shows an example of the relationship of word count to human rater scores for one prompt from the Automated Student Assessment Prize (ASAP) Kaggle competition (see Shermis & Hamner, 2012). The results show a correlation of 0.79 between word count and raters scores, which is close the agreement level between human raters. For the Kaggle competition of eight items, two sets of human scores correlated with word count above 0.8 and all correlations were above 0.5. Indeed, many of the top performing models used some kinds of word count features. While using this feature in a machine learning model may account for much of the variance, features that tend to rely on word count will often tend to overshadow other variables that may assess more construct relevant aspects such as the use of appropriate language, proper grammar, and so forth. Thus, automated scoring best practice requires using more construct relevant approaches to predicting score with features less obviously tied to length than unadorned measures such as word count.

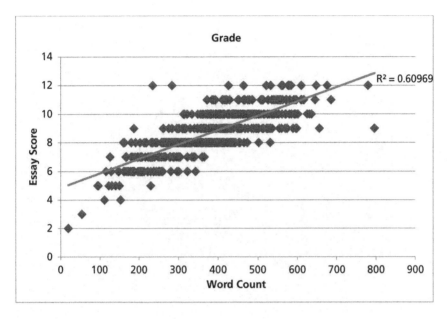

Figure 5.1 Correlation of word count to essay length in an ASAP essay set.

In addition, overall length is a quite easy parameter to pad in bad-faith attempts by students who can lard essays with content irrelevant words.

Understand Non-Linearities in Features

A typical approach to automated scoring is to apply machine learning methods such as linear regression. Indeed, almost all modeling of essay performance from the 1960s to the 1990s tended to use linear regression (see Foltz, Laham, & Landauer, 1999; Page, 1967). As a simplifying assumption, it makes intuitive sense; the presence of more (or less) of a feature indicates better performance. For example, fewer grammar errors means the essay is better; more relevant content means the essay is better. However, some construct relevant features do not have simple linear relationships with the quality of an essay. Coherence of an essay can be measured by examining the semantic overlap of one sentence to the next (see Foltz, Kintsch, & Landauer, 1998; Hearst, 1997). Figure 5.2 shows the relationship of sentence to sentence coherence in the same Kaggle prompt as used in Figure 5.1. The density of the responses are shown by the range from white to blue. The green line shows the linear regression fit of the feature to the prediction of human score. The red line shows a locally-weighted regression fit. In the mid-range, a linear model provides a reasonable approximation, but at the

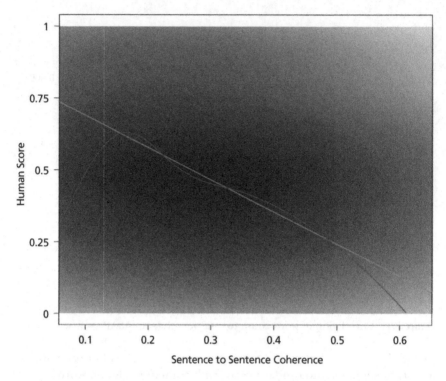

Figure 5.2 Sentence to Sentence coherence in a Kaggle essay set.

ends of the spectrum of coherence, there is a divergence from the human ratings. This is because essays that are too coherent, are just repetitive. Essays that are not at all coherent don't hold together. Both of these results correspond to poorer performance. While a linear model may provide a potentially effective approximation, using nonlinear modeling would better capture the subtle aspects of the construct of coherence. Thus, modelling such data requires both an understanding of the nature of how the variables perform within the algorithm, how the features are related to the constructs, and what kind of modeling may be most effective at accounting for their performance.

DETECTING BIAS IN MODELS

Machine learning models can be biased by training on non-construct relevant features (measurement bias) or by making inappropriate assumptions about the algorithms used to model those features (algorithm bias). But the models can also be biased by being trained on biased data (sample bias) or by not sampling subgroups appropriately (prejudice bias). Machine learning can leverage massive amounts of data to draw inferences. By "learning" from examples, and extracting patterns, it derives rules of what features in human behavior correspond to complex tasks. But if those examples contain bias, then the machine learning may infer that same bias. Three critical best practices in avoiding bias are to (a) select a broad sample of training examples to cover the range of possible input, (b) evaluate bias across subgroups and set criteria for effective performance, and (c) protect the model from scoring inappropriate input.

As an example, if students are given a writing prompt which asks: "Write an essay about a hero and describe why this person is a hero to you," there may be many ways for a student to describe what kind of a person fits their view of being a hero. Thus, it is important to capture the range of potential types of answers and not differentially penalize responses for the choice of their hero, instead of the quality of their explanation. This can be done by broadly selecting writing samples across the intended population, ensuring that responses from different subgroups are represented as well as using both high and low quality essays within the training sets.

Then, when a model is built, it should be tested against held-out data representing the various subgroups to ensure that different subgroups are not scored differently. For each of these subgroups, it is important to calculate various agreement indices (e.g., r, Kappa, Quadratic Kappa, Exact agreement, and standardized mean differences (SMDs) comparing human–human results and with IEA-human results (see Williamson, Xi, & Breyer, 2012) . Significant differences between subgroups should be flagged and should determine whether the model is appropriate or needs additional training data before it is used.

Protecting the Model

Once a model is finally operationally deployed, it is important to ensure that the model only scores examples that are within the range of the assumptions that were made by the model. This can be considered protecting the model from inappropriate input, or maybe more properly, protecting the results from models that are not built for that kind of input. The features used to analyze the essays provide a means to ascertain how well any essay falls within the distributional confines of the training set. By analyzing the features of the essays from the training set, we can therefore derive an expected range of essay features. The system can then determine if the value for a particular feature or the combined values for a group of features are beyond the training range. Those that fall outside the confidence interval of this range may indicate potential violations of the assumptions of the scoring model and may cause instabilities in the model. These violations may be due to students writing too much or too little, being off-topic or using a topic that is not represented in the training set, using language that is structured highly differently from what was in the training set, or intentional acts to game the system (e.g., Lochbaum, Rosenstein, & Foltz, 2013) such as larding of large words, copy-pasting material, or repeating content. In all such cases, the essays should not be scored by the model, but should be flagged for human evaluation.

CONCLUSION: KEEPING HUMANS IN THE LOOP

Finally, a best practice in automated scoring involves knowing that not all automated scoring should be automatic. Human oversight is needed to continually monitor and evaluate the performance of models as data comes in, to evaluate essays that fall outside the bounds of what can be scored by the models, and to update models if there is evidence of bias, drift, or declines in performance (see Way, Lochbaum, & Zurkowsky, 2016). For operational scoring, policies and procedures can be established to have humans score some or all essays using a variety of criteria based on the stakes of the assessment, the variability in the quality of the responses, and the need to validate performance. For example, for many summative assessments, a random subsample should be held out for validation by human scorers in order to detect drift of both human and computer scoring. In addition, essays that appear to violate the assumptions of the model, or appear to have gaming-like features should be detected and sent for human evaluation. For very high-stakes assessments, essays can be scored by one human and by the computer. If the two agree, the score is set. If they disagree, the essay can be adjudicated by an additional human. For formative writing, all essays may be automatically scored as students iterate over drafts (Foltz & Rosenstein, 2015). Unusual essays can be sent to the instructor and potentially the final draft of the essay can be evaluated by the instructor.

Keeping humans in the loop recognizes that there are strengths and weaknesses in both human and automated scoring. Automated scoring provides a fast, accurate, consistent scoring for essays that fall within the assumptions of the model. Human scoring provides deliberate careful analyses that can capture subtle nuances in language that the computer may not detect and can give better directed feedback that can connect to the students. Best practices in automated scoring ensures that we understand these strengths and weaknesses and establish procedures to use it to its greatest effectiveness.

REFERENCES

Beigman-Klebanov, B., Madnani, N., Burstein, J. C., & Sumasundaran, S. (2014). Content importance models for scoring writing from sources. In *Proceedings of the 52 Annual Meeting of the Association for Computational Linguistics* (pp. 247–252). Baltimore, MD.

Bunch, M. B., Vaughn, D., & Miel, S. (2016). Automated scoring in assessment systems. In Y. Rosen, S. Ferrara, & M. Mosharraf (Eds.), *Technology tools for real-world skill development* (pp. 611–626). Hershey, PA: IGI Global.

Burstein, J., Chodorow, M., & Leacock, C. (2004). Automated essay evaluation: The Criterion Online writing service. *AI Magazine, 25*(3), 27–36.

Carbonnel, J. R. (1970). AI in CAI: An artificial-intelligence approach to computer-assisted instruction. *IEEE Transactions on Man-Machine Systems, 11*(4), 190–202.

Chodorow, M., & Burstein, J. (2004). *Beyond essay length: Evaluating e-rater's performance on TOEFL essays* (Research Report 73). Princeton, NJ: Educational Testing Service.

Foltz, P. W., Gilliam, S., & Kendall, S. (2000). Supporting content-based feedback in online writing evaluation with LSA. *Interactive Learning Environments, 8*(2), 111–129.

Foltz, P. W., Kintsch, W., & Landauer, T. K. (1998). The measurement of textual coherence with Latent Semantic Analysis. *Discourse Processes, 25*(2&3), 285–307.

Foltz, P. W., Laham, D., & Landauer, T. K. (1999). The intelligent essay assessor: Applications to educational technology. *Interactive Multimedia Education Journal of Computer Enhanced Learning, 1*(2).

Foltz, P. W., & Rosenstein, M. (2015). Analysis of a large-scale formative writing assessment system with automated feedback. In G. Kiczales, D. M. Russel, & B. Woolf (Eds.), *Proceedings of the 2nd ACM conference on Learning@Scale* (pp. 339–342). New York, NY: ACM.

Foltz, P. W., Rosenstein, M., Lochbaum, K. E., & Davis, L. (2012, April). *Improving reliability throughout the automated scoring process.* Paper presented at the National Council on Measurement In Education Conference, Vancouver, BC.

Foltz, P. W., Streeter, L. A., Lochbaum, K. E., & Landauer, T. K (2013). Implementation and applications of the Intelligent Essay Assessor. In M. Shermis & J. Burstein (Eds.), *Handbook of automated essay evaluation* (pp. 68–88). New York, NY: Routledge.

Franzke, M., Kintsch, E., Caccamise, D., Johnson, N., & Dooley, S. (2005). Computer support for comprehension and writing. *Educational Computing Research, 33*(1), 53–80.

Friend, T. (2018, May 14). How frightened should we be of A.I.? *New Yorker Magazine.* Retrieved from https://www.newyorker.com/magazine/2018/05/14/how-frightened-should-we-be-of-ai

Gerbner, G., Holsti, O. R., Krippendorff, K., Paisley, W. J., & Stone, Ph. J. (Eds.). (1969). *The analysis of communication content: Development in scientific theories and computer techniques.* New York, NY: Wiley.

Hearst, M. (1997). TextTiling: Segmenting text into multi-paragraph subtopic passages. *Computational Linguistics, 23*(1), 33–64.

Higgins, D., Brew, C., Hellman, M., Ziai, R., Chen, L., Cahill, A.,...Blackmore, J. (2014) Is getting the right answer just about choosing the right words? The role of syntactically-informed features in short answer scoring. arXiv: 1404.0801,v2.

Krippendorff, K., & Bock, M. A. (2009). *The content analysis reader.* Thousand Oaks, CA: SAGE.

Landauer, T. K., Laham, D., & Foltz, P. W. (2001). The intelligent essay assessor, the debate on automated essay grading. *IEEE Intelligent Systems, 15,* 27–31.

Lochbaum, K. E., Rosenstein, M., & Foltz, P. W. (2013, April). *Detection of gaming in automated scoring of essays with the IEA.* Paper presented at the 75th Annual meeting of National Council of Measurement in Education.

Mislevy, R. J., Behrens, J. T., Dicerbo, K. E., & Levy, R. (2012). Design and discovery in educational assessment: Evidence-centered design, psychometrics, and educational data mining. *Journal of Educational Data Mining, 4*(1), 11–48.

Page, E. B. (1967). The imminence of grading essays by computer. *Phi Delta Kappan, 47,* 238–243.

Perelman, L. (2018). *Why and how automated essay scoring doesn't work (most of the time) & the perils and promise of automated essay evaluation.* Retrieved from http://lesperelman.com/writing-assessment-robo-grading/presentation-on-automated-essay-scoring/

PwC. (2018). *Sizing the prize: What's the real value of AI for your business and how can you capitalise?* Retrieved from http://preview.thenewsmarket.com/Previews/PWC/DocumentAssets/476830.pdf

Rupp, A. A. (2018). Designing, evaluating, and deploying automated scoring systems with validity in mind: Methodological design decisions. *Applied Measurement in Education, 31*(3), 191–214. https://doi.org/10.1080/08957347.2018.1464448

Shermis, M.D., & Burstein, J. (2013). *Handbook of automated essay evaluation: Current applications and future directions.* New York, NY: Routledge.

Shermis, M., & Hammer, B. (2012, April). *Contrasting state-of-the-art automated scoring of essays: Analysis.* Paper presented at National Council of Measurement in Education Annual Meeting, Vancouver, CA.

Smith, T. (2018, June 30). More state opting to 'Robo-Grade' Student Essays by Computer. *NPR.* Retrieved from https://www.npr.org/2018/06/30/624373367/more-states-opting-to-robo-grade-student-essays-by-computer

Thurlow, M. M., Hermann, A., & Foltz, P. W. (2010, November). *Preparing MSA science items for artificial intelligence scoring.* Talk presented at the Maryland Assessment Group Conference, Ocean City, MD.

Way, D., Lochbaum, K. E., & Zurkowsky, J. (2016, June). *Continuous flow scoring of prose constructed responses: A hybrid of automated and human scoring.* Session presented at the National Conference on Student Assessment, Philadelphia, PA.

Williamson, D. M., Bennett, R., Lazer, S., Bernstein, J., Foltz, P. W., Landauer, T. K.,...Sweeney, K. (2010, June). *Automated scoring for the assessment of common core standards.* Retrieved from https://www.ets.org/s/commonassessments/pdf/AutomatedScoringAssessCommonCoreStandards.pdf

Williamson, D. M., Xi, X., & Breyer, F. J. (2012). A framework for evaluation and use of automated scoring. *Educational Measurement: Issues and Practice, 31*(1), 2–13. https://doi.org/10.1111/emip.2012.31.issue-1

Wilson, J., & Andrada, G. N. (2013, April). *Examining patterns of writing performance of struggling writers on a statewide classroom benchmark writing assessment.* Paper presented at the annual meeting of the American Educational Research Association, Classroom Assessment SIG, San Francisco, CA.

Wilson, J., & Andrada, G. N. (2016). Using automated feedback to improve writing quality: Opportunities and challenges. In Y. Rosen, S. Ferrara, & M. Mosharraf (Eds.), *Handbook of research on technology tools for real-world skill development* (pp. 678–703). Hershey, PA: IGI Global.

CHAPTER 6

ITEM POOL DESIGN AND ASSEMBLY

The State of the Art

Jeffrey M. Patton[1]
Financial Industry Regulatory Authority (FINRA)

Ray Y. Yan
Financial Industry Regulatory Authority (FINRA)

Historically, technology has dictated that test developers craft a small number of test forms and host relatively infrequent administrations. But in recent decades, the testing industry has made a major shift to so-called "continuous" testing in which a candidate can make an appointment at a testing center at a time that is convenient for them. The test form is administered on a computer, and the test form can be generated on demand from a large set of items, often referred to as an item bank.

In response to this shift, test developers have increasingly utilized an item "pool" as a middle layer between the item bank and test forms. The idea is that the item bank contains all items, in all stages of development, whereas the item pool contains a subset of only operational items, and it is

Application of Artificial Intelligence to Assessment, pages 115–124
Copyright © 2020 by Information Age Publishing
All rights of reproduction in any form reserved.

from this pool that items are drawn to assemble a candidate's test form. The details of this process can differ quite a bit among testing programs, but the basic structure is the same.

Why have testing programs opted for this more complex structure? One reason may be to better organize test items. Items cannot be classified into one of only a few development categories. Instead of simply being an operational or pretest item, an item might be under review, being edited, or temporarily removed from operational use due to overexposure. Having a pool makes clearer to everyone involved which items are eligible for operational use.

Another benefit of item pools is the increasing importance of test security. In contrast with a paper-and-pencil test that may have infrequent, large-scale administrations, a program with continuous testing might expose hundreds or thousands of items. Within a short time frame, an organized group of candidates could memorize and distribute a large portion of these items. An item pool serves as a "buffer" between the item bank and the public by only exposing a portion of the bank at any point in time. Akin to paper-and-pencil testing, where a backup test form might be made in case the primary form is compromised, a new item pool can be assembled from the item bank if any efforts to steal the active pool are successful. In addition, the developer can periodically "rotate" through active pools to help prevent high exposure rates and mitigate attempts to steal content.

A third (and perhaps the most convincing) reason for item pools is the ability to "design" the pool so as to best support the desired properties of test forms. For example, a mismatch between the distribution of item difficulty in the bank and the distribution of ability in the candidate population can lead to very uneven item exposure rates. By explicitly choosing the set of items from which test forms can be assembled, it can be much easier to control exposure rates.

Unfortunately, the literature on item pools is quite sparse. Much research has focused on methods for item selection and test assembly, but much less research exists to inform the design of item pools and methods to assemble pools from an item bank. Thus the goals of this chapter are to explore issues specific to the design of item pools and to present some practical pool assembly methods. Our background and focus is on the context of continuous, computer-based testing in which no two candidates see the same form (e.g., computerized adaptive testing or linear-on-the-fly testing). Nonetheless, we seek to present guidance and strategies that can be applied to many kinds of testing programs.

DESIGN OF A SINGLE ITEM POOL

The term "pool design" has no precise definition in the literature. In this chapter, it refers to the process of establishing the desired categorical and quantitative attributes of the items making up a pool. Some common categorical attributes of items include content area (e.g., algebra, geometry, trigonometry) and cognitive complexity (e.g., factual recall, synthesis, application), whereas quantitative attributes might include the value of Fisher information at a given ability value, the average time required to answer the item, or the item's word count.

In this section, we will often find it useful to distinguish between the categorical and quantitative attributes of items. Alternatively, it may be simpler to refer to item attributes in a more general way introduced by van der Linden (2005). Suppose there are K relevant attributes for all items in the bank, whether categorical or quantitative. Also suppose that all quantitative attributes have been discretized into a reasonable number of categories. Rather than visualizing the item bank as a matrix with K columns and a row for each item, we could instead visualize a K-dimensional array where each cell contains the frequency count of items possessing that particular combination of attributes. This array is referred to as the "design space," and each individual cell is referred to as a "design point." For example, if there are three attributes that contain four, six, and eight categories respectively, there are $4 \times 6 \times 8 = 192$ design points in the space, and these points can be indexed by $d = 1, 2, \ldots, D$, where $D = 192$.

Aside from containing at least one complete test form, it is not necessarily obvious what properties a good or "optimal" pool should have. The design of test forms is (arguably) more straightforward. Usually there are specifications for the distribution of content, item types, and/or cognitive complexity. If the goal of testing is to make a pass/fail decision or to achieve a sufficiently precise test score, common choices are to maximize Fisher information at the pass point or to adopt some form of adaptive testing, respectively. The composition of the item pool will have a large impact on the success of these goals; as stated by van der Linden (2005, p. 292), "The composition of the item pool is 'our most important constraint on test-assembly problems.'" In the following sections, we describe two approaches to pool design: a straightforward heuristic method and a more rigorous approach termed "optimal pool design" (van der Linden, 2005).

A Heuristic Method for Pool Design

An intuitive way to conceptualize an item pool is as a large test form that is, say, N times the size of a normal test form. In this way, we can be assured that the available distribution of items across design points mirrors the desired distribution for test forms. As an example, refer to the hypothetical math test described in Table 6.1. The items can be described by two different categorical attributes (content area and cognitive complexity) which contain two and three categories, respectively, yielding six design

TABLE 6.1 Design of a Hypothetical Mathematics Test Form and Item Pool[a]

Design Point	Content Area	Cognitive Complexity	Form Count	Desired Pool Count	Bank Count	Actual Pool Count
1	Algebra	Recall	2	10	19	10
2	Algebra	Synthesis	4	20	18	18
3	Algebra	Application	4	20	33	20
4	Geometry	Recall	4	20	21	20
5	Geometry	Synthesis	8	40	31	31
6	Geometry	Application	8	40	59	40
Total			**30**	**150**	**181**	**139**

[a] In this example, the size of the item bank (relative to the item pool) is probably too small to justify the use of pools. These item counts are for illustrative purposes only.

points. The column labeled "Form Count" lists the number of items from each design point required for a test form, and the adjacent column ("Pool Count") lists the number of items required for the item pool for $N = 5$. (We consider the choice of N later in this section.) A test form should have 30 items, and accordingly, the item pool should contain 150 items.

However, unless the test developer has anticipated a pool of this size, the existing item bank may not contain the desired number of items for all design points. In Table 6.1, we can see that the bank contains a surplus of items for four of the design points but falls short for two of the design points (see the column labeled "Bank Count"). So the actual pool will contain (at most) 139 items. This shortage brings up a larger issue: When designing an item pool, the existing item bank may not be able to support it. But design should not be overly constrained by the available bank. It is during pool assembly that we may need to temporarily adjust pool specifications to accommodate the bank, whereas pool design should reflect long-term goals and inform future item-writing assignments so that the bank can eventually support the desired pools.

Next, how should an item pool be designed if test forms are intended to be optimal in some way? Suppose that our hypothetical math test is designed to make a pass/fail decision and forms must have maximum Fisher information at the passing point. If we continue to think of an item pool as a large test form, the pool should also have maximum information at the passing point. Intuitively, this is an appropriate choice: If test forms should have large numbers of items located near the passing point, the pool should make available large numbers of items near the passing point.

However, the "large test form" analogy is not always the best guide. van der Linden (2005, p. 311) provides an example where the goal is to design a pool for a computerized adaptive testing (CAT) program. The goal of CAT is to obtain a sufficiently precise estimate of each candidate's ability, so items are chosen to maximize information (or a similar criterion) at the candidate's current ability estimate (roughly speaking). In this situation, the definition of an "optimal" test form is different for every candidate, and it is unclear what a single, optimal[2] pool might look like.

One idea is to have the distribution of item difficulty in the pool match the distribution of ability in the candidate population. But van der Linden (2005) points out that this is incorrect. Having a large number of items located near a given candidate's ability level does not ensure that his or her test form will have sufficient information. This is because test forms cannot be assembled based on item difficulty alone; forms must also meet a variety of non-statistical constraints (e.g., content distribution, item exposure control). For a given candidate, what we actually want is a full test form that has maximum information at his or her ability level. So van der Linden (2005) suggests designing a pool as a set of test forms such that their locations of maximum information have a distribution resembling that of the candidate population.

This example makes clear that the definition of "optimal" for a test form depends on the purpose of testing (e.g., a sufficiently precise test score, or a pass/fail decision). In contrast, an optimal item pool is one that is "best" able to support the construction of optimal forms. For our hypothetical math test, the two definitions imply similar designs for test forms and for the pool. But in the CAT example, the definition of an optimal test form cannot be applied to pools.

Finally, how might one go about choosing the size of the item pool? That is, how to choose the value of N? Policy may dictate a minimum size for the pool, but otherwise, there is no straightforward answer to this question. In the context of continuous testing, the use of one item pool almost certainly implies the use of multiple, "rotating" item pools. Thus the size of the pools depends on the size of the available item bank, the frequency of pool rotation (e.g., monthly, quarterly), and the amount of overlap allowed (if any) among pairs of pools.

Assuming the rotation frequency and bank size are fixed, there is a direct tradeoff between pool size and pairwise pool overlap. A large item pool will yield relatively low item exposure rates while it is active, but the overlap among pools will be higher. In contrast, small pools will have lower overlap but yield higher exposure rates. Suffice to say, an acceptable compromise between pool size and overlap can be found via simulation, and the result very much depends on the particulars of the testing program.

Optimal Pool Design

The heuristic procedure described in the previous section is a straightforward, robust method to design an item pool. However, it is a method based on intuition, and there is not necessarily a clear answer to what an optimal pool looks like. Optimal pool design, introduced by van der Linden (2005), offers a more principled approach with several advantages: a priori control of item exposure rates, a pool design that is explicitly optimized for a given testing program, and even potential to minimize the cost of item production.

This method is rather complex and van der Linden (2005) covers it in some detail, so here we provide a conceptual overview. To begin, the power of optimal pool design stems from its use of linear programming (LP), a mathematical method for constrained optimization. Perhaps the most popular use of LP in psychometrics is the assembly of test forms. As an example, suppose we want to build a 30-item test from a pool of 200 items. We must express the desired test specifications as linear equations, as well as the criterion to be optimized (e.g., maximum information at a passing score). Then the LP solver software efficiently searches among all sets of 30 items that meet the constraints and finds one that optimizes the criterion. LP has been successfully applied to a wide variety of test assembly problems over the past several decades, and LP has numerous advantages over traditional, sequential methods of test assembly (e.g., Diao & van der Linden, 2011; van der Linden, 2005).

The application of LP to pool design is a bit more complex. We begin by assuming that the item bank is infinite and is composed not of a list of items, but a list of design points. Essentially, one simulates the administration of test forms (assembled using LP) and keeps track of how many items are used from each design point. In this way, one uses empirical evidence (albeit simulated) to obtain a distribution of design points (and pool size) that is optimal for the particular test and candidate population.

In addition, there are two distinct advantages proposed by van der Linden (2005). First is the ability to control item exposure rates. We will not delve into the details, but it is straightforward to adjust the output of the LP simulation to ensure that no exposure rate is above a particular value. Second, van der Linden (2005) illustrated the use of a cost function as the function to be optimized. Specifically, we can estimate the cost of developing an item at a particular design point and favor design points that favor lower costs. Estimating the cost of development for many different types of items may seem like a big challenge, but see van der Linden (2005) for some practical methods to do this.

ASSEMBLY OF A SINGLE ITEM POOL

Having presented some approaches to item pool design, we now address the topic of pool assembly. Although pool assembly itself has not received much attention in the literature, much of the research on test assembly can be generalized to the assembly of pools. As such, we do not go into much detail here but instead refer the reader to other sources.

First, LP is a powerful, flexible tool for item pool assembly. Most LP research is focused on test assembly, but there are some helpful sources concerned specifically with item pools including Ariel, Veldkamp, and van der Linden (2004); Han and Rudner (2014); van der Linden (2005); and van der Linden, Ariel, and Veldkamp (2006). Though the up-front costs of setting up an LP model can be high (e.g., translating design constraints into linear equations), the benefits are clear for highly constrained or complex assembly problems. For an in-depth treatment of the advantages of LP, see van der Linden (2005).

Instead, we might choose to employ a heuristic method for pool assembly. Many methods have been proposed for the sequential selection of items for test forms, including the maximum priority index (Cheng & Chang, 2009) and the weighted deviations model (Stocking & Swanson, 1993). These methods could be adapted for pool assembly, and they have the advantage of being (somewhat) easier to understand than LP. However, any change in a pool's design may require a large change in the selection algorithm.

Finally, the most optimistic option is available when optimal pool design is used and all required items are available in the item bank. In this case, no optimization is needed because the counts of items at each design point are already optimized. So we need only to collect the required items that form the pool. As pointed out by van der Linden (2005) however, this situation is quite unlikely given the difficulty in controlling the statistical or other quantitative attributes of items.

Regardless of the methods used for pool design and assembly, the use of one item pool almost certainly implies the use of multiple, "rotating" item pools (as mentioned previously). In this situation, there is the risk of using the most desirable items in the first few pools, resulting in suboptimal pools later on. Instead, it is much preferred to keep the properties of pools constant over time; this is to ensure the consistency of measurement reliability and validity over time, as well as to ensure a consistent candidate experience. We address this important issue in the next section.

ASSEMBLY OF MULTIPLE ITEM POOLS

As mentioned previously, if a testing program has decided to use item pools, this almost certainly implies the use of a system of rotating item pools. If a given pool is designed to be optimal in some way, there is the danger that all "good" items will be used in earlier pools, leading to suboptimal pools later. Thus it is essential to ensure the consistency of pools over time. However, even if a pool is not designed to be optimal, we may still want to ensure consistency so as to ensure a uniform candidate experience, regardless of the particular pool in use. Little research has explored this issue, but some practical methods have been proposed.

Before describing these methods, we should point out that typically, a testing program's item bank is not a static thing—items are constantly being added, removed, evaluated, and so on. Therefore, it is unlikely that a developer will assemble several pools at a time with the intention of activating all of them at some point in the future. Rather, it is more likely that each pool will be assembled as needed. Additionally, we assume in this section that pool assembly is done using LP. Heuristic methods may very well be useful here, but for simplicity, we assume that LP is used.

van der Linden (2005) suggests a few different approaches to this problem. One option is to assemble several pools simultaneously using LP. By using the same constraints across pools, we can ensure an even spread of the most desirable items across pools. And if only one pool is needed, the remaining pools can be returned to the item bank.

A simpler alternative is to employ the "Big Shadow Test" method (van der Linden, 2005). Essentially, we simultaneously assemble the desired pool along with a "big" pool that is, say n times the size of a normal pool. By proportionally aggregating the constraints for the larger pool, we can ensure that the most desirable items are also distributed proportionally between the two pools. Similar to the previous method, the large "shadow" pool is then returned to the item bank.

Rather than assembling several pools at the same time, it is also possible to build pools in isolation but still ensure the even spread of the best items over time. This situation is analogous to when item exposure control is implemented in the assembly of individual test forms. Two simple options entail keeping track of the composition of all prior pools. When building a new pool, we can set explicit overlap constraints with several previous pools. An alternative is to use selection penalties; with this method, we can prefer to use items that have not appeared in a pool for some time, whereas those items used more recently can be "penalized."

Perhaps a more straightforward option is analogous to "randomesque" exposure control (Kingsbury & Zara, 1989). Suppose we want to assemble a pool with maximum information at a passing score. Instead of simply maximizing information, which would lead to the overly "greedy" selection of the best items, we can maximize a stochastic function of information. For example, we might multiply information by a random number drawn from a uniform distribution between zero and one. This method ensures that the best items are not all concentrated in one pool. By "tuning" the stochastic variable, we can control the degree of overlap between subsequent pools.

SUMMARY AND CONCLUSION

Although relatively little psychometric research has focused on issues specific to item pools, it is clear that the large body of existing research on test assembly can be leveraged to great benefit. Accordingly, we have presented and summarized a number of practical methods for both the design and assembly of a system of rotating item pools.

It is also clear that the use of item pools holds great promise for operational testing programs. First, item pools are a convenient way to better organize the items of a testing program. Second, rotating through operational pools offers a relatively low-cost approach to help prevent or mitigate the attempts of unscrupulous candidates to steal content or cheat. And lastly, crafting a "middle layer" between the item bank and test forms allows us the valuable opportunity to optimize the set of items available for operational use.

It is our hope that this chapter will inspire more widespread use of item pools; we also hope to make clear the need for additional research in this area.

NOTE

1. The views and analysis expressed herein are those of the authors and do not necessarily reflect those of FINRA or of the author's colleagues. FINRA, as a matter of policy, disclaims responsibility for any private publication or statement by any employee.
2. The term "optimal" is applied to pools only loosely in this section. It reflects the fact that a pool might be assembled to optimize some criterion, even if a heuristic design method is used. This is distinct from the term "optimal pool design" (described in the next section) which seeks to optimize the pool design itself.

REFERENCES

Ariel, A., Veldkamp, B. P., & van der Linden, W. J. (2004). Constructing rotating item pools for constrained adaptive testing. *Journal of Educational Measurement, 41,* 345–359.

Cheng, Y., & Chang, H.-H. (2009). The maximum priority index method for severely constrained item selection in computerized adaptive testing. *British Journal of Mathematical and Statistical Psychology, 62,* 369–383.

Diao, Q., & van der Linden, W. J. (2011). Automated test assembly using lp_Solve version 5.5 in R. *Applied Psychological Measurement, 35,* 398–409.

Han, K. T., & Rudner, L. M. (2014). *Item pool construction using mixed integer quadratic programming* (GMAC Research Report 14-01). Retrieved from gmac.com

Kingsbury, G. G., & Zara, A. R. (1989). Procedures for selecting items for computerized adaptive tests. *Applied Measurement in Education, 2,* 359–375.

Stocking, M. L., & Swanson, L. (1993). A method for severely constrained item selection in adaptive testing. *Applied Psychological Measurement, 17,* 277–292.

van der Linden, W. J. (2005). *Linear models for optimal test design.* New York, NY: Springer.

van der Linden, W. J., Ariel, A., & Veldkamp, B. P. (2006). Assembling a computerized adaptive testing item pool as a set of linear tests. *Journal of Educational and Behavioral Statistics, 31,* 81–99.

CHAPTER 7

AUTOMATED TEST ASSEMBLY

Case Studies in Classical Test Theory and Item Response Theory

Siang Chee Chuah
The College Board

Donovan Hare
University of British Columbia

Luz Bay
The College Board

Thomas Proctor
The College Board

Selecting items for an item pool to constitute a test form can be a relatively simple task. However, complex test specifications, item enemies, strict statistical requirements, and other constraints can make it challenging to manually assemble test forms. There could be multiple moving components to consider and making one change can impact other components.

Application of Artificial Intelligence to Assessment, pages 125–140
Copyright © 2020 by Information Age Publishing
All rights of reproduction in any form reserved.

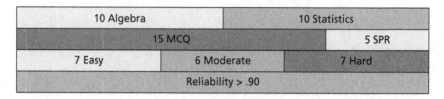

10 Algebra		10 Statistics	
15 MCQ			5 SPR
7 Easy	6 Moderate	7 Hard	
Reliability > .90			

Figure 7.1 Example of layers of test specifications.

One way to illustrate test constraints is as a series of layers. Let us say that we are selecting 20 items to build a math test form. The hypothetical specifications for the test form are as follows (see Figure 7.1 for illustration):

- 10 items from algebra,
- 10 items from statistics,
- 15 items are multiple-choice items (MCQ),
- 5 items are student produced response (SPR),
- 7 easy items,
- 6 moderate difficulty items,
- 7 hard items, and
- reliability of the test form should be over .90.

Each layer constitutes specifications that have items that are mutually exclusive. In the example, an algebra item cannot be a statistics item. On the other hand, an algebra item can be an MCQ item or an SPR item. In this case the constraints are not mutually exclusive.

The degree to which each layer is independent from the other layers can add to the challenge of assembling the test form. For example, if 7 of the algebra items must be MCQ items and 3 of the algebra items must be SPR, then it may be more difficult to meet the narrower specifications (see Figure 7.2 as an example). The item pool would need to support items that meet specific combinations of content, format, and difficulty.

The irony is that the narrower the specifications, the easier it is to manually select items for an item pool. There are fewer moving components, thereby simplifying the assembly process.

10 Algebra			10 Statistics		
7 MCQ		3 SPR	8 MCQ		2 SPR
3 Easy	3 Moderate	4 Hard	4 Easy	3 Moderate	3 Hard
Reliability > .90					

Figure 7.2 Example of layers of test specifications that are more rigid.

The specificity of the requirement may not be necessary for the test, nor might it be supported by the item pool as items with some combinations of characteristics may be scarce. For example, it may be more difficult to develop algebra MCQ items that are difficult. Disconnecting some of the layers of the test specifications may be appropriate, as it will provide more flexibility in the assembly of forms. Unfortunately, greater flexibility may mean that there are more moving components to consider when assembling the form, making it more challenging to do it manually. Furthermore, the scarcity of some types of items may mean that we must be more judicious in selecting them, to more efficiently distribute them amongst the test forms being assembled.

AUTOMATED TEST ASSEMBLY (ATA)

Fortunately, computers are adept at following rules and balancing multiple assembly specifications or constraints (van der Linden, 2005, 2017). As such, software to assemble test forms can be a boon for test form assembly. The number of constraints and the size of the item pool is only limited by the capacity of the computer and software. ATA software is not perfect. It can only assemble forms based on the specifications that are programmed into the software. This issue can be illustrated as an ice cream truck problem. In this situation, let us say that three passages are selected to be on a test. However, all three passages are about ice cream trucks. There are no test specifications that prohibit more than one passage being selected that pertain to ice cream trucks. Moreover, the items and passages are not tagged to identify ice cream trucks. However, the form was rejected for having three passages that are about ice cream trucks. This example is meant to illustrate there are sometimes specifications that are not defined, nor are they coded in the item metadata, but arise when test forms are reviewed. In such situations, human intervention is necessary, and it may be better to think of ATA forms as a starting point for manual form assembly.

FORM ASSEMBLY FOR COMPUTERIZED TESTS

Form assembly using computers is not new. If we think of it, there are many instances of tests that are fully assembled by computers. Linear-on-the-fly test (LOFT) forms are fixed length forms that are assembled on-demand by a computer (van der Linden, 2005). It is an instance of ATA with little if any human intervention for form assembly. By extension, computer adaptive tests are an example of ATA, albeit with the added function that the test adapts based on the examinee's response. Similarly, ATA could also be used to build multi-stage adaptive tests (Melican, Breithaupt, & Zhang, 2010). It has the capacity to assure that whatever route an examinee takes through a multi-stage adaptive test, that all the constraints are met.

COMPONENTS IN ATA

There are three basic components to ATA: the item pool, the test specifications, and the ATA software (see Figure 7.3). The item pool is a list of the items available for selection for the test form. This would typically include item identifier code, metadata of the item content, and item statistics. The test specifications or constraints are the rules for test assembly. This might include the number of items on a test, the number of items by content, and the desired difficulty profile of the test items on the form. Finally, the ATA software is used to assemble the items together based on the test constraints.

CHARACTERISTICS OF ATA SOFTWARE

Heuristic or Optimal

There are two basic methods for ATA software to assemble test forms. One is the heuristic method, which utilizes general rule-of-thumb strategies to assemble the form. See van der Linden (2005) and van der Linden and Li (2016) for a comprehensive description of heuristic methods. They are

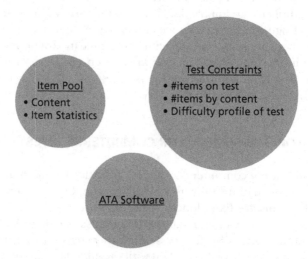

Figure 7.3 Components for form assembly.

extremely fast and efficient, and therefore can be scaled-up very easily. One drawback with heuristic methods is that it is not known if the solution is optimal, or how far from optimality the solution is. At least not without doing additional analysis. In contrast, using the optimization method, such as linear optimization, we can gauge the degree of optimality of the solution. Optimality in this case is the best combination of items for the test form, that is based on the available item pool and the test constraints. The unit of measure defining optimality is defined by the user, as expressed in the ATA software.

Sequential or Simultaneous

Test forms can be assembled in sequential order or all at once. Each build strategy has its benefits and costs. Sequential building can be thought of as building one test form at a time until all the forms are built or building a subset of forms first before moving onto the next set, up until the end. Technically, you could conceive of sequential building as selecting one item at a time until you have a complete form, and then continue until you have built all the test forms. This would be akin to a computer adaptive test (CAT). The benefit of assembling smaller units is that fewer computer resources are required at any one time, and the net result can be faster assembly times. As the unit size increases, the computational resources asymptotically increase, thereby potentially lengthening the build time.

Soft or Hard

There are two basic types of test constraints, soft constraints and hard constraints. Hard constraints are constraints or rules that are inviolable. For example, for a fixed length test, the number of items on a test is a hard constraint. It is not acceptable to have a test form with an extra item or an item short. As a consequence of this requirement, ATA software will not generate a test form if it violates a hard constraint.

In comparison, soft constraints are more of a "would like to have" rather than a must have. In this case, the program will try to get the test forms as close to the desired constraint but will still generate the form even if it violates the preference. Both hard constraints and soft constraints can apply to the same content. For example, a test might have a soft constraint to have seven items about algebra, and a hard constraint to have a minimum of five algebra items and a maximum of ten algebra items. As a result, the ATA software will strive to produce a test form that has seven algebra items but may produce a test form with nine algebra items. In the context of linear optimization, this is expressed in the objective function of the program (van der Linden, 2005). The objective function can be setup to minimize or maximize the certain values, which for convenience we will call penalty points in the context of this chapter.

Let us say that every deviation from the desired seven algebra items is a penalty point. Picking nine items would mean that there are two penalty points. We can program the ATA software to minimize the number of penalty points in the objective function, thereby prompting the ATA software to try and pick seven items. There can only be one objective function in the program, so if you have more than one constraint, changing the size of the penalty points allows the user to prioritize some constraints over others. If each deviation for picking a trigonometry is worth ten penalty points, then the ATA software would choose to make more deviations for algebra, in comparison to trigonometry. In this manner, the ATA software is setup to prioritize some constraints over others.

HOW DOES LINEAR PROGRAMMING WORK?

The following example illustrates a linear programming problem (see Table 7.1). Let us say that you run a factory making two models of hibachis. You would like to know what combination of the two hibachis would gather the most profit. There are limits to how many cast iron ingots and labor hours available in a day and you decide how many of each to build, within the constraints of your limited resources.

The goal of the example in Table 7.1 is to maximize profit. Therefore, the objective function would be to maximize

$$\text{Profit} = 2.00x + 1.50y$$

There is a limited amount cast iron ingots available, so one constraint for selecting the two units of hibachi's is

$$3x + 4y \le 1,000$$

TABLE 7.1 Hibachi Model Constraints

Hibachi Model	x	y	Maximum per Day
Profit	$2.00	$1.50	
Cast Iron Ingots	3	4	1,000
Labor Hours	6	3	1,200

There is a limited amount of labor available to build the hibachis. The constraint for labor units is

$$6x + 3y \leq 1{,}200$$

There are also logical constraints to the hibachi problem. You can't make negative numbers of hibachis, so there are constraints for only positive numbers of hibachis.

$$x \geq 0$$
$$y \geq 0$$

Note, that the objective function for linear optimization problems can only be expressed in terms of addition and subtraction. Also, the constraints cannot be expressed as strict inequality (i.e., no less than or greater than). Which is why all constraints are expressed as less than or equal to, or greater than or equal to.

Figure 7.4 illustrates the possible combinations of hibachis that could be produced in a day given the constraints. Each point on the grid within the quadrilateral is a possible combination of hibachis. The objective function represents the amount of profit. With the goal of the problem to identify the maximum profit that could be made during the day, we can find the maximum profit level by pushing the objective function out as far as we can within the quadrilateral. In this example, the maximum point is one hundred and twenty x and one hundred and sixty y hibachis. This is a maximum of $480 profit per day.

For the assembly of test forms, it is not plausible to select half of an item to be administered on a test. Rounding solutions to the closest integer is not a guarantee that the solution is optimal, or even if the solution is viable.

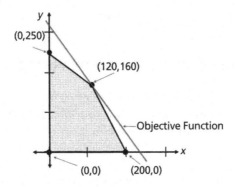

Figure 7.4 Hibachi problem feasibility set.

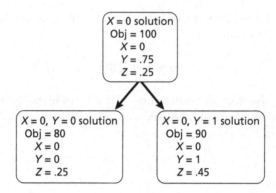

Figure 7.5 Branch and bound.

To resolve this, ATA utilizes mixed integer programs (Nemhauser & Wolsey, 1999), which is a special case of linear programing that have some of the variables restricted to integers. It guarantees that any solution produced is consistent with the constraints.

This leads us to the branch-and-bound search tree (van der Linden, 2005). Let us say that we would like to maximize the objective function, and we have three dichotomous variables (X, Y, Z) that we must identify either as a 0 or 1 (see Figure 7.5). The program has determined that the maximum possible objective function, otherwise known as the upper bound, is 100 when $X = 0$, but have not identified the values for Y and Z. This is not a viable solution, as both Y and Z are not integers. So as part of the search, the program can branch into $Y = 0$ and $Y = 1$. In either case the upper bound of the objective function when $Y = 0$ is 80, and the upper bound of the objective function when $Y = 1$ is 90. At first glance we might be tempted to only consider the path down $Y = 1$ because it has the higher bound value. However, there is no guarantee that it will lead to a viable solution or the optimal solution. So, it is possible that the algorithm goes down one path but must backtrack down a different path.

ELEMENTS OF AN ATA SOFTWARE PROGRAM

An ATA program consists of a few different elements. Below is a description of how we structure those elements with *IBM ILOG CPLEX* as the base program (International Business Machine Corporation, 2019). Those elements include:

1. *A section to read in data.* While it is possible to express information such as item pool metadata in the program, it is more efficient

to keep it as an external file and read in the data. This keeps the program more compact and makes it easier to apply the same code to a different item pool.

2. *Test constraint parameters and definitions.* Keeping the constraint parameters and definitions separate make the program more comprehensible and allows us to make changes to the constraints faster.

3. *Time or Gap limit.* The *CPLEX* program allows us to specify how long the program runs. Without a limit, the program would keep running until it finds the optimal solution. However, for larger problems, this could be impractically long, and the improvements may be negligible. By specifying a time limit, the program will output the best available solution at the end of the time limit, if one is available. Or, one can set a gap limit, which is the difference between the best available solution and the theoretically best solution, as expressed by the optimization function.

4. *The objective function or linear optimization function.* It is a linear expression of the profit or cost associated with a solution, and the relative weight attributed to each soft constraint. The program can be set to either maximize or minimize the values of the objective function.

5. *Constraints.* These are the rules by which the program must follow in order to assemble the test form.

6. *Output results.* The method by which the program outputs the results.

EXAMPLES OF ATA IMPLEMENTATION

The implementation of the ATA system will depend on one's situation and requirements. Things to consider include: whether the ATA system has to keep building test forms over and over again, or if it is a one off, would you build multiple tests using the same constraints or if the constraints are changed frequently, how complex are the rules and how many rules are there, and how user friendly or flexible should the ATA system be for the end user. We also include a description of the types of constraints that you might consider using.

The following is a description of three ATA implementations. It includes a description of the functionality and circumstances that led us to implement the system as it is currently. We hope this information is useful when considering how best to implement a system of your own.

ACCUPLACER® COMPANION FORMS

The ACCUPLACER suite of exams has a set of paper-and-pencil test forms. An ATA system is used to assemble the test forms. It is a relatively simple implementation of ATA because:

- There are only a relatively small number of test forms to build.
- Test forms are assembled using an IRT framework.
- It is a linear test form.
- The constraints are relatively simple and stable.

For this instance, we did not build a complicated ATA system. We use *IBM OPL CPLEX* for the base program and all coding is done in OPL (Optimization Programming Language) which is a language developed for *CPLEX* optimization software. The constraints are relatively straightforward and include:

- number of items on a test form;
- number of overlap items between test forms;
- setting a requirement that the TIF (test information function) is higher than a target;
- a mechanism to keep the TIF across test forms as parallel as possible;
- a mechanism to maximize TIF overall or at cut-score;
- a constraint to keep item sets together;
- content requirements;
- dependencies (e.g., if an item can only be administered if another item is also administered); and
- enemy Items.

ACCUPLACER ORDERED ITEM BOOKLETS

The same ATA technology can also be applied to assist in the standard setting process. The bookmark method for standard setting utilize an ordered item booklet. For linear test forms, the process typically involves taking a test form and ordering the items by difficulty. For computerized adaptive tests, ATA could be used to assemble a test form based on the specifications of the test. It is a straight forward application and each instance is typically only used once. As such we did not build a complex system and programmed the implementation in OPL.

The constraints are relatively straightforward and include:

- Items can only appear once on the booklet.

- Items are proportionally representative of the content specifications of the test.
- Items are ordered by item difficulty (RP67).
- Select items that cover a broad range of item difficulties.
- Select items that are distributed evenly across difficulty.
- Select items to minimize items with similar content information in adjacent positions.
- There is a degree of manual adjustment at the top and bottom of the scale. There is often sparse item selection, and one may have to decide which constraints are more important to meet, for example, competing requirements such as requiring alternating items by content and spacing items by difficulty.

SAT

In the case for the assembly of the SAT forms, it required a more substantial ATA system to support form assembly. The reason for added functionality has to do with several factors. The first reason is the sheer number of constraints. The system was developed to summarize information regarding each test form and to ease comparisons between forms. The second is the need to summarize the content and psychometric information efficiently so that we could perform form reviews efficiently and standardize the information so that test forms could be compared to previously assembled forms. The third reason is a requirement to efficiently document and archive builds so that pertinent information can be reviewed and audited if necessary. The final reason is that the interface was designed with a more user-friendly interface, so that users unfamiliar with the *IBM ILOG CPLEX* platform could operate the program.

Classical Framework

The test forms assembled are for a linear test format, which is simpler. However, the use of a classical framework for form assembly, that is, p-values and reliability, adds to the complexity of form assembly. A limiting factor in linear optimization is that it does not support optimization with division or multiplication. Using the test information function to constraint reliability is straightforward from an ATA perspective and computationally efficient in linear optimization because the values are additive. However, in a classical framework, the formulas are not additive or subtractive, so workarounds are needed. For example, in order to compute reliability, there is multiplication and division. The formula is as follows:

$$\alpha = \frac{n}{n-1}\left[1 - \frac{\sum_{i=1}^{n}\sigma^2}{\left(\sum_{i=1}^{n}\sigma_i \rho_i x\right)}\right]$$

(van der Linden 2005, p. 117)

There are several workarounds. The simplest workaround is to compute the point biserial correlation of the item with the construct, and constraint the sum of the values to a target. You could get the value of the target sum from previously assembled forms with good statistical properties, or extrapolate it based on the expected distribution of items p-values. It is not a perfect measure, but based on our experience it performs well, and it is computationally efficient for the ATA software. A second workaround is to constraint the numerator and denominator values in the reliability formula (see van der Linder, 2005). We found it to be computationally efficient. However, as a practical issue, we did not know how to set the numerator or denominator. Setting it to the values from previously assembled forms worked. However, we thought it was overly restrictive, and may hider form assembly, particularly if the statistical characteristics of the items in the pool shift.

A solution was to use quadratic optimization to compute reliability. This allowed to calculation of division, however it was computationally expensive and slowed down the assembly of test forms. The solution was a hybrid of quadratic optimization and constraining the numerator and denominator. The first step was for the ATA software to assemble one test form with using quadratic optimization, then based on that one form, the numerator and denominator is computed, and set as a constraint for form assembly. This process can be automated and done by the ATA software, so that the process is seamless to the user.

A second issue is how to control the difficulty of the test form. In an IRT framework this can be done by constraining the test characteristic curve. In a classical framework it can be done by constraining the average p-value of the items selected. However, if the distribution of the items across difficulty also needs to be controlled, then using the average p-value may not be sufficient. In our experience, this can lead to mean p-value target being met, but some unforeseen circumstances occurring. For example, most of the items selected are bunched up around the p-value target, or large number of difficult items with a few extremely easy items to balance them out. Neither of these outcomes were acceptable so several workarounds were developed.

One method is to divide up the items into difficulty bins. Then set targets for how many items from each bin the ATA program should select. This method was computationally efficient. However, in practice if the bin targets could not be met, the average p-value of the test form would drift

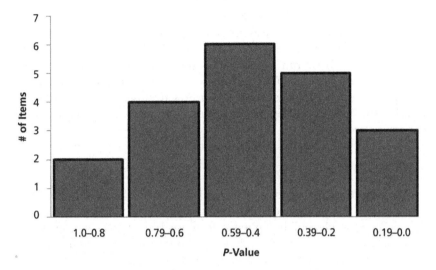

Figure 7.6 Bin targets of item *p*-values.

away. This required manual adjustment of the bin targets to get a desired outcome. Combining an average *p*-value target and the bin method lead to better results but still required manual adjustment if there were deviations.

Another method is to space out the items by difficulty so that the desired distribution of items is selected. By setting a constraint for the distance, in terms of difficulty, between items it is possible to specify a desired distribution of items. For example, if a uniform distance is specified between adjacent items, then the ATA program will attempt to select a uniform distribution of items across difficulty. Similarly, by setting wider distances at the ends of the test and narrower distances in the middle of the test, you can specify a normally distributed test form by difficulty. This method proved to be computationally expensive and while it worked, it proved to be cumbersome when building multiple test forms.

The method that proved to be a compromise between manual adjustment and computational efficiency was to use quadratic optimization to control the difficulty of the items. The distribution of item *p*-value could be expressed as a standard deviation and an average *p*-value. The standard deviation was expressed as a quadratic optimization target. While computationally more expensive than linear optimization, it proved to be robust and the computational load was manageable when building multiple test forms.

ATA System Features

The ATA system we developed in-house was designed as a general-purpose ATA application that takes standardized files. It allows a user to specify the constraints to assemble a test without having to program in *CPLEX ILOG*. This also allows us to use the system on other tests without having to build a new ATA system. It operates on a set of files and basic functions. The combination of basic functions enables the expression of more complex rules and specifications. This allows more users to manage and execute the application, without having to learn how to program in *ILOG CPLEX*. It also allows the wider deployment of the software without having to pay expensive licensing fees.

The ATA system has the following features that you may want to consider for your own use.

1. It has the capacity to build multiple tests and sub-tests simultaneously. This feature could be used to build vertically related test forms. For example, building one test form for 10th graders and one for 12th graders simultaneously, where both forms are related by common items or constrained by a non-overlapping enemy items.
2. The system has been developed to build many test forms either simultaneously or sequentially. This feature allows us to either build all the forms simultaneously, one at a time, or in sequential sets. This feature may be helpful if you have multiple tests to build, and each test has a different specification. However, the tests share the same item pool and there are restrictions as to item reuse across test forms.
3. The system also summarizes and standardizes information about each form assembled so that test forms can more easily be compared to previous builds.
4. The ATA system also has a clean and clear system for managing the test constraints. From a data management perspective, having a standardized data format and friendly user interface reduces the potential for human error.
5. There are also features to aid in quality control. A system feature is to highlight any manual adjustments made by the user, so that there was not an accidental alteration of the test constraints. The core systems are also archived separately to avoid accidental tampering to the ATA system files.
6. The archival and documentation process are also an important feature. Records of every build and iteration of ATA build are generated by the system and saved so that they could be reviewed. In addition, a final summary about the build is archived. This summary is useful for conveying information about the status of the build and item bank to relevant parties.
7. Functionality to troubleshoot failed builds can be useful to identify shortcomings in the pool, or over constriction of the constraints.

When building test forms with hard constraints, if the ATA program cannot meet all the hard constraints it will not generate any test forms. It can be difficult to identify which constraint or item type is not being met, particularly if there are a lot of constraints. A debug functionality that runs when the build fails can be useful in this instance. This can be done by systematically turning the hard constraints into soft constraints and identifying where the deviations are. The constraints with too many or too few items indicate which hard constraints cannot be met.

8. When dealing with large numbers of test forms and constraints, it may be necessary to make enhancements to the efficiency and speed of the program. Some of the features that we incorporated are the use of warm starts and general improvements in the algorithm. Warm starts are a function in *IBM ILOG CPLEX* that allows the user to provide a starting set of items for the test form. This allows the program to use the items as a starting point for which to do the search. The selected items do not need to meet all or any of the constraints, but it has more advantages if they do.

9. The ATA system can handle discrete and item sets. This is useful when there are sets of items that must be selected together.

10. It can also handle complex dependencies. A feature of the program is the modular design of the software. This allows us to rapidly add functions that allow dependencies between items that were not originally conceived of. That is to say, the program is flexible enough to handle unforeseen requirements.

11. And finally, the ATA system can handle builds using both classical or IRT based statistics.

OTHER ISSUES

Some issues to consider that were not previously described include item inventory prediction and item exposure control. The same software used to assemble test forms can be used for non-test assembly purposes. Item inventory development can have a very long development schedule. As such, predicting the types of item that you want is useful for item development planning. The ATA software could be used to predict the types of items that you most frequently need from the item pool. One way to do this is to reinsert retired items back into the item pool and associate a high penalty if the ATA program selects it. This has the effect of telling the program to avoid selecting those retired items unless absolutely necessary. Retired items selected by the program indicate high usage types and are prime item types for development. Another method for item inventory prediction is to build test forms and allow reuse of items. However, associate a high penalty for reused items. Items that are reused despite the penalty, indicate high usage item types that should be targeted for development.

This technology can also be applied to item exposure control. One item exposure strategy for a large testing programs is to divide an item pool into parts and only use items from each part at any one administration. An ATA program can aid this task by doing the splitting in a calculated manner so that the pools are divided equally. For example, one could specify that the ATA program divide a test into three parts equally by item content and item statistics. In that manner, each part would have an equal number of items and the basic properties of each part are similar, so that no one administration is deficient compared to another. Another strategy could be to build as many test forms as possible, and then randomly divide those test forms into each part.

We hope this description of ATA may provide some utility for the reader in deciding if ATA is useful for them. If you do decide to implement ATA technology we hope that our experiences and suggestions prove helpful.

REFERENCES

International Business Machine Corporation. (2016). *IBM ILOG CPLEX CP Optimizer user's manual.* Retrieved from https://www.ibm.com/support/knowledge center/SSSA5P_12.7.0/ilog.odms.studio.help/pdf/usrcplex.pdf

Melican, G. J., Breithaupt, K., & Zhang, Y. (2010). Designing and implementing a multistage adaptive test: The uniform CPA exam. In W. J. van der Linden & C. A. W. Glas (Eds.), *Elements of adaptive testing* (pp. 31–55). New York, NY: Springer.

Nemhauser, G. L., & Wolsey, L. A. (1999). *Integer and combinatorial optimization.* New York, NY: Wiley.

van der Linden, W. J. (2005). *Linear models for optimal test assembly.* New York, NY: Springer.

van der Linden, W. J. (2017). Optimal test design. In W. J. van der Linden (Ed.), *Handbook of item response theory* (Vol. 3). Boca Raton, FL: CRC.

van der Linden, W. J., & Li, J. (2016). Comment on three-element item selection procedures for multiple forms assembly: An item matching approach. *Applied Psychological Measurement, 40,* 641–649.

CHAPTER 8

MULTISTAGE TESTING IN PRACTICE

Duanli Yan
Educational Testing Service

Being in the current digital age, schools, students, teachers, researchers, and practitioners have begun using more innovative technologies to support educational activities. New technologies are being incorporated in school curricula and new data collection methods are being developed to offer new options for ongoing formative, culminating summative and alternative assessments. There are also needs to separately track the performance of students with disabilities and develop plans to improve it. Thus, there are the emerging needs to develop and implement new and innovative methods to support students, teachers, schools, researchers, and practitioners using technology for learning, instructions, feedback, evaluation, personalized learning and assessment, and progression evaluations.

In order to improve our educational measurement and evaluation processes, we need to increase their efficiency and accuracy and solve real world problems. We strive to address questions such as: "How can we improve students' learning?"; "How can we evaluate progression?"; "How can we evaluate more accurately and efficiently?"; and "How can we give more

Application of Artificial Intelligence to Assessment, pages 141–160
Copyright © 2020 by Information Age Publishing
All rights of reproduction in any form reserved.

instructional feedback?" The answers to these questions include: We need to know students better, obtain more information about the students, give tailored shorter and targeted evaluations and feedback, use evidence-based evaluations and assessments, give quick follow-up feedback instruction and evaluations, develop new innovative methods and applications to improve measurement and evaluation efficiency and accuracy, incorporate computerized adaptive and multistage tests, develop adaptive learning and training, develop and use both human and AI automated scoring to support operational assessment scoring, diagnoses, evaluations, assessments, and provide more information to inform policy makers.

To meet the emerging needs, the traditional one-size-fits-all lesson plan and assessment are limited, the evaluations and assessments need to be tailored and personalized to improve teaching and assessment efficiency and accuracy. Computerized adaptive testing (CAT) and computerized multistage testing (MST) have become the important frameworks of tailored testing, given their advantages on efficiency, accuracy, and practical implementation. The idea of CAT and MST started more than 50 years (Angoff & Huddleston, 1958), and educational research and measurement community became interested in CAT research operational implementations. CAT became a very popular method of administering questionnaires, collecting data and on-the-fly scoring (van der Linden & Glas, 2010; Wainer, 2000), and has been used in many large scale assessments over the last decades. In addition to CAT when the adaptation is at item level, researchers began to explore MST when the adaptation proceed from stage to stage with a group of items at each stage. Lord (1970, 1971a, 1971b, 1971c) polished the MST idea with detailed illustrations (Wainer, 2015). MST got increased popularity in recent years (Yan, von Davier, & Lewis, 2014).

Both CAT and MST has been shown to have advantages over traditional linear testing for more efficient and precise measurement of test takers' performance (Hendrickson, 2007; Lord, 1980; Wainer, 2000). In traditional linear testing, measurement precision may vary across the ability levels of the test takers. On the other hand, CATs and MSTs focus measurement at an individual test taker's ability level, so they can provide equally precise measurement for all test takers including those of average ability and those near the ends of the measurement scale (Hendrickson, 2007; Lord, 1974; Mills, Potenza, Fremer, & Ward, 2002; Wainer, Kaplan, & Lewis, 1992). MST incorporating most of the advantages from CAT and linear testing to offer features include testing efficiency and accuracy, greater control of test content, more robust item review, as well as simplified test assembly and administration. Thus, MST becomes of more and more interest to researchers and practitioners as technology advances.

In the last few years, many large scale operational testing programs have adopted MST to offer flexible, efficient, and accurate tailored evaluation and assessment of educational outcomes. These include the National Assessment of Educational Progress (NAEP), the survey of student and adult skills—the Programme for the International Assessment of Adult Competencies (PIAAC), the Graduate Record Examination (GRE), the American Institute of Certified Public Accountants (AICPA), and Educational Record Bureau (ERB). Many higher education and K–12 are moving toward computer-based, and computerized adaptive and multistage testing. Some states have already implemented CAT/MST alternative assessment (e.g., CA), and other states are in the process of developing and implementing CAT/MST.

The following sections describe and discuss the MST basics and features, MST implementation considerations, MST applications in large-scale assessment, and R packages for MST simulations to support operational MST design, assembly, statistical methods, and scoring.

MST BASICS

Similar to CAT, items are administered sequentially and selected optimally according to the current responses to the administered items. While in CAT, items are selected one after each other and the ability of the test taker is estimated after the administration of each item. In MST, however, items are selected in groups or modules, and the selection of the subsequent modules is based on the performance on the previously administered modules, not on the single items (Yan, von Davier, & Lewis, 2014). Thus, it can be an effective compromise between CAT and linear testing, embedding features and benefits from both designs. Yan, von Davier, and Lewis (2014) provides a thorough overview of the many aspects of MST design and application. It illustrates and discusses many practical issues and considerations for the whole operational MST process from design to application.

MST Design

When an MST has only one stage, it is basically a linear test; when an MST has as many stages as the number of items a test taker is administered, it is equivalent to an item-level CAT. Most commonly, MSTs have two or three stages. Figure 8.1 illustrates a two-stage and a three-stage MST.

Item/Module Pool

Item or module pool is an essential part of an MST. Items can be grouped into categories based on item difficulties and discriminations estimated

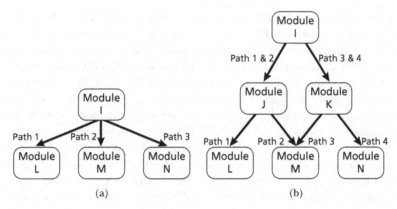

Figure 8.1 Examples of (a) two-stage (1-2 MST) and (b) three stage (1-2-3 MST) MST Structures.

TABLE 8.1 The 2 × 2 Table of Items Based on P+ and r_{bi} for a Calibration Sample

	r_{bi}				
P+	**0–.20**	**.20–.40**	**.40–.60**	**.60–1.00**	**Marginal**
.84–.96	0	3	6	1	10
.70–.84	0	3	10	7	20
.51–.70	1	4	28	7	40
.36–.50	1	8	11	0	20
.20–.35	2	2	6	0	10

based on item response theory (IRT) or classical test theory (CTT). Table 8.1 is an example of an item pool with 100 items based on CTT.

Module Designs

Module design is an important part of MST design to determine the test length, difficulty, discrimination, content, and so forth. The lengths of modules can be varied at different stages. For example, all modules can have the same length or the same number of items; the initial module at stage one can have a shorter length, and the last modules can have a longer length; the initial module can have a longer length and the last modules can have a shorter length. The module difficulty can be estimated with IRT or CTT. Modules with average difficulty at low, medium, or high levels can be considered to be low, medium, or high level difficulty modules, respectively.

Module discrimination can be estimated with IRT or CTT. Modules with average discrimination at low, medium, or high levels can be considered to be low, medium, or high level discriminating modules, respectively. Commonly, medium difficulty modules are used for the initial stage of testing; lower, medium, and higher difficulty modules are used for the middle or final stage, respectively.

Module Assembly

Modules are assembled to meet the test target specifications. The target specifications for MST designs and their modules can be set based on the properties of the item pool, including the total number of available items in the pool and the number of items required for each design. The specifications of combinations of requirements for module length, module difficulty, and module discriminations, and content specifications depend on the item pool. The items selected for modules should be in the range represented by the operational assessment.

Routing

MST routing is the process that routes or classifies test takers to different paths or next stage modules based on their performance on the previous module(s) using selected rules, which can be quite different depending on the purpose and design of the MST. Unlike the item-by-item adaptation in CAT, MST has fixed paths along which an examinee may move through the test. Along these paths are sets of items (modules) that are administered as intact units. The rules that determine which modules are administered to an examinee are called routing rules.

Statistical Model

Current operational MSTs generally use IRT as a basis for item calibration, pool design, module assembly, routing algorithms, and scoring. There are also non-IRT-based alternatives, including a tree-based methodology for MST.

MSTs have similar features as CATs; they can be much shorter in test lengths compared to linear tests. They are shown to have equal or higher predictive and concurrent validity compared to linear tests (Betz & Weiss, 1974; Linn, Rock, & Cleary, 1969; Wainer, 1995). Test developers can design and assemble the modules before the test administration, which allow them greater control over the content balance, quality of the test structure and administration of the test in comparison to a CAT. Given modules being designed and administered adaptively, MSTs can maintain the measurement advantages of CATs (Patsula & Hambleton, 1999; van der Linden & Glas, 2010). Since MST modules are presented to the test taker as a unit, which allows test takers to review their items during testing. MSTs can also be used for small volume testing, especially if there exists strong assumptions violation such as data and model fitting, dimensionality, and local independence, which makes the test more extensive.

MST IMPLEMENTATION CONSIDERATIONS

When it comes to implementing MST for operational assessments, many practical issues and considerations arise for the whole operational MST process from designs to applications including achievement testing, classification testing, and survey assessments, for higher education and for K–12 assessment. MST, in reality, requires of their designers a number of important decisions. These decisions define the compromise that a given test strikes between each of a set of competing priorities. Designers naturally want their test to be short, reliable, secure, economical, robust, and efficient. However, each of these priorities can be fully achieved only at the expense of the others. The priorities of a test's design are expressed through the answers to a series of practical questions: "Should the test incorporate only two stages or are three or more needed?"; "How long should each stage be?"; "How many alternative test levels or sections are needed within each stage?"; "What measurement properties should each test section possess?"; "How should routing decisions among stages and sections be made?"; and "Should final scores be based on IRT ability estimates or simple transformations of number of correct scores?" In order to address these most important issues in designing and implementing MSTs, researchers and practitioners put much effort to explore these practical considerations.

Yan, von Davier, and Lewis (2014c) gave an overview of MSTs. They discussed the key processes and considerations for designing MST for operational assessment implementations. For the different purposes of assessment, MST designs will need to be tailored differently to address questions regarding stages, modules, and constraints for assembly. Routing and scoring methodologies also will need to be tailored to address these different purposes. For example, MSTs for achievement testing should focus on estimation accuracy for a range of test takers' proficiency levels, while MSTs for classification testing will focus on the accuracy of classifying test takers into appropriate groups. They listed the advantages and disadvantages of linear, CAT, and MST.

Test Design, Item Pool, and Maintenance

Lord (1971a) described the major issues in designing a two stage testing procedure, including the method of scoring the routing test, the cut off points for routing the test takers to the second stage, and the method of scoring the entire two stage procedure. Since 1990, researchers explored various MST designs and design complexity, including 1-3, 1-2-2, 1-3-3, 1-2-3, 1-5-5-5-5, 1-1-2-3-3-4, and 5-5-5-5-5-5; test and module length given the various designs; item banks, statistical targets, and test assembly associated with the designs; routing and scoring methodologies and decisions, as well as security and exposure control. The determination of the test structure also requires consideration of the feasibility and economy of the test. In general, the more stages, the more modules are available at different levels, the easier it is to adapt to the candidate level and the measurement error, but the more stages, the more modules per stage implied for MST expenses. Zenisky and Hambleton (2014) provided a thorough history of MST designs from research results into practice.

With test design in hand, a quality item pool dictates the quality of the test, and it depends on many things such as the quality items, how to design an optimal item pool blueprint to guide item writing process, and evaluate an existing item pool. Models for blueprint design such as integer programming, item generation, generating modules, and maintenance. Veldkamp (2014) discussed MST item pool design and maintenance. Kim and Dodd (2014) added considerations for mixed format MST when tests containing both dichotomous (e.g., multiple-choice) and polytomous (e.g., constructed-response) items, given each format's advantages and drawbacks, and discussed their implications for MST design, the item pool, and test assembly.

MST implementation process began by systematically evaluating the performance of different design options in a theoretical context. Then, those designs that appeared to strike the right compromise among the various competing priorities were identified. These designs were then subjected to a series of data collection studies that evaluated the extent to which theory translated to the real world. Luecht (2014) has advised many early MST operational implementations. He also illustrated the design and implementation considerations on how to design and implement larger-scale MST including measurement information targeting, item bank inventory issues, test assembly, item exposure and security issues, routing and scoring precision, and system performance and data management issues.

Test Assembly

After deciding the basic MST structural design and the construction of the item bank, it is time for test assembly process. There are many test assembly considerations, such as information function, assembly methods, content balance, and test exposure control. Designers need to balance multiple constraints and considerations, and make a series of decisions. This process requires intensive computation and real-time data processing capabilities, as well as a large amount of data simulations. From the common automated test assembly methods using mixed-integer programming (Adema, 1990; Luecht & Nungester, 1998; van der Linden, 1998), the heuristic method (Stocking & Swanson, 1993), and the Monte Carlo statistical sampling method (Belov & Armstrong, 2008), researchers explore MST module assembly designs, and identified the primary questions to be answered. These include deciding on the optimal number of stages and range of module difficulty within stages, and research on the differences between scores and decisions based on number-correct score routing versus using IRT score routing (Luecht, Brumfield, & Breithaupt, 2006). Ariel, Veldkamp, and Breithaupt (2006) also studied transforming a discrete item pool into an MST module pool with optimal module pool assembly.

In a typical MST practice, multiple parallel panels need to be preassembled before test administration. Each panel consists of several stages and each stage contains one or more modules assembled at different difficulty levels. This complex structure generates new challenges for test assembly because of the following multifaceted demands: (a) modules in one stage must have distinct information curves to sufficiently differentiate pathways through the test, (b) all pathways must be sufficiently parallel across the parallel panels, and (c) all pathways in all parallel panels must meet all non-statistical design constraints (such as content balancing and enemy items). Zheng, Wang, Culbertson, and Chang (2014) synthesize the last decades research studies on test assembly and gives an overview of various test assembly methods for MST. van der Linden and Diao (2014) demonstrated a universal shadow-test assembler method for MST. Han and Guo (2014) demonstrated an MST module-shaping on the fly assembly method, which replaces the preassembled test module with a test module assembled on the fly after each stage with test modules shaped to come as close as possible to the normal density function of the interim proficiency estimate and its standard error. They have implemented the method in *MSTGen* (Han, 2013) software. Verschoor and Eggen (2014) also discussed some operational content and routing implications on assembling to optimize the test assembly and routing for MST.

Routing, Scoring, and Equating

Many methods are considered in MST routing, including IRT-based and CTT-based MST routing algorithms, as well as the approaches for classification, mastery testing, diagnostic testing, and approaches for content optimizations in practice. As in CAT, IRT, and CTT can be applied to MST. Weissman (2014) described the commonly used IRT-Based MST routing. Yan, Lewis, and von Davier (2014a) introduced a tree-based MST routing with simplicity, lack of restrictive assumptions, and the possibility of implementation based on small samples. Their tree-based MST design and routing is an extension of the tree-based CAT design described by Yan, Lewis, and Stocking (2004).

While most work in MST has focused on achievement testing, MST has also been applied to classification testing. Smith and Lewis (2014) extended the work by Lewis and Sheehan (1990) on computerized mastery test and discussed MST for categorical decisions with multistage testing combined with Wald's sequential probability ratio test to make categorical decisions more efficiently. By adopting an adaptive stopping rule, their approach has most of the efficiency of an adaptive test which can limit item exposure. Glas (2014) discussed an MST classification using multi-dimensional model and Bayesian sequential decision to take into account the cost of test administration and the distance between the test takers' proficiencies and cutoff points. von Davier and Cheng (2014) also discuss MST using diagnostic models.

Parameter estimation, scoring, and linking is common to both MST and CAT. The estimation methods include IRT-based using maximum likelihood and Bayesian methodologies, CTT-based MST approaches using regression trees, the approaches for classification testing, other models using multi-dimensional IRT, and models for diagnostic testing. Moreover, item calibration, scoring and linking all need to be monitored and adjusted as quickly as possible if any deviation from the expected results is identified. MST calibration and linking involves data collection in conventional test administrations for building initial modules and routing rules for MST administrations. Once MST administrations begin, data are collected to establish scoring rules, develop new test modules, equate the cut-scores for routing, and ensure comparability of tests over time. Comparability of tests involves both comparability of reported scores and comparability of test performance. Thus, routing rules for modules must be comparable for different administrations. When many administrations are involved, special procedures are considered for maintenance of stable linkage. Haberman and von Davier (2014) discussed considerations for proficiency estimation, or scoring, in MST.

Reliability, Validity, Fairness, and Security

Like in any other practice, MST's reliability, validity, and security need to be tested and demonstrated. When performing such an inspection, again, both CTT-based method and IRT-based method may be employed. MST reliability from the perspective of CTT is similar to the traditional single value reliability that describes the average error variance for all scores. MST reliability from an IRT perspective deals with standard errors for theta estimates as well as for scale scores. Livingston and Kim (2014) discussed test reliability using a CTT framework. van Rijn (2014) discussed the test reliability in an IRT framework and illustrated the estimation method on an actual multistage mathematics test that was used in a special study in the National Assessment of Educational Progress (NAEP).

Zwick and Bridgeman (2014) discussed many validity and fairness considerations and implications in MST operational implementations, these include content balancing, item review, skipping strategies, routing algorithms, computer platforms, accommodation for disabilities, and differential item functioning.

Although MST is more secure than linear testing, it is still a serious challenge to effectively control the exposure of the test, especially for high-stakes tests. With a CAT, when a pool is used for a period of time, complex algorithms have been developed to avoid overuse of some items relative to others in the pool (Stocking & Lewis, 1998; Sympson & Hetter, 1985). Lee, Lewis, and von Davier (2014) discussed the practical considerations about content balance and exposure control.

LARGE SCALE ASSESSMENT APPLICATIONS

MST has become an assessment design of choice for many operational assessments including real world large scale international achievement and survey assessments. The applications in this section present the many tailored aspects of the MST for these applications. The details of the assessment development processes when implementing operational MSTs are described, including the specifications and design options, priorities, constraints, simulation studies, and the many challenges and critical issues that need to be considered from theory to practice.

Robin, Steffen, and Liang (2014) described the MST application for the Graduate Entrance Examination (GRE®), including the practical psychometric considerations in designing and implementing an operational MST including design, scales, assembly, calibration, and linking.

Breithaupt, Zhang, and Hare (2014) shared some practical models for MST administration based on two operational certification testing programs: the American Institute of Certified Public Accountants which is an examination required for licensure in accounting, and a Medical Council of Canada examination required for the licensure of physicians in Canada. They discussed the comparability, content coverage, expected score precision, item bank development and inventory planning, challenges and practical solutions for exposure control and test security, as well as other implications for operational implementation.

There are a lot of MST applications for K–12 assessments, including: The Multi-State Alternate Assessment (MSAA) administered in the spring as a summative assessment for federal accountability purposes. MSAA is administered for ELA and mathematics in Grades 3–8 and Grade 11, and students are classified into one of four performance levels: Level 1, Level 2, Level 3, and Level 4; The *Winsight®* Assessment System, a fully integrated comprehensive flexible and interactive set of tools for K–12 that measures students' knowledge, skills, and abilities; state subject tests (e.g., science test); state alternative assessments; and primary school test. Wentzel, Mills, and Meara (2014) discussed the processes and considerations to transition a K–12 assessment—Comprehensive Testing Program (CTP) Online to MST application.

U.S. and international survey assessments have played important roles in reporting the educational progresses, such as the National Assessment of Educational Progress (NAEP), the Programme for the International Assessment of Adult Competencies (PIAAC), and the Programme for the International Student Assessment. Oranje, Mazzeo, Xu, and Kulick (2014) illustrated how an MST is designed and implemented for NAEP and how to address the practical issues differently in survey assessment. Chen, Yamamoto, and von Davier (2014) discussed the many differences in MST designs and applications for two international survey assessments: the PDQ, an assessment of adult literacy for prose, document, and quantitative literacy; and the PIAAC which is the most comprehensive international survey of adult skills in numeracy and literacy, and the problem solving in technology rich environments. PIAAC is linked to previous surveys of adult skills including the International Adult Literacy Survey (IALS) and Adult Literacy and Life Skills Survey (ALL). Maintaining this link has made it possible to look at changes in skill levels, as well as the distribution of those skills, over time. PIAAC is adaptive to respondents in two ways: One is the modal adaptation—for respondents without an experience of using computer, traditional paper and pencil booklet can be administered; and the other is the proficiency adaptation—a cluster of items from a single scale at a time based on the background information and the performances on the preceding items based on a variant of matrix sampling.

Yamamoto, Shin, and Khorramdel (2018) discussed the MST application for the survey of student skills—the Programme for the International

Student Assessment (PISA). They illustrate the unique features of the implemented designs in PISA and the expected gains in test efficiency and accuracy, as well as limitations and challenges of MST designs for cross-country surveys. Practical aspects and insights into utilizing MST to measure complex constructs in cross-cultural surveys are provided.

Yan, Lewis, and von Davier (2014b) also compared the different MST module designs for optimality, and illustrated the designs using a tree-based approach with small sample calibration. This is especially useful for small volume assessments when there are limitations including sample data, IRT model assumption violations.

RECENT RESEARCH FOR PRACTICAL ISSUES AND SOLUTIONS

As the number of MST implementations increases, researchers and practitioners seek information about the most recent practical applications, their practical considerations, their challenges, and solutions for practical assessments using MST. The following lists a small subset of the current MST research activities:

- investigation on computerized adaptive multistage testing panels for multidimensional assessment,
- using IRT and MIRT models for item parameter estimation with multidimensional MST,
- item calibration in incomplete testing designs to address the missing data issues development of multistage tests based on teacher ratings,
- evaluating the content validity of multistage tests,
- differential item functioning in adaptive multistage testing,
- multistage testing in secondary school,
- misrouting effect given false positive and false negative responses,
- comparisons of MST and CAT in simulations and operational assessment,
- MST classification using probability-based approaches,
- using different routing blocks to different levels and different contents of reading proficiency assessment,
- systematically search across design elements and parameterized information targets and analytical evaluation of MST measurement properties to find optimized objective statistical functions, and
- adaptive multistage test design with inter-sectional routing method.

R PACKAGES

Implementing real-world CAT and MST is quite complicated. Researchers and practitioners often struggle to decide what the best design, assembly, estimation, scaling, and scoring for their assessment. They put tremendous amount of effort doing simulations in hope to find their optimal decision in various programing languages and platforms.

In order to explore the various designs, assembly, estimations, and scoring models to find the optimal solution for their situation, researchers developed software tools for CAT and MST. In CAT, several commercial software (e.g., CATSim, Adaptest) exist and some open-source solutions for simulation studies exist, such as R packages *catR* (Magis & Barrada, 2017; Magis & Raîche, 2012), mirtCAT (Chalmers, 2015), and the R-based software Firestar (Choi, 2009). In MST, MSTGen (Han, 2013) exists. Very recently, the R package *mstR* was developed to provide a tool for simulations in the MST context, similarly to the *catR* package for CAT framework.

Now, there are open source R software packages free to all other researchers. The goal is to help researchers and practitioners to save their efforts to simulate, implement, and compare CAT and MST. The R packages consist of *catR* and *mstR*, where *catR* stands for CAT with R; and *mstR* stands for MST with R.

The package *catR* (Magis & Barrada, 2017; Magis & Raiche, 2012) consists of basic functions to compute item response probabilities, item information, ability estimations, standard errors, expected information, and numerical integration, and functions to generate item banks, select items and item exposure control, check stopping rules, simulate respondents and perform adaptive testing. The estimation and scoring methods include Bayes modal (BM), maximum likelihood (ML), weighted likelihood (WL), and expected a posteriori estimation (EAP). The package *mstR* (Magis, Yan, & von Davier, 2018) is a sister-like of *catR* but in the context of multistage testing (MST). It also consists of the *catR* similar functions listed above. Instead of optimally selecting one item after each other, MST administers blocks or modules of items at each stage and determines the best path between modules from one stage to the next one. With respect to CAT, MST holds less rules for next module selection. However, it requires appropriate setting of the modules, module assembly of accurate items, and suitable paths between modules from two successive stages.

Both packages *catR* and *mstR* share many similar settings and options, *catR* requiring more focus on the suitable setting of the CAT scenario, and *mstR* needing more attention to the definition of the modules, the MST structure and the various paths. But they both generate many response patterns under pre-specified CAT or MST scenarios and perform adaptive testing. Both support a variety of common and specialized parameter estimation techniques, ability estimation techniques, and item selection algorithms, both for dichotomous and polytomous item types. They include dichotomous and polytomous unidimensional IRT models including 1PL, 2PL, 3PL, 4PL, GRM, MGRM, PCM, GPCM, RSM, NRM, MIRT, Testlet IRT, and Response-Time IRT.

The following are some examples of R codes from catR and mstR:

The `randomCAT()` function

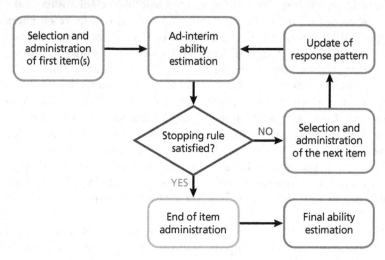

Using `randomCAT()`:

Full code:
```
R> res <- randomCAT(trueTheta=0, itemBank=bank,
        start=start, test=test,
        stop=stop, final=final)
```

To see the output as displayed in the console:
```
R> res
```

To see the output as a list of elements:
```
R> str(res)
```

To show the path of ability estimates (with confidence intervals):
```
R> plot(res, ci=TRUE)
```

Using `randomMST()`:

Full code for MST simulation:
```
R> res4 <- randomMST(trueTheta=0, itemBank=it, modules=modules,
            transMatrix=trans, response=x,
            start=start, test=test3, final=final)
```

A simulation example:

Code:
```
R> res <- simulateRespondents(thetas=theta, itemBank=bank,
       rmax=0.2, start=start, test=test, stop=stop,
       final=final)
```
Output:
```
R> res
R> plot(res)
```

Currently, Both *catR* and *mstR* packages are used in the R community and can be downloaded from CRAN: https://cran.r-project.org/web/packages/catR/index.html and https://cran.r-project.org/web/packages/mstR/mstR.pdf.

In addition to the creation and the development of the online open source R packages *catR* and *mstR*, a user-oriented book *Computerized Adaptive and Multistage Testing with R* was written (Magis, Yan, & von Davier, 2017). This book is in the Springer UseR! Series, and its goals are: (a) provide a detailed, complete and illustrated description of the two packages, their architecture, internal functions, and main characteristics; and (b) illustrate their uses in both simulation studies for empirical research and concrete simulations to solve real-life or concrete experimental research questions on adaptive administration.

The book is structured to take the reader through all key aspects of CAT and MST simulations, from data generation, item banking, item parameter generation for simulations, to estimation and scoring by using *catR* and *mstR*. It starts with an introduction to IRT (the foundation stone for the packages), then provide overviews of CAT and MST, and discuss the important concepts associated with CATs and MSTs. It then introduces the R open source software packages *catR* and *mstR* for CAT and MST simulations, and provide illustrative examples using real item parameters from real test administrations and various realistic and plausible scenarios set and tried through intensive simulation studies.

SUMMARY

There are more and more international operational testing programs considering MST for practical administrations for best practices in testing and assessment. There are always many practical issues that arise when it comes to real world applications. MSTs require of their designers a number of important considerations and decisions. These considerations and decisions include the assessment design, implementations and test assembly, item pool development and maintenance, routing and scoring methodologies, test equating, test security, validity and fairness, as well as many challenges and compromises due to competing priorities for operational implementation and applications.

Currently, the R packages are helpful toolkits adapted by operational CAT and MST implementations. They are being used by researchers and practitioners, and the catR package is the core for the Open-source Online R-based Adaptive Testing Platform, Concerto, developed by the Psychometric Center at the University of Cambridge. It allows users to create various online assessments, from simple surveys to complex IRT-based adaptive tests. *Concerto* is free for academic and commercial use: http://concertoplatform.com/

Computerized Adaptive and Multistage Testing with R (Magis, Yan, & von Davier, 2017) extends the authors award-winning volume *Computerized Multistage Testing: Theory and Applications* (Yan, von Davier, & Lewis, 2014). Both books and the R packages are textbooks and toolkits for graduate school courses. Applications of CAT/MST, and these R packages are numerous. They can be used:

- in intensive simulation studies with real item banks or MST structures, in order to extract valuable information for potential real-time applications;
- for theoretical psychometric research, such as comparing the statistical accuracy of new item selection rules (in CAT) with respect to currently existing ones;
- to compare CAT versus MST scenarios based on the same pool of calibrated items;
- to test various adaptive architectures to determine which scenario is the optimal choice; and also
- pieces of the package (such as specific R functions) can be extracted and used in research contexts that are independent of adaptive testing, for example, to estimate ability or compute related standard errors.

REFERENCES

Adema, J. J. (1990). The construction of customized two-stage tests. *Journal of Educational Measurement, 27,* 241–253.

Angoff, W. H., & Huddleston, E. M. (1958). *The multi-level experiment: A study of a two-stage system for the College Board Scholastic Aptitude Test* (Statistical Report 58-21). Princeton, NJ: Educational Testing Service.

Ariel, A., Veldkamp, B. P., & Breithaupt, K. (2006). Optimal testlet pool assembly for multistage testing designs. *Applied Psychological Measurement, 30,* 204–215.

Belov, D. I., & Armstrong, R.D. (2008) A Monte Carlo approach to the design, assembly, and evaluation of multistage adaptive tests. *Applied Psychological Measurement, 32,* 119–137.

Betz, N. E., & Weiss, D. J. (1974). *Simulation studies of two-stage ability testing* (Research report 74-4). Minneapolis: University of Minnesota.

Breithaupt, K. J., Zhang, Y., & Hare, D. R. (2014). The multistage testing approach to the aicpa uniform certified public accounting examinations. In D. Yan, A. A. von Davier, & C. Lewis (Eds), *Computerized multistage testing: Theory and applications.* London, England: Chapman and Hall.

Chambers, J. M., & Hastie, T. J. (1992). *Statistical models.* Pacific Grove, CA: Wadsworth and Brooks/Cole Advanced Books and Software.

Chen, H., Yamamoto, K., & von Davier, M. (2014). Controlling multistage testing exposure rates in international larger-scale assessments. In D. Yan, A. A. von Davier, & C. Lewis (Eds), *Computerized multistage testing: Theory and applications* (pp. 391–437). London, England: Chapman and Hall.

Choi, S. W. (2009). Firestar: Computerized adaptive testing simulation program for polytomous item response theory models. *Applied Psychological Measurement, 33*, 644–645.

Glas, C. A. W. (2014). Adaptive mastery multistage testing using a multidimensional IRT model. In D. Yan, A. A. von Davier, & C. Lewis (Eds), *Computerized multistage testing: Theory and applications* (pp. 205–218). London, England: Chapman and Hall.

Haberman, S.J., & von Davier, A.A. (2014). Considerations on parameter estimation, scoring, and linking in multistage testing. In D. Yan, A. A. von Davier, & C. Lewis (Eds), *Computerized multistage testing: Theory and applications* (pp. 229–248). London, England: Chapman and Hall.

Han, K. T. (2013). MSTGen: Simulated data generator for multistage testing. *Applied Psychological Measurement, 37*, 666–668.

Han, K.T., & Guo, F. (2014). Multistage testing by shaping modules on the fly. In D. Yan, A. A. von Davier, & C. Lewis (Eds), *Computerized multistage testing: Theory and applications* (pp. 119–134). London, England: Chapman and Hall.

Hendrickson, A. (2007). An NCME instructional module on multistage testing. *Educational Measurement: Issues and Practice, 26*, 44–52.

Kim, J., & Dodd, B.G. (2014). Mixed-format multistage tests: Issues and methods. In D Yan, A. A. von Davier, & C. Lewis (Eds), *Computerized multistage testing: Theory and applications* (pp. 55–68). London, England: Chapman and Hall.

Lee, Y.-H., Lewis, C., & von Davier, A. A. (2014). Test security and quality control for multistage tests. In D. Yan, A. A. von Davier, & C. Lewis (Eds), *Computerized multistage testing: Theory and applications* (pp. 285–300). London, England: Chapman and Hall.

Lewis, C., & Sheehan, K. (1990). Using Bayesian decision theory to design a computerized mastery test. *Applied Psychological Measurement, 14*(4), 367–386.

Linn, R. L., Rock, D. A., & Cleary, T. A. (1969). The development and evaluations of several programmed testing methods. *Educational and Psychological Measurement. 29*, 129–146.

Livingston, S. A., & Kim, S. (2014). Multistage test reliability estimated via classical test theory. In D. Yan, A. A. von Davier, & C. Lewis (Eds), *Computerized multistage testing: Theory and applications* (pp. 265–270). London, England: Chapman and Hall.

Lord, F. M. (1970). Some test theory for tailored testing. In W. H. Holtzman (Ed.), *Computer-assisted instruction, testing, and guidance* (pp. 139–183). New York, NY: Harper & Row.

Lord, F. M. (1971a). A theoretical study of two-stage testing. *Psychometrika, 36,* 227–242.

Lord, F. M. (1971b). Robbins-Munro procedures for tailored testing. *Educational and Psychological Measurement, 31,* 3–31.

Lord, F. M. (1971c). The self-scoring flexilevel test. *Journal of Educational Measurement, 8,* 147–151.

Lord, F. M. (1974). *Practical methods for redesigning a homogenous test, also for designing a multilevel test* (RB-74-30). Princeton, NJ: Educational Testing Service.

Lord, F. M. (1980). *Applications of item response theory to practical testing problems.* Hillsdale, NJ: Erlbaum.

Luecht, R. (2014). Design and implementation of large-scale multistage testing, systems. In D. Yan, A. A. von Davier, & C. Lewis (Eds), *Computerized multistage testing: Theory and applications* (pp. 69–84). London, England: Chapman and Hall.

Luecht, R. M., & Nungester, R. (1998). Some practical examples of computer-adaptive sequential testing. *Journal of Educational Measurement, 35,* 229–249.

Luecht, R. M., Brumfield, T., & Breithaupt, K. (2006). A testlet assembly design for adaptive multistage tests. *Applied Measurement in Education, 19*(3), 189–202.

Magis, D., & Barrada, J. R. (2017). Computerized adaptive testing with R: Recent updates of the package catR. *Journal of Statistical Software, 76*(1), 1–19.

Magis, D., & Raîche, G. (2012). Random generation of response patterns under computerized adaptive testing with the R package catR. *Journal of Statistical Software, 48,* 1–31.

Magis, D., Yan, D., & von Davier, A. A. (2017). *Computerized adaptive and multistage testing with R.* New York, NY: Springer.

Magis, D., Yan, D., & von Davier, A. A. (2018). *mstR: Procedures to generate patterns under multistage testing* (R package version 1.2). Retrieved from https://cran.r-project.org/web/packages/mstR/mstR.pdf

Mills, C., Potenza, M. T., Fremer, J. J., & Ward, W. C. (2002). *Computer-based testing: Building the foundation for future assessments.* Mahwah, NJ: Erlbaum.

Oranje, A., Mazzeo, J., Xu, X., & Kulick, E. (2014). A multistage testing approach to group-score assessments. In D. Yan, A. A. von Davier, & C. Lewis (Eds), *Computerized multistage testing: Theory and applications* (pp. 371–390). London, England: Chapman and Hall.

Patsula, L. N. (1999). *A comparison of computerized-adaptive testing and multi-stage testing* (Unpublished doctoral dissertation). University of Massachusetts at Amherst, Amherst, MA.

Robin, F., Steffen, M., & Liang, L. (2014). The multistage test implementation of the GRE revised general test. In D. Yan, A. A. von Davier, & C. Lewis (Eds). *Computerized multistage testing: Theory and applications* (pp. 325–342). London, England: Chapman and Hall.

Smith, R., & Lewis, C. (2014). Multistage testing for categorical decisions. In D. Yan, A. A. von Davier, & C. Lewis (Eds), *Computerized multistage testing: Theory and applications* (pp. 189–204). London, England: Chapman and Hall.

Stocking, M. L., & Lewis, C. (1998). Controlling item exposure conditional on ability in computerized adaptive testing. *Journal of Educational Measurement, 23,* 57–75.

Stocking, M. L., & Swanson, L. (1993). A method for severely constrained item selection in adaptive testing. *Applied Psychological Measurement, 23,* 57–75.

Sympson, J. B., & Hetter, R. D. (1985). Controlling item-exposure rates in computerized adaptive testing. In *Procedings of the 27th Annual Meeting of the Millitary testing Association* (pp. 973–977). San Diego, CA: Navy Personnel research and Development Center.

van der Linden, W. J. (1998). Optimal assembly of psychological and educational tests. *Applied Psychological measurement 22,* 195–211.

van der Linden, W. J., & Glas, C. A. W. (2010). *Elements of computerized adaptive testing.* New York, NY: Springer.

van der Linden, W. J., & Diao, Q. (2014). Using a universal shadow-test assembler with multistage testing. In D. Yan, A. A. von Davier, & C. Lewis (Eds), *Computerized multistage testing: Theory and applications* (pp. 101–118). London, England: Chapman and Hall.

van Rijn, P. W. (2014). Reliability of multistage tests using item response theory. In D. Yan, A. A. von Davier, & C. Lewis (Eds), *Computerized multistage testing: Theory and applications* (pp. 251–264). London, England: Chapman and Hall.

Veldkamp, B. P. (2014). Item pool design and maintenance for multistage testing. In D. Yan, A. A. von Davier, & C. Lewis (Eds), *Computerized multistage testing: Theory and applications* (pp. 39–54). London, England: Chapman and Hall.

Verschoor, A., & Eggen, T. J. H. M. (2014). Optimizing the test assembly and routing for multistage testing. In D. Yan, A. A. von Davier, & C. Lewis (Eds), *Computerized multistage testing: Theory and applications* (pp. 135–150). London, England: Chapman and Hall.

von Davier, M., & Cheng, Y. (2014). Multistage testing using diagnostic models. In D. Yan, A. A. von Davier, & C. Lewis (Eds), *Computerized multistage testing: Theory and applications.* London, England: Chapman and Hall.

Wainer, H., Kaplan, B., & Lewis, C. (1992). A comparison of the performance of simulated hierarchical and linear testlets. *Journal of Educational Measurement, 29,* 243–251.

Weissman, A. (2014). IRT-based multistage testing. In D. Yan, A. A. von Davier, & C. Lewis (Eds), *Computerized multistage testing: Theory and applications* (pp. 153–168). London, England: Chapman and Hall.

Wentzel, C., Mills, C. M., & Meara, K. C. (2014). Transitioning a K–12 assessment from linear to multistage tests. In D. Yan, A. A. von Davier, & C. Lewis (Eds), *Computerized multistage testing: Theory and applications* (pp. 355–370). London, England: Chapman and Hall.

Yamamoto, K., Shin, H., & Khorramdel, L. (2018). Multistage adaptive testing design in international large-scale assessments. *Educational Measurement: Issues and Practice. 37*(4), 16–27.

Yan, D., Lewis, C., & von Davier, A. A. (2014a). A tree-based approach for multistage testing. In D. Yan, A. A. von Davier, & C. Lewis (Eds), *Computerized multistage testing: Theory and applications* (pp. 169–188). London, England: Chapman and Hall.

Yan, D., Lewis, C., & von Davier, A. A. (2014b). Multistage test design and scoring with small samples. In D. Yan, A. A. von Davier, & C. Lewis (Eds), *Computerized multistage testing: Theory and applications* (pp. 301–324). London, England: Chapman and Hall.

Yan, D., Lewis, C., & von Davier, A. A. (2014c). Overview of computerized multistage tests. In D. Yan, A. A. von Davier, & C. Lewis (Eds), *Computerized multistage testing: Theory and applications* (pp. 3–20). London, England: Chapman and Hall.

Yan, D., Lewis, C., & Stocking, M. (2004). Adaptive testing with regression trees in the presence of multidimensionality. *Journal of Educational and Behavior Statistics, 29,* 293–316.

Yan, D., von Davier, A. A., & Lewis, C. (Eds.). (2014). *Computerized multistage testing: Theory and applications.* London, England: Chapman and Hall.

Zenisky, A. L., & Hambleton, R. K. (2014). Multistage test designs: Moving research results into practice. In D. Yan, A. A. von Davier, & C. Lewis (Eds), *Computerized multistage testing: Theory and applications* (pp. 21–38). London, England: Chapman and Hall.

Zheng, Y., Wang, C., Culbertson, M. J., & Chang, H.-H. (2014). Overview of test assembly methods in multistage testing. In D. Yan, A. A. von Davier, & C. Lewis (Eds), *Computerized multistage testing: Theory and applications* (pp. 87–100). London, England: Chapman and Hall.

Zwick, R., & Bridgeman, B. (2014). Evaluating validity, fairness, and differential item functioning in multistage testing. In D. Yan, A. A. von Davier, & C. Lewis (Eds), *Computerized multistage testing: Theory and applications* (pp. 271–284). London, England: Chapman and Hall.

CHAPTER 9

AN INTELLIGENT CAT THAT CAN DEAL WITH DISENGAGED TEST TAKING

Steven L. Wise
NWEA

As applications of artificial intelligence (AI) become increasingly common in everyday life, it is natural to explore its potential role in achievement measurement. This idea is reinforced by the ubiquitous presence of computers in our schools and organizations, and in the increased role they have played in the development, administration, and scoring of tests. The general notion of administering "smarter" achievement tests is attractive to educators who desire an efficient collection of valid information about what test takers know and can do.

However, the application of AI in achievement testing is not a particularly new idea. It started nearly 50 years ago, as the principles of *tailored testing* were introduced and investigated (Green, 1970; Linn, Rock, & Cleary, 1969; Lord, 1970; Owen, 1969; Weiss & Betz, 1973). This type of test eventually became known as a *computerized adaptive test (CAT)*. Around that time, two major developments were influencing the field of measurement. First, item

Application of Artificial Intelligence to Assessment, pages 161–174
Copyright © 2020 by Information Age Publishing
All rights of reproduction in any form reserved.

response theory (IRT) was emerging and just beginning its transformative impact on the field of measurement. Second, the possibility of computer-based testing was rapidly becoming a reality, as computers were becoming smaller and less expensive, and could support laboratories containing multiple computer terminals.

A CAT uses the computer's decision-making capability to employ two basic IRT concepts. The first is the principle of *invariance*—the idea that test takers' expected scores are invariant regardless of which subsets they receive from a calibrated set of items. The second is the concept of *item information*—that the amount of psychometric information provided by an item response varies across ability and is highest when the item's difficulty matches the test taker's ability. This implies that (a) if test takers received different sets of items, their scores would be comparable because they were on the same scale; and (b) test information would efficiently accrue if test takers were administered items well matched to their ability levels. This is what a CAT does: It uses an intelligent item selection algorithm that continually strives to adapt item difficulty to match the test taker's ability. As a result, using far fewer items, a CAT can attain measurement precision equivalent to that from a traditional fixed-item test.

It is useful to conceptualize a CAT test event as a series of items being selected, administered, and scored. With each successive item, we gain more psychometric information about the test taker. The basic CAT algorithm was intended to maximize the accumulated information, which is equivalent to selecting item difficulty as to minimize the resulting test score's standard error. The primary goal of the CAT has been efficient measurement, focused on maximizing test score reliability (i.e., precision).

In practice, however, it quickly became evident that while adapting solely on item difficulty maximizes reliability, score validity could be compromised. Most operational tests are based on blueprints with specific item content requirements, and maximum-information item selection ignores these requirements. In addition, strict adherence to maximum-information item selection often led to some items being overexposed, which could lead to undesirable drift in item difficulty parameters. To address these types of concerns, a number of constraints to the item selection algorithm have been proposed by researchers and implemented to control issues such as content alignment, exposure control, and item enemies. Such constraints are intended to ensure test score validity, albeit at the expense of some tolerable amount of testing efficiency.

Even though the CAT algorithm has evolved since its inception, its evolution represents primarily refinements of the basic idea of adaptation though adjusting item difficulty. This has led to a simplistic conceptualization of an adaptive test as one that "adapts" solely through item difficulty. For example, the online *Glossary of Education Reform* contains a typical definition of a CAT: "Computer-adaptive tests are designed to adjust their level of difficulty—based on the responses provided, to match the knowledge and ability of a test taker" ("Computer-adaptive Test," n.d.). There are, however, many ways a test could potentially adapt to the behavior of a test taker. The purpose of this chapter is to discuss one of those ways and to argue for an expanded view of adaptive tests—one that promotes validity through multiple types of adaptation.

Why have CATs shown restricted evolution over the years? A plausible explanation is that CATs have often been developed as computerized versions within established paper-and-pencil testing programs. In these circumstances, the testing *standards* (AERA, APA, & NCME, 2014) recommend that test givers provide evidence of score comparability across testing modes. This has resulted in researchers and test givers devoting considerable attention to establishing score comparability between computerized and paper-and-pencil test modes. In one sense, this is reasonable, as it follows the *standards'* recommendations. On the other hand, the emphasis on comparability has likely had the unintended effect of discouraging the development of computer-based tests (CATs included) whose features were markedly different from their paper-and-pencil counterparts. This has been changing as more capable CATs have recently begun to emerge that are not tethered to a paper-and-pencil version. This invited the development of more innovative CATs.

Re-Conceptualizing Adaptation More Broadly

The idea that a computer-based test can intelligently adapt to a test taker's behavior is powerful, and our traditional CATs which adapt item difficulty—with suitable item-selection constraints—provide a strong example of the power of adaptation to improve measurement. It can be argued, however, that item difficulty-based adaptation has evolved to the point that further refinements are unlikely to materially increase a traditional CAT's ability to improve measurement. That is, we now have established a reasonably good understanding of how to operationally develop, administer, and score difficulty-adapting CATs.

A CAT, however, could potentially adapt to test taker behavior in ways other than adapting item difficulty. CATs can collect many types of data during test events about test taker behavior, and these data could provide information about the presence of construct-irrelevant factors whose presence can diminish test score validity (Haladyna & Downing, 2004; Messick, 1989). If a CAT could adapt to a test taker in such a way that the impact of these factors was reduced or eliminated, the validity of the resulting test score would be improved. This suggests an expanded definition of adaptive testing—one that goes beyond difficulty-based adaptation:

A Computerized Adaptive Test (CAT) is a type of computer-based test that can adapt, during a test event, to test taker behavior in ways that can improve test efficiency and the validity of the scores produced.

To illustrate this broader definition of CATs, I will focus on test taker *disengagement*, which is a frequently observed construct-irrelevant factor that can seriously diminish test score validity (Wise & DeMars, 2005).

Our contemporary measurement models assume that, during a test event, all of the item responses reflect what the test taker knows and can do regarding the domain of interest. This assumption requires that each of the item responses comes from an engaged test taker who devotes effort in applying his or her knowledge, skills, and abilities to respond to each item presented. In reality, however, a test taker can become disengaged while taking a test. When this happens, score validity is threatened, because disengagement constitutes a construct-irrelevant behavior that tends to induce a negative bias on test scores. Disengaged test taking occurs most often with low-stakes tests, for which test takers are most likely to perceive an absence of personal consequences associated with their test performance (Knekta, 2017; Wolf & Smith, 1995).

A commonly observed form of disengaged test taking can be identified based on how quickly a test taker submits a response to an item. This is useful with computer-based tests, which can readily measure and record item response time. Schnipke (1995) first noted the presence of *rapid-guessing behavior*, in which a test taker responds to an item much faster than it generally takes under *solution behavior* to read the item, solve its challenge, and select an answer. Rapid guesses represent instances of a test taker's choice to "opt out" of being measured, because they reflect a response process that provides little, if any, psychometric information for the construct or domain being measured (Wise & Kuhfeld, in press). The presence of rapid guessing therefore impairs the measurement process, and it is desirable to reduce its prevalence.

The Psychometric Impact of Disengagement on CAT

Test taker disengagement, exhibited as rapid guessing during a CAT, has three negative consequences that affect the quality of measurement. While two of the consequences are common to both adaptive and traditional fixed-item tests, the third is unique to CAT.

First, as noted earlier, rapid guessing tends to negatively bias test scores. The reason for this can readily be seen when a CAT is administered. A CAT continually tries to select items that are matched to the test taker's ability level, which implies that correct answers ought to result about 50% of the time.[1] But the accuracy rate of rapid guesses tends to be far lower, typically 15%–35%.[2] This suggests that when test takers rapidly guess, they are momentarily responding as if they were of markedly lower ability. The result of this behavior is a negatively biased ability estimate, with the degree of bias a function of both the number of rapid guesses that occur during a test event and how lucky the test taker's rapid guesses are.

Second, when rapid guessing is present, IRT-based estimates of the standard error of ability will be too low. Rapid guesses have been shown to yield little to no actual psychometric information (Wise, 2017; Wise & Kuhfeld, in press), but traditional IRT scoring—which assumes engaged test taking—aggregates the information theoretically provided by all of the item responses when estimating the standard error of ability. For example, if a test taker exhibits rapid guessing on 10 items of a 40-item test, informative responses were obtained on only 30 of the 40 items. Traditional IRT scoring, however, would presume there were 40 informative responses, resulting in the standard error of ability being underestimated.

The third consequence of rapid guessing became evident as we better understood rapid-guessing behavior during a CAT. Wise and Kingsbury (2016) observed that CAT test takers will sometimes resume solution behavior after they had exhibited a series of rapid guesses. Because rapid guesses are predominantly incorrect, the item selection algorithm is likely to be misled into administering less difficult items, that are progressively less targeted to the test taker's actual ability level. Then, once re-engagement occurs, even though the test taker is again exhibiting solution behavior, the initial item responses can provide only a fraction of the psychometric information they would have had they been more accurately targeted. Moreover, it may take quite a few engaged responses before item difficulty begins to be well targeted again. As a result, multiple solution behaviors may occur upon re-engagement that yield little psychometric information, resulting in ability estimates with diminished precision (i.e., larger standard errors).

To illustrate this mis-targeting problem, Figure 9.1 shows item-by-item information about a test event from NWEA's MAP® Growth™ assessment in math. MAP Growth is a multiple-choice computerized adaptive testing system that administers interim achievement tests to K–12 students. MAP Growth calculates scores on its RIT achievement scale, for which 10 points equals one logit. Because MAP Growth test events can be considered low-stakes and unspeeded, rapid guessing sometimes occurs, which reflects unmotivated test taking. The main body of Figure 9.1 shows the difficulty level of each item administered and each of these difficulty levels closely matched the test taker's Bayesian-based provisional achievement estimate at that point in the test event. Additionally, along the horizontal axis there are two types of symbols indicating, for each item response, when the response was correct and when it was a rapid guess.

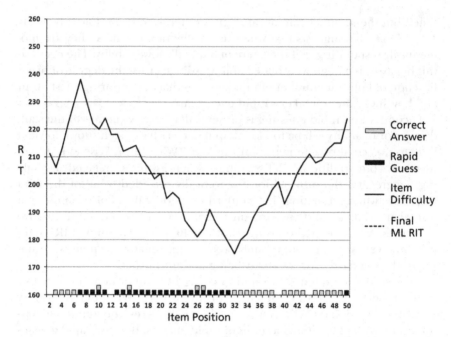

Figure 9.1 A Map Growth CAT test event in which a test taker re-engaged after a period of disengagement. This illustrates how item difficulty can become mis-targeted because of disengagement. On the RIT achievement scale, one logit equals 10 RIT points.

In this example, the test taker started out well, passing his first four items and moving his provisional RIT score from its initial value (near 210) to a value exceeding 230. At the fifth item his test-taking behavior dramatically changed, and he exhibited rapid guesses to 24 of the next 25 items, while passing only four. As a result of this change in behavior, his provisional RIT scores (and correspondingly, item difficulty) steadily decreased down to a value below 180. At this point in the test event, his behavior changed again, and he exhibited solution behavior to 18 of the remaining 19 items, passing 16 of them. Correspondingly, his provisional RIT scores and item difficulties steadily increased back up to their final values above 210. If one accepts the premise that this test taker's actual achievement level was in the region of 220, then when the test taker re-engaged at the 32nd item, he received an item whose difficulty was more than *four logits* below his achievement level. A response to an item this far away provides minimal item formation— less than 5% of that from a well-targeted item. Moreover, it took a dozen subsequent items for item difficulty to gradually move back to within two logits of his actual achievement level, a difference that still reflected considerable mis-targeting. This illustrates how low information can be provided by initial item responses after re-engagement, resulting in reduced precision of the test score. Essentially, this test event reflected two different test takers: the engaged student whose achievement level appeared to be well above 200, and a disengaged version of that student who mostly failed to correctly answer items whose difficulties were well below 200.

MANAGING THE CONSEQUENCES OF DISENGAGEMENT

Given the three consequences of disengagement on CAT, what can be done about the problem? One option would be simply to report engagement information on score reports, so the degree of test taker engagement would be communicated to individuals who interpret that score. A second option is to statistically adjust the test taker's score for the amount of rapid guessing that had occurred (Wang & Xu, 2015; Wise & Kingsbury, 2016). Both of these options represent actions that can be taken after a test event (and therefore any rapid guessing) had already occurred.

Effort Monitoring

A more proactive approach would be to intervene, in real time, during a test event in an attempt to curtail the amount of subsequent disengagement. The logic for this idea is straightforward; a computer-based test could monitor item response time during the test, which would permit the identification of rapid guesses as they occurred. Then, if a specified amount or pattern of rapid guessing occurred, some sort of intervention would be initiated that was intended to re-engage the test taker.

Effort monitoring was first investigated with a low-stakes university outcomes assessment by Wise, Bhola, and Yang (2006). For this traditional (i.e., fixed-item) computer-based test, if a test taker exhibited three consecutive rapid guesses, the following message would appear on their computer screen:

> Your responses to this test indicate that you are not giving your best effort.
>
> It is very important that you try to do your best on the tests you take on Assessment Day. These assessment data are used by <the university> to better understand what students learn at <the university>, and what improvements need to be made. In addition, <the university's> assessment data are reported to the state as evidence of what <the university's> students know and can do.

Wise et al. conducted an experiment in which test takers were randomly assigned to either receive the warning message, or not, if it was deserved it (i.e., if they exhibited three rapid guesses in a row). In addition, Kong, Wise, Harmes, and Yang (2006) conducted a follow-up study that used the same experimental conditions.

The results of these studies, which are summarized in Table 9.1, show that the warning messages had positive effects on both subsequent engagement and test performance. Averaging across the two studies, sending messages to deserving test takers had the effect of increasing the proportion of solution behaviors—termed *response time effort* (RTE; Wise & Kong, 2005)—by a full standard deviation. Correspondingly, test performance was also found to increase by about a half standard deviation. In addition, the positive impact of the messages on test score validity was supported by the correlations of test scores with external variables for which positive correlations would be expected (i.e., convergent validation evidence). In each study, these correlations for test takers deserving messages showed a marked increase. It is especially interesting that the correlations increased when messages were provided even though test score variability decreased, a finding that is consistent with the interpretation that warning messages had the effect of removing disengagement-related construct-irrelevant variance.

It is important to note that effort monitoring represents a novel type of computer-based test adaptation. The test detects rapid-guessing behavior and adapts to its presence by displaying warning messages. In contrast, test takers who do not exhibit rapid guessing receive no messages. Hence, the test adapts to test-taker behavior in a new way—one that does not involve adjusting item difficulty.

TABLE 9.1   Results From Two Studies Investigating the Impact of Effort Monitoring With a University General Education Assessment

	Study	
Study Findings	**Wise, Bhola, & Yang (2006)**	**Kong, Wise, Harmes, & Yang (2006)**
Test-Taking Engagement	RTE significantly increased ($ES = .78$)	RTE significantly increased ($ES = 1.37$)
Test Performance	Nonsignificant test performance increase ($ES = .32$)	Significant test performance Increase ($ES = .61$)
Correlations With External Variables	Higher squared correlations of test performance with SAT scores and GPA (r^2 increase ranged from .05 to .11)	Higher squared correlations of test performance with SAT scores (r^2 increase ranged from .07 to .09)

Note: The results summarized in the table are based on those test takers who deserved a warning message. The findings for test-taking engagement and test performance refer to test taker behavior after a warning message had been deserved. ES = standardized mean difference effect size.

A More Intelligent CAT

Beginning in 2016, NWEA released new versions of its MAP Growth assessments designed to address the three consequences of disengaged test taking. Along with the traditional item difficulty adaptation, MAP Growth now incorporates two additional types of adaptation. First, it uses effort monitoring to detect disengaged test taking. MAP Growth does not, however, send warning messages directly to test takers. It instead sends a notification to the computer of the test proctor, who is encouraged to personally intervene with the test taker to re-engage them. When these interventions are successful, the test taker will cease rapid guessing, which will result in scores that are less negatively distorted by rapid guessing and will have lower standard errors.

The second adaptation is that item selection in MAP Growth now ignores item responses resulting from rapid guessing as it identifies the items to select for test takers. We have found that this relatively simple modification can prevent the item selection algorithm from being "confused" by rapid guesses (Wise & Kingsbury, 2016), because it helps avoid the mis-targeting consequence described earlier.

Both of these adaptations can positively address the three consequences of disengaged test taking on a CAT by responding to test taker behavior. Proctor notification can decrease the amount of rapid guessing that occurs, while the item selection modification helps ensure that the CAT can provide well-targeted items to each test taker. Together, these adaptations promise to promote test score validity by alleviating the impact of a common construct-irrelevant factor.

The initial investigation from the proctor notification feature in CAT indicates that its impact is similar to that observed with effort monitoring that directly sends messages to test takers. After proctor notification, mean test taker engagement increased, as did mean test performance. Moreover, the scores from test events that elicit notifications showed increased convergent validation evidence.

Expanded Methods of Effort Monitoring

There are numerous additional methods by which effort monitoring might potentially be used to detect disengagement and intervene during a test event. These methods vary in both the indicator(s) of disengagement that could be used, and the types of interventions that could result from its occurrence.

Beyond response time, a variety of *process data* might be collected during computer-based tests that could serve as useful indicators of disengagement. Goldhammer and Zehner (2017) defined process data as "empirical information about the cognitive (as well as meta-cognitive, motivational, and affective) and related behavior that mediate the effect of the measured construct(s) on the task product (i.e., item score)" (p. 128). Examples of process data that have shown potential useful for identifying test-taking disengagement include eye tracking (Oranje, Gorin, Jia, & Kerr, 2017), gestures or verbalizations during a test event (Maddox, 2017), facial recognition (Grafsgaard, Wiggins, Boyer, Weibe, & Lester, 2013), and whether or not the item response was reviewed by the test taker (Wise & Gao, 2017). Additionally, research using physiological information such as biometric measures (e.g., heart rate), body movement, or brain waves might be found useful in identifying disengagement.

Harmes and Wise (2016) investigated a method for detecting disengagement on an item based on the degree to which a test taker exhibited the actions expected to be completed by an engaged test taker. For example, if the test taker did not scroll through a lengthy reading passage or did not open important tabbed information needed to understand the item's challenge, one might infer disengagement. A computer-based test could record these types of test-taker behavior on each item and evaluate the extent to which engagement was indicated.

Hence, there are numerous types of indicators of disengagement that could be considered by a CAT. To be useful in effort monitoring, however, an indicator would need to have several characteristics. First, its collection should be unobtrusive. It would probably interfere with measurement, for instance, if we were to ask test takers to report, after each item response, how engaged they were on that item. Second, the indicator must be able to be quickly evaluated by the CAT, so that a timely intervention could be implemented. Third, there needs to be empirical evidence of a clear and unambiguous link between the indicator and disengagement (including the indicator criteria used to infer disengagement).

Just as there are different indicators of disengagement that could be used, there are multiple types of interventions that could be implemented by an effort monitoring CAT. Some interventions will be overt, from the test taker's perspective, while others will be less obvious. As with indicators of disengagement, the effectiveness of a given intervention should be empirically validated.

It was noted earlier that displaying messages to test takers can increase engagement. However, there are various types of messages that could be used. Messages warning test takers that their rapid-guessing behavior has been noticed, such as those used by Wise et al. (2006) with university students, are especially direct. With younger test takers, gentler messages of encouragement may prove more effective. In addition, Kong et al. (2006) investigated the use of messages praising test takers who had *not* exhibited rapid guessing rather than warning those who had. More research is needed to better understand the most effective types of messages to display to various types of test takers.

An alternative approach to intervention would be for the CAT to alter the way the test was administered. Pausing the test event and providing a short break might serve to re-engage the test taker. More subtly, altering the difficulty of the items administered may improve engagement, even though this would come at the cost of somewhat diminished test information. Similarly, some types of items tend to receive fewer rapid guesses, such as those that are less mentally taxing (Wolf, Smith, & Birnbaum, 1995), those requiring less reading (Wise, Pastor, & Kong, 2009), and those containing pictures, figures, or graphs (Lindner, Lüdtke, Grund, & Köller, 2017; Wise et al., 2009). Finally, just as *gamification* has been shown to increase student motivation in learning environments, gamification elements are likely to find a role in adaptive testing. A CAT may, for example, begin to offer a game-like challenge to a disengaged test taker, particularly if that challenge can be adapted to the particular interests (e.g., hobbies, activities, sports teams, etc.) of the test taker (Kingsbury & Wise, 2012).

CONCLUDING COMMENTS

Each month seems to bring news of some new application of AI that will affect our lives. But while there is a clear role for AI in computer-based testing, the science of incorporating AI into CAT is still in its infancy. What is needed to encourage the development and incorporation of additional AI elements to improve measurement? I would argue that the answer largely requires a greater understanding of the psychology of test taking and the ways in which construct-irrelevant factors threaten the validity of test scores. Essentially, I am encouraging measurement researchers and practitioners to conceptualize adaptive testing as a general method for maximizing test score validity rather than maximizing score reliability. In this view, for example, the validity benefits of reducing the distortive effects of some construct-irrelevant factor will sometimes outweigh the psychometric benefits accrued through improvements in the efficiency of difficulty-based item selection.

The idea that the goal of a CAT should be directed toward maximizing validity rather than maximizing psychometric information might be questioned on the grounds that it violates the fundamental ideal of standardized testing. That is, if some test takers receive an intervention, while others do not, doesn't this departure from standardization confound our interpretation of test performance differences among test takers? I have two responses to this concern. First, the interventions discussed here are intended to address the presence of a construct-irrelevant factor, such as disengagement, that may affect some test takers, but not others. If such a factor is differentially present, then it already represents a confounding factor that is affecting the test data, and the point of the intervention is to reduce that confound. Second, it is worth noting that a traditional CAT already is less standardized than a fixed-item test, because test takers receive different sets of items. Any adaptation, by definition, implies less standardization. It is therefore important to differentiate between departures from standardization that serve to enhance validity, and those that diminish validity.

A useful model for future AI developments in CAT is provided by individually-administered tests of achievement or ability. Administrators of these sorts of tests are typically trained to monitor a test taker's behavior during the test event, and to take action if they observe that score validity is threatened by some construct-irrelevant factor (e.g., low motivation, anxiety, illness, etc). With the rise of group-based testing a century ago, such individualized test administration was rendered impractical. The promise of AI-based CATs is that they can help us return to individualized testing practices that will maximize test score validity.

AUTHOR'S NOTE

The views expressed in this chapter are solely those of the author and they do not necessarily reflect the positions of NWEA. Correspondence concerning this chapter should be addressed to Steven L. Wise, NWEA, 121 NW Everett St, Portland, Oregon 97209. Email: steve.wise@nwea.org

NOTES

1. A 50% accuracy rate is characteristic of CAT based on a one- or two-parameter IRT model. Under a three-parameter model, the accuracy rate will tend to be somewhat higher—closer to 60%.
2. The accuracy of rapid guesses is affected largely by the option position of the correct answer. They tend to be higher for middle options and lower for the first and last option positions (Wise & Kuhfeld, in press).

REFERENCES

American Educational Research Association, American Psychological Association, & National Council on Measurement in Education. (2014). *Standards for educational and psychological testing*. Washington, DC: American Educational Research Association.

Computer-adaptive Test. (n.d.). In *The Glossary of Education Reform*. Retrieved from http://edglossary.org/computer-adaptive-test/

Goldhammer, F., & Zehner, F. (2017). What to make of and how to interpret process data. *Measurement: Interdisciplinary Research and Perspectives, 15*(3/4), 128–132.

Grafsgaard, J., Wiggins, J. B., Boyer, K. E., Wiebe, E. N., & Lester, J. (2013, July). Automatically recognizing facial expression: Predicting engagement and frustration. In *Proceedings of the Sixth International Conference on Educational Data Mining*. Memphis, TN: International Educational Data Mining Society.

Green, B. F. (1970). Comments on tailored testing. *Computer-assisted instruction, testing, and guidance*. New York, NY: Harper & Row.

Haladyna, T. M., & Downing, S. M. (2004). Construct-irrelevant variance in high-stakes testing. *Educational Measurement: Issues and Practice, 23*(1), 17–27.

Harmes, J. C., & Wise, S. L. (2016). Assessing engagement during the online assessment of real-world skills. In Y. Rosen, S. Ferrara, & M. Mosharraf (Eds.), *Handbook of research on technology tools for real-world skill development* (pp. 804–823). Hershey, PA: IGI Global.

Kingsbury, G. G., & Wise, S. L. (2012). Turning the page: How smarter testing, vertical scales, and understanding of student engagement may improve our tests. In R. W. Lissitz & H. Jiao (Eds.), *Computers and their impact on state assessments: Recent history and predictions for the future* (pp. 245–269). Charlotte, NC: Information Age.

Knekta, E. (2017). Are all pupils equally motivated to do their best on all tests? Differences in reported test-taking motivation within and between tests with different stakes. *Scandinavian Journal of Educational Research, 61*(1), 95–111.

Kong, X. J., Wise, S. L., Harmes, J. C., & Yang, S. (2006, April). *Motivational effects of praise in response-time based feedback: A follow-up study of the effort-monitoring CBT*. Paper presented at the annual meeting of the National Council on Measurement in Education, San Francisco, CA.

Lindner, M. A., Lüdtke, O., Grund, S., & Köller, O. (2017). The merits of representational pictures in educational assessment: Evidence for cognitive and motivational effects in a time-on-task analysis. *Contemporary Educational Psychology, 51*, 482–492.

Linn, R. L., Rock, D. A., & Cleary, T. A. (1969). The development and evaluation of several programmed testing methods. *Educational and Psychological Measurement, 29*, 129–146.

Lord, F. M. (1970). Some test theory for tailored testing. In W. H. Holtzman (Ed.), *Computer-assisted instruction, testing, and guidance*. New York, NY: Harper & Row.

Maddox, B. (2017). Talk and gesture as process data. *Measurement: Interdisciplinary Research and Perspectives, 15*(3/4), 113–127.

Messick, S. (1989). Validity. In R. L. Linn (Ed.), *Educational measurement* (3rd ed., pp. 13–103). New York, NY: American Council in Education & Macmillan.

Oranje, A., Gorin, J., Jia, Y., & Kerr, D. (2017). Collecting, analyzing, and interpreting response time, eye tracking and log data. In K. Ercikan & J. W. Pellegrino (Eds.), *Validation of score meaning for the next generation of assessments* (pp. 39–51). New York, NY: Routledge.

Owen, R. J. (1969). *A Bayesian approach to tailored testing* (Research Report 69-92). Princeton, NJ: Educational Testing Service.

Schnipke, D. L. (1995). *Assessing speededness in computer-based tests using item response times* (Unpublished doctoral dissertation). Johns Hopkins University, Baltimore, MD.

Wang, C., & Xu, G. (2015). A mixture hierarchical model for response times and response accuracy. *British Journal of Mathematical and Statistical Psychology, 68,* 456–477.

Weiss, D. J., & Betz, N. E. (1973). *Ability measurement: Conventional or adaptive?* (Research Report 73-1). Minneapolis, MN: University of Minnesota, Psychometric Methods Program, Department of Psychology.

Wise, S. L. (2017). Rapid-guessing behavior: Its identification, interpretations, and implications. *Educational Measurement: Issues and Practice, 36*(4), 52–61.

Wise, S. L., Bhola, D., & Yang, S. (2006). Taking the time to improve the validity of low-stakes tests: The effort-monitoring CBT. *Educational Measurement: Issues and Practice, 25*(2), 21–30.

Wise, S. L., & DeMars, C. E. (2005). Low examinee effort in low-stakes assessment: Problems and potential solutions. *Educational Assessment, 10,* 1–17.

Wise, S. L., & Gao, L. (2017). A general approach to measuring test-taking effort on computer-based tests. *Applied Measurement in Education, 30,* 343–354.

Wise, S. L., & Kingsbury, G. G. (2016). Modeling student test-taking motivation in the context of an adaptive achievement test. *Journal of Educational Measurement, 53,* 86–105.

Wise, S. L., & Kong, X. (2005). Response time effort: A new measure of examinee motivation in computer-based tests. *Applied Measurement in Education, 18,* 163–183.

Wise, S. L., & Kuhfeld, M. R. (in press). A cessation of measurement: Identifying test taker disengagement using response time. In M. J. Margolis & R. A. Feinberg (Eds.), *Integrating timing considerations to improve testing practices.* New York, NY: Routledge.

Wise, S. L., Pastor, D. A., & Kong, X. J. (2009). Understanding correlates of rapid-guessing behavior in low stakes testing: Implications for test development and measurement practice. *Applied Measurement in Education, 22,* 185–205.

Wolf, L. F., & Smith, J. K. (1995). The consequence of consequence: Motivation, anxiety, and test performance. *Applied Measurement in Education, 8,* 227–242.

Wolf, L. F., Smith, J. K., & Birnbaum, M. E. (1995). Consequence of performance, test motivation, and mentally taxing items. *Applied Measurement in Education, 8,* 341–351.

CHAPTER 10

DIFFERENCES IN THE AMOUNT OF ADAPTATION EXHIBITED BY VARIOUS COMPUTERIZED ADAPTIVE TESTING DESIGNS

Mark D. Reckase
Michigan State University

Unhee Ju
Riverside Insights

Sewon Kim
Michigan State University

Computerized adaptive testing (CAT)[1] is a widely used approach to customize the items administered to each examinee during a test. The item selection is made to optimize a criterion such as maximizing the amount of Fisher information at the most recent estimate of proficiency or maximizing

Application of Artificial Intelligence to Assessment, pages 175–187
Copyright © 2020 by Information Age Publishing
All rights of reproduction in any form reserved.

decision accuracy for placement above or below a cut score (e.g., see Thompson, 2009). CAT designs have been successfully used in a variety of settings from military testing (ASVAB; Pommerich, Segall, & Moreno, 2009), placement in 2-year college courses (COMPASS; ACT, 2006), licensure and certification (NCLEX; NCSBN, 2016), and so forth. In recent years, there has been interest in using CAT designs for evaluating student achievement within the context of state testing programs (e.g., Minnesota; Minnesota Department of Education, 2017). Like any other approach to test design, there is not a single approach to CAT. There are many alternative designs using different options related to item selection, proficiency estimation, exposure control, item pool composition, content constraints, item types, and so forth. Our own previous work (Reckase, Ju, & Kim, 2018, 2019), plus observations of operational CATs, have shown that all designs are not equally adaptive. That is, two test designs for the same purpose may both be labeled as a CAT, but the amount of customization of the test for each examinee for the two designs might not be the same. The purposes of this chapter are to suggest some descriptive measures of adaptation, summarize previous research on amount of adaptation for some CAT designs, and show the differences in the amount of adaptation that result from the use of some common CAT designs.

For the research reported here, the basic unconstrained CAT (UCAT) will serve as a basis for comparison. This is a CAT that selects individual items to maximize the information at the current proficiency estimate and uses maximum likelihood estimation to obtain the proficiency estimate after each item is administered. The other designs that are considered are the a-stratified approach with b-blocking (Stratified; Chang, Qian, & Ying, 2001) and two multi-stage designs (MST; Yan, von Davier, & Lewis, 2014). Previous work concentrated on CAT designs that used the Rasch model for item calibration and scoring (Reckase, Ju, & Kim, 2018, 2019). The work reported here extends previous research to CATs based on the three-parameter logistic (3pl) model.

DEFINITIONS OF ADAPTATION

The ideal case for an adaptive test designed to accurately estimate the location of an individual on the latent construct that is the target for the test is that each individual would receive a set of items that was specifically targeted to their true location on the scale. That is, if the Rasch model was the method for scaling and scoring the CAT, then all items would be selected that had b-parameters equal to the true location (θ) on the Rasch-based scale. In that case, individuals with different true locations would get different sets of items. The mean b-parameters for each individual would be perfectly correlated with their location and the variance of the *b*-parameters for each individual would be 0.

However, the true location is never known so a typical CAT uses the current estimate of location for selecting items. But a well adapted test should still have a high correlation between the mean *b*-parameters for the items selected for individuals and their final estimates of θ. Also, the variance of *b*-parameters for individuals should be small relative to the amount of variation in the item pool. When the 3pl model is used for scaling and scoring, the conception of adaptation is the same, but the point of maximum information for an item is usually substituted for the *b*-parameter when selecting items. That is the method for item selection that was used in this research.

Given this conceptualization of the desired characteristics of a CAT, three indexes of adaptation have been proposed and evaluated. The first is the correlation between the mean item location parameter for those items administered to examinees and the final estimate of the examinees' locations on the item response theory (IRT) scale, $r_{\zeta\hat\theta}$, where ζ is a symbol indicating the item characteristic used for selecting the items—*b*-parameter or point of maximum information. The second index is the ratio of the standard deviation of the mean item location indicator for items administered to examinees to the standard deviation of the proficiency estimates for the examinees, $s_{\bar\zeta_j}/s_{\hat\theta_j}$, where the subscript j indicates the specific examinee. This index shows if the spread of the item location indicators for the selected items matches the spread of examinee proficiency estimates. The third index is the proportion reduction in variance of the item locations administered to the examinee relative to the variance of the item locations in the item pool,

$$PRV = \frac{s_\zeta^2 - \text{pooled } s_{\zeta_j}^2}{s_\zeta^2}.$$

All three of these indexes were used in this research to evaluate the adaptability of the CAT designs considered here.

ADAPTIVE TESTING PROCEDURES USED IN THE STUDY

The research reported in this chapter compares the amount of adaptation that results from the use of three different adaptive test designs. The comparisons use a common item pool and a common goal for the test. Because simple labels often mask important details of CAT designs, the details of the designs used in our research are given below.

Basic Unconstrained CAT (UCAT)

The basic unconstrained CAT (UCAT) has the goal of obtaining an accurate estimate of the location of each examinee on the continuum for the hypothetical construct that is the target of the test. This CAT uses an item pool that has items that have been well calibrated using the 3pl model. The UCAT assumes an initial estimate of proficiency for the examinee of 0.0 and selects items to provide maximum Fisher information at the current estimate of proficiency. The proficiency is estimated using maximum likelihood when the set of item scores for an examinee contains both an incorrect and a correct score. Before both correct and incorrect responses are present, the proficiency estimate is increased by .7 after a correct response and is decreased by .7 after an incorrect response. The UCAT terminates when a test length of 40 items has been reached.

a-Stratified With *b*-Blocking

The *a*-stratified with *b*-blocking design (stratified) was originally proposed to make sure that the most discriminating items were not overused and low discriminating items were not underused (Chang, Qian, & Ying, 2001). The original method selected items based on the *b*-parameter rather than maximizing information. For the research reported here, items were selected using maximum information so the comparisons with other procedures would be consistent. However, selection based on the *b*-parameter was also done and showed little difference so those results are not reported here to save space. To implement the stratified procedure, the item pool for the test was divided into parts (strata) based on the magnitude of the *a*-parameters for the items. However, if there is a relationship between the *a* and *b* parameters, the strata will have different distributions of difficulty. To counter this problem, the strata were "blocked" on the *b*-parameter to ensure that the spread of difficulty for each stratum was about the same.

For the research reported here, the item pool was divided into four strata. To insure the proper distribution of difficulty for the four strata, the item pool was first sorted according to the value of the *b*-parameters. Then, starting with the lowest *b*-parameters, for each set of four items (a "block" of items), the item with the lowest *a*-parameter is placed in the lowest stratification level, the item with the next lowest *a*-parameter in the second stratum, and so on. This is done for each set of four items to yield four item pools (strata) that varied in the level of *a*-parameters, but also spanned the range of *b*-parameters.

The simulated tests using this design administered items sequentially, selecting the first ten items from the first stratum using maximum information item selection and maximum likelihood proficiency estimation, then the next ten from the next stratum, and so on, to administer the 40-item test. This process selects the last ten items from the stratum with the highest *a*-parameters. In all cases, the proficiency is estimated using maximum likelihood as was described for UCAT.

Multi-Stage 1-3-3 Design

The multi-stage test (MST) administered fixed modules of items according to decision rules. For the design used here, there was a single first-stage module called the routing test that used two decision points to route examinees to one of three second stage modules. The second stage modules were designed to make accurate classifications into the three modules at the third stage. The easiest second stage module was designed with one decision point to route to the easy and medium difficulty modules at the third stage. The medium second stage module had two decision points to route to all three third stage modules. The difficult second stage module had a single decision point to route examinees into the medium or difficult module at the third stage. In all cases, the routing rules were designed to send roughly equal numbers of examinees to each of the three modules at a stage. Items for the third stages were selected to give final estimates of proficiency based on as close an approximation to uniform information across the proficiency range as possible.

Two different configurations of sizes of modules were used for this research. One design is based on the belief that it is important to do accurate routing at the beginning of the test. That design has a 20-item routing test and the modules for the second and third stages have ten items—80 items for the full set of modules. The second design is based on the belief that it is more important to have a good set of items in the third stage and that the first two stages will adequately route examinees to the best third stage test for them (Zheng, Nozawa, Gao, & Chang, 2012). This design had ten items in each module for the first two stages and 20 items in the modules at the third stage—100 items for the full set of modules.

ITEM POOL

The research reported here is based on simulations of the three types of test designs using the same sample of simulated examinees. Such a study is impossible except in simulation because it is unlikely that individuals would be willing to take three tests, and even if they were, a constant level of motivation across all three tests would be unlikely. Using simulations of the tests makes a direct formal comparison of the results possible. However, to make the results of the simulation generalizable to real situations, the simulations must be as realistic as possible.

One challenge is to create a simulated item pool that is very like an item pool that could be produced in reality. In this case, the simulated item pool was modeled after the multivariate distribution of the a-, b-, and c-parameters from a test developed by CTB-McGraw Hill. The observed multivariate distribution was used to generate 3,000 sets of item parameters that had means, standard deviations, and intercorrelations like the empirical set. This 3,000-item pool was considered the master pool from which operational pools were selected. Table 10.1 summarizes the characteristics of the actual item pool and the item pool generated to have similar characteristics.

The operational item pool was determined through simulation of the UCAT. The UCAT was simulated using the 3,000-item pool to determine a range-optimal item pool for that CAT design (see Reckase [2010] for the background on this procedure). This process tallied the ability estimates used to select items into bins with a width of .6 on the θ scale with the middle bin centered on the 0 point of the scale. This process resulted in a target distribution for items over bins that called for 488 items for the item pool for the UCAT. Then, items were selected to fill out the requirements of the distribution over bins from the 3,000-item master pool. This process showed that there were insufficient items in the 3,000-item pool to fill the most extreme bins. The final pool consisted of 319 items that met the requirements for the bins in the middle range of the IRT scale. These 319 items were considered as the final operational item pool for the UCAT. The characteristics of that item pool are summarized in the bottom section of Table 10.1. The process of selecting the 319 items was replicated five times yielding slightly different sets of items in each bin for each replication.

Once the operational pool was developed, the stratified and MSTs designs were developed from the same operational pool. For the Stratified test design, the items in the pool were first sorted from low to high on the b-parameter. Then sequentially in sets of four, the items were placed in the four levels of stratification based on the a-parameters for each set. The results were strata with 80 items each, except for the last one that had 79 items.

Items were selected for the MST designs using the same pool of items. Those designs needed 80 or 100 items out of the 319. For the first two stages, items were selected to have maximum information at the routing decision points. This approach for item selection was used to maximize classification accuracy. Also, items for the second stage modules were selected to minimize the overlap in difficulty for the modules. To do this, twice as many items as were needed for the second stage modules were selected

TABLE 10.1 Summary Statistics for the Real and Generated Item Pools							Correlation		
Item Parameters		Mean	SD	Min	Max	Median	a	b	c
CTB Pool (n = 302)	a	0.91	0.32	0.20	1.99	0.89	1.00	—	—
	b	−0.48	0.91	−3.34	2.08	−0.47	0.29	1.00	—
	c	0.15	0.06	0.03	0.40	0.15	0.37	0.34	1.00
Generated Item Pool (n = 3,000)	a	0.90	0.30	0.29	2.01	0.87	1.00	—	—
	b	−0.49	0.90	−3.49	2.16	−0.48	0.28	1.00	—
	c	0.15	0.06	0.01	0.45	0.14	0.37	0.35	1.00
Selected Item Pool (n = 319) *	a	0.92	0.31	0.30	1.90	0.88	1.00		
	b	−0.50	1.43	−3.49	2.16	−0.49	0.40	1.00	
	c	0.15	0.07	0.01	0.42	0.14	0.46	0.56	1.00

* The pool selection was replicated five times. The values presented here are the median values from the replications.

to maximize information at the decision points for the easy and difficult models. Then the final sets of items were selected so that the second-stage modules would have non-overlapping distributions of difficulty. The items for the third stage were selected to give the approximately equal amount of measurement precision over the range of examinee's proficiencies routed to the modules at Stage 3, taking into account the amount of information obtained from the previous two stages.

The results of these development processes were three test designs based on the same item pools. These test designs were used in simulations using the same set of simulated examinees, so the results are directly comparable.

RESULTS

For the simulation, 500 examinee θ values were randomly sampled from a standard normal distribution. The same set of values was used for the simulation of each test design. The results were replicated 100 times so that the stability of the results could be determined.

UCAT

Results for the UCAT design are presented in Tables 10.1, 10.2, and 10.3. The information in Table 10.1 summarizes the item parameters for the operational item pool. The means and standard deviations for each of the parameters are presented along with the intercorrelation between the

TABLE 10.2 Comparison of True and Estimated θ for the Four Designs

Design	Estimated θ		RMSE	Correlation
	Mean	SD		
UCAT	0.01	1.03	0.21	0.98
Stratified	0.01	1.03	0.22	0.98
20-10-10	0.00	1.09	0.33	0.95
10-10-20	0.01	1.06	0.30	0.96

Note: In all cases, true θ had a mean of .00 and a *SD* of 1.0.

TABLE 10.3 Median Measures of Adaptation for Designs

Design	Adaptation Statistic		
	$r(\overline{\zeta}_j, \hat{\theta}_j)$	$s_{\overline{\zeta}_j}/s_{\hat{\theta}_j}$	PRV
UCAT	0.98	0.91	0.89
Stratified	0.96	0.92	0.87
20-10-10	0.84	0.64	0.54
10-10-20	0.86	1.07	0.65

parameters. Note that the item pool selected for the UCAT has a much larger standard deviation of *b*-parameters than the original CTB pool or the master pool because items were chosen for the operational pool to give adequate information over the full range of θ used in the simulation. As a result, the correlation between item parameters is greater than for the CTB pool and the generated pool.

The first row of Table 10.2 gives descriptive information about the true and estimated θs for the UCAT simulation, including the mean, standard deviation, root mean squared error (RMSE), and correlation. These results show that the θs were well estimated by the UCAT. Finally, the first row of Table 10.3 gives the values of the measures of adaptation for this test to serve as a baseline for evaluating the other test designs. These are the median values from the five replications of the operational item pools. Observed values from each replication differed at most by .01 from the values in the table. All three measures of adaptation show that the UCAT administered items that were well adapted to the final θ estimates.

Stratified

The results for the stratified design are presented in Tables 10.2, 10.3, and 10.4. Table 10.4 shows descriptive information about the

TABLE 10.4	Item Parameters for the Levels in the Stratified Design				
		a-Stratified CAT With *b*-Blocking			
Statistics	Total	Level 1	Level 2	Level 3	Level 4
N	319	80	80	80	79
a					
Mean	0.92	0.65	0.81	0.99	1.23
SD	0.31	0.17	0.19	0.23	0.27
b					
Mean	–0.50	–0.49	–0.50	–0.50	–0.53
SD	1.43	1.44	1.44	1.45	1.42
c					
Mean	0.15	0.13	0.14	0.16	0.17
SD	0.07	0.07	0.07	0.07	0.07

characteristics of the items allocated to each of the four strata. These results show that all four strata had about the same range of *b*-parameters and *c*-parameters. Also, the mean *a*-parameters increased from strata 1 to 4 as intended. However, there is some overlap between the distributions of *a*-parameters for the strata. This results from the fact that the *a* and *b* parameters are correlated.

The second row of Table 10.2 gives information about the estimation of θ for the stratified test design. The values for the true values of θ are the same as for the UCAT. Overall, proficiency was well estimated using this design. Differences with the results from UCAT were small.

The second row of Table 10.3 shows the measures of adaptation for the stratified test design. The results show that the median adaptation statistics are slightly lower than those for the UCAT for the correlation and the PRV. A possible explanation is that at any point in the test, items are selected from only ¼ of the full item pool. However, the differences are small, and the stratified approach gives better control over the exposure of items. The improved exposure control may justify slightly reduced adaptation. Further the ratio of the standard deviations is slightly higher for the stratified design than for UCAT. That may be because selecting from ¼ of the full pool results in the selection of more extreme items and the *b*-blocking insures that extreme items are available for selection in each stratum.

Multi-Stage Design

Tables 10.2, 10.3, 10.5 and 10.6 show the results for the MST designs. Table 10.5 provides a summary of the item parameters for each module in the

TABLE 10.5	Item Parameter Summary for the MST Designs							
			Median Over Five Replications					
			a		b		c	
Design	Stage	Type	Mean	SD	Mean	SD	Mean	SD
20-10-10	1	Routing	1.39	0.21	–0.11	0.54	0.17	0.06
	2	Easy	1.07	0.19	–1.06	0.21	0.13	0.05
		Medium	1.17	0.12	–0.08	0.67	0.16	0.05
		Difficult	1.21	0.16	0.86	0.13	0.17	0.06
	3	Easy	0.79	0.28	–3.13	0.11	0.09	0.04
		Medium	0.79	0.15	–0.38	0.05	0.14	0.05
		Difficult	1.14	0.33	2.01	0.10	0.20	0.07
10-10-20	1	Routing	1.46	0.20	–0.11	0.51	0.17	0.04
	2	Easy	1.08	0.16	–0.92	0.21	0.13	0.06
		Medium	1.31	0.15	–0.18	0.66	0.15	0.05
		Difficult	1.26	0.15	0.79	0.16	0.18	0.06
	3	Easy	0.73	0.25	–2.98	0.23	0.09	0.05
		Medium	0.78	0.18	–0.38	0.10	0.14	0.05
		Difficult	1.10	0.32	1.86	0.18	0.22	0.06

designs. The values in the Table 10.5 are the median values from the five replications of selections of items from the item pool. The most notable result in the table is that the difficulty parameters show the expected pattern for the easy, medium, and difficult modules at stages two and three. There is also a pattern of declining values for the a-parameters from the first to the third stages. This pattern is a result of the module assembly process which selects the items for the first stage, then those for the second stage and then finally for the third stage. As a result, the higher a-parameter items tend to get used in the earlier stages.

Table 10.6 shows the proportion of examinees routed to each module for each design. The goal of the routing was to have ⅓ of the examinees routed to each module so that each item would have approximately equal usage. Overall, the results came close to achieving that goal. Most of the percents of examinees routed to the modules were near 33%. However, the easy modules tended to get slightly fewer administrations than desired and the difficult modules had slightly more administrations than desired. The 20-10-10 design had slightly higher classification accuracy than the 10-10-20 design. This is likely because the former design was making routing decisions with 50 items (20 items at the first stage and 30 at the second stage) targeted at the decision points and the latter design was making the same

TABLE 10.6 Percent Routed to Each Module for the Two MST Designs: Median Values From Five Replications

Design	Stage	Module			Classification Accuracy
		Easy	Medium	Difficult	
20-10-10	2	30.17	30.94	38.83	80.37
	3	30.22	34.40	35.44	83.26
10-10-20	2	32.56	29.47	37.22	78.18
	3	31.12	32.75	36.11	81.17

Note: Routing points were −.44 and .44. Values in rows do not sum exactly to 100 because of rounding when taking the medians.

decisions with 40 items (10 items at the first stage and 30 at the second stage). The differences are very small, however.

The last two rows of Table 10.2 summarize the accuracy of the θ estimates for the MST designs. These results are not quite as good as for the other two designs. The RMSE values are slightly larger and the correlations with the true values are slightly lower. However, they are still very good as would be expected for a 40-item adaptive test.

The last two rows of Table 10.3 summarize the measures of adaptation for the MST designs. The values for the correlation and PRV statistics for these two designs are notably lower than those for the UCAT and Stratified designs. This is because the adaptation for MST is at the module level rather than at the item level. All examinees who take the same path through the stages will have the same set of items, so the amount of adaptation is somewhat restricted. However, the 10-10-20 design was much better on the ratio of standard deviations statistic. Having 20 items in the last stage results in greater spread in the mean difficulty level for the items administered to examinees. The 10-10-20 design is also better than the 20-10-10 design on the other two adaptation statistics. The fact that there are only 10 items in the routing test that are taken by all examines rather than 20 makes it possible to do more adaptation with the other 30 items in the MST design, increasing the overall level of adaptation.

DISCUSSION

The purpose for the research reported in this chapter was to extend our understanding of the amount of adaptation that is present in various adaptive testing designs. Previous work investigated the amount of adaptation for item-level computerized adaptive tests that were based on the one-parameter (Rasch) item response theory model and looked at the influence of item pool size and distribution of difficulty on the amount of adaptation. The research reported here focused on adaptive testing designs using the three-parameter logistic item response theory model. The specific designs considered were the simple item-level adaptive test, the a-stratified adaptive test with b-blocking, and two variations of three-stage multi-stage testing. All tests were 40 items in length and used maximum likelihood ability estimation. The items for the tests were all selected from the same item pool.

There were two notable results from the research. The first was that the quality of estimation and adaptation for the adaptive test using the stratified item pool were practically the same as these for the simple item level adaptive test. The stratified approach gives better control over item usage, but the added constraints do not seem to have negative consequences for the quality of estimation and adaptation.

The second notable result was that the multi-stage test designs were less adaptive than the other designs and had somewhat larger errors of estimation for the proficiency estimates. An unanticipated result was that the 10-10-20 design performed better than the 20-10-10 design. It had been hypothesized that accurate routing at the beginning of the test (a 20 item routing test) would result in better adaptation overall. That was not the case. Although the routing was slightly more accurate for the longer routing test, the overall adaptation was less because half of the test was the same for all examinees.

The evaluation of the amount of adaptation for adaptive tests is a relatively new concept. The methods were developed because of a concern that some tests labeled as adaptive tests were not very adaptive because of overly constrained item selection or poor quality item pools. The research presented here shows that the methods are also useful to compare alternative adaptive test designs. However, there are many different variations for adaptive test designs. The work reported here investigates only a limited number of the possibilities. It is hoped that others will begin reporting the amount of adaptation for the tests that are of interest to them. Over time, the research community will have a better sense of how well the alternative adaptive testing procedures work. This should lead to better adaptive test designs and more accurate estimates of proficiency than those obtained from some of the commonly used designs.

NOTES

1. CAT procedures have been developed over many years, so it is difficult to attribute the method to a single source. A useful reference to the procedures is van der Linden & Glas (2007).

REFERENCES

ACT, Inc. (2006). *COMPASS/ESL reference manual.* Iowa City, IA: Author.

Chang, H.-H., Qian, J., & Ying, Z. (2001). *a*-stratified multistage computerized adaptive testing with *b* blocking. *Applied Psychological Measurement, 25*(4), 333–341.

Minnesota Department of Education. (2017). *Technical manual for Minnesota standards-based accountability and English language proficiency assessments – for the academic year 2015–2016.* Roseville, MN: Author.

National Council of State Boards of Nursing. (2016). *NCLEX-RN examination: Detailed test plan for the National Council Licensure Examination for Registered Nurses.* Chicago, IL: Author.

Pommerich, M., Segall, D.O., & Moreno, K.E. (2009). The nine lives of CAT-ASVAB: Innovations and revelations. In D. J. Weiss (Ed.), *Proceedings of the 2009 GMAC Conference on Computerized Adaptive Testing.* Minneapolis, MN.

Reckase, M. D. (2010). Designing item pools to optimize the functioning of a computerized adaptive test. *Psychological Test and Assessment Modeling, 52*(2), 127–141.

Reckase, M. D., Ju, U., & Kim, S. (2018). Some measures of the amount of adaptation for computerized adaptive tests. In M. Wiberg, S. Culpepper, R. Janssen, J. González, D. Molenaar (Eds.), *Quantitative Psychology, IMPS 2017, Springer Proceedings in Mathematics & Statistics 233* (pp. 25–40). Charm, Switzerland: Springer.

Reckase, M. D., Ju, U., & Kim, S. (2019). How adaptive is an adaptive test? Are all adaptive tests adaptive? *Journal of Computerized Adaptive Testing, 7*, 1–14. doi:10.7333/1901-0701001

Thompson, N. A. (2009). Item selection in computerized classification testing. *Educational and Psychological Measurement, 69*(5), 778–793.

van der Linden, W. J., & Glas, C. A. W. (2007). Statistical aspects of adaptive testing. In C. R. Rao & S. Sinharay (Eds.), *Psychometrics.* Amsterdam, Netherlands: Elsevier.

Yan, D., von Davier, A. A., & Lewis, C. (Eds.). (2014). *Computerized multistage testing: Theory and applications.* Boca Raton, FL: CRC Press.

Zheng, Y., Nozawa, Y., Gao, X., & Chang, H. H. (2012). *Multistage adaptive testing for a large scale classification test: The designs, automated heuristic assembly, and comparison with other testing modes* (ACT Research Report 2012-6). Iowa City: ACT Inc.

CHAPTER 11

AUTOMATIC ITEM GENERATION WITH MACHINE LEARNING TECHNIQUES

A Pathway to Intelligent Assessments

Jaehwa Choi
The George Washington University

ABSTRACT

The conventional assessments on the Internet (AoI) face the challenges of maintaining the desired level of quality and security from increasing demands of online applications, which is called the AoI trilemma. Although automatic item generation (AIG) has been proposed to address these issues, it is not fully "automated" or "intelligent" yet to provide a variety of high-quality assessment services on a large scale in the AoI environment. In this manuscript, I firstly review several important new technological infrastructures (e.g., digital assessment platforms and machine learning techniques) for AIG in the AoI environments. Then, I propose few strategies of using machine learning techniques to maximally utilize AIG for intelligent assessment services.

Application of Artificial Intelligence to Assessment, pages 189–209
Copyright © 2020 by Information Age Publishing
All rights of reproduction in any form reserved.

Assessments on the Internet

The developments of science and technology have had widespread impacts on the society as a whole. Information or intelligent communication technology (ICT), which has developed rapidly in the 21st century, has had wide range of and even destructive impacts on various fields. Such developments of ICT, also called the fourth industrial revolution of the 21st century, differs from the previous ones. Some of the concepts reflecting such differences are automation, intelligence, cloud, and peer-to-peer (P2P) with/of big data.

The core functions of assessments (also called testing or measurement) are collecting and analyzing such data. From classroom exams to professional licensure or certification, assessments play a major role in knowing how one learns and how to facilitate to learn. Therefore, among various areas, assessments would be an integral part under the influence of such ICT developments. As the importance of data is increasingly emphasized with the developments of ICT, the importance of assessments is increasing. Even the whole system is evolving centered on assessment functionality, so it can be called, assessment-centric system.

Assessments on the Internet (AoI; Choi, 2017, 2019), for example, computer-based testing (CBT) or internet-based testing (iBT), has become prolific in the last few decades because of its known advantages: flexible administrations, capability of adding additional layer for enhancing security, automatic scoring/grading, adaptive assessment, or supporting innovative assessment formats (e.g., interactive or multimedia-based assessments). Although CBT and iBT are the concepts that focus on the delivery aspects of assessment, AoI presents the overall assessment process (creation, field-testing, delivery, or analysis, etc.) on the Internet. As assessee (a person who is assessed, e.g., test-taker, examinee, or candidate) populations have been familiar with digital devices and environments, their experiences on AoI has also significantly been enhanced. As digital technology continues to advance, AoI is becoming the standard format for many assessment services and programs (e.g., the TOEFL test by Educational Testing Service). Nowadays, more than one million assessments are delivered worldwide via the internet per month, and the number is increasing gradually.

Assessments on the Internet Trilemma

When the cycle of the administration is long enough and not often (e.g., once a year), there seems to be little need for changing the traditional assessment production process. However, as more assessments can be digitally delivered, it is clear that there is a steady increase in the need to provide assessments more often. Due to the advantages of being able to administer more frequently and flexibly, AoI triggers much higher demand than the paper-and-pencil based assessments. However, the traditional assessment item and test development approaches are having difficulty in meeting these demands. Due to this nature, the traditional production method yields various concerns as follows.

Firstly, it is "slow and expensive." The required cost associated with individual and manual item production procedure substantially limits the number of items ready for operation. Secondly, it requires "extensive field-test." Because items were individually developed, the statistical outcomes (e.g., difficulty) of items are unpredictable. This field-test (also called as validation or calibration) includes an empirical data analysis in order to assess and improve the quality of items and the assessment (e.g., exam) as a whole. Therefore, a field-test, entails significant cost and effort, is needed before operational test administrations for all items. Thirdly, it exposes to the "risk of item exposure." The above-mentioned aspects, costs and time, limit the number of operational items to be developed/provided. It is natural that test security risk may increase as the insufficient numbers of items are being exposed to more assessees. Although algorithmic procedure (e.g., randomizing item selection) can be integrated to control the security issues, excessive exposure beyond the level of such preventive tools can be devastating to the fairness and integrity of an assessment. Fourthly, it is "difficult to balance difficulty levels." As Drasgow, Luecht, and Bennett (2006) mentioned, with the traditional approach, "It is notoriously hard to hit difficulty targets, which results in having too many items at some levels and not enough at other levels." Lastly, it typically produces "items with static elements." The traditional approach primarily produces items with static elements (i.e., all elements of the items are fixed), and it is not friendly with innovative digital items such as dynamic, multimedia, simulation, and interactive items.

In the AoI environments, it is difficult to achieve all three goals—exposure control, field-test, and online delivery—because it is faced with a phenomenon that requires a choice among three alternatives that are mutually exclusive. This difficulty in maintaining a high level of assessment quality and security while delivering online in large scale is called the "AoI trilemma" (Choi, 2017), as Figure 11.1 depicts.

Figure 11.1 includes four different assessment scenarios around the three goals. The first scenario is that exposure control is highly emphasized against empirical validation (i.e., field-test) and online delivery. In this case, we can maintain a high level of assessment security, whereas we sacrifice a certain degree of quality and convenience of assessments on a large scale through online delivery. The second scenario is that field-test is maximally emphasized over exposure control and online delivery. In this case, there

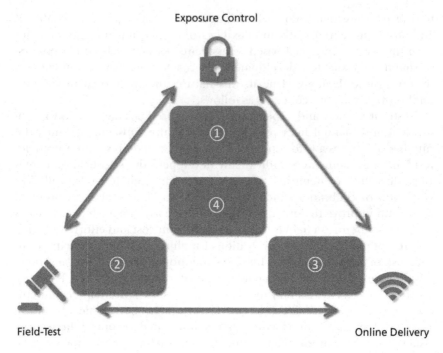

Figure 11.1 Assessments on the Internet (AoI) trilemma.

could be a risk of item leakage during a field-test and it might be difficult to produce enough items for online delivery on a large scale. But, it is possible to maintain a high level of quality through intensive empirical validation. The third scenario emphasizes online delivery rather than field-test and exposure control. In this case, the quality and the security of assessment could be low, but massive online delivery is much more possible. Due to the nature of Internet-based assessments, there is virtually no limit to the delivery side unless quality and security are considered. The fourth situation is that all three goals are achieved and balanced. Although this case is an ideal situation to be pursued, the conventional test development approach has obvious limitations to realize it.

The fundamental reason of this challenge is, in the traditional approach, each item is individually and manually crafted—drafted, reviewed, edited, field-tested, and revised by item writers who are typically content or subject matter experts (SMEs). In the era of AoI, the limitations of manually producing assessment inventory become obvious—they are both expensive and time-consuming, they motivate assessment developers to seek efficient ways of producing a large number of items. The purpose of this chapter is to propose a solution to this trilemma using various new technologies. In the next section, we will look at what technologies are available to solve the trilemma, how these technologies are strategically used, and what new infrastructure is needed to fully exploit these technologies.

AUTOMATIC ITEM GENERATION

New Technology: Automatic Item Generation

Automatic Item Generation (AIG; Bejar, 1993; Choi, Kim, & Yoon, 2012; Embretson & Yang, 2007; Gierl & Haladyna, 2013; Irvine & Kyllonen, 2002) is one of the various solutions that have been provided to overcome slow and expensive assessment development issues. Researchers, psychometricians, item writers, and assessment service providers increasingly find themselves facing a new paradigm where the assessment item production process is no longer manual, but rather can be a massive production automatized by technology. AIG is an emerging research area and an innovative assessment development strategy where cognitive and psychometric theories are integrated together into a digital framework, especially in ICT environments. The number of content areas and the number of applications of AIG are exploding: from early childhood to higher education levels, from math to intelligence assessments. As such, this new reality raises important issues in effective and scientific assessment development by integrating ICT advancements (Choi, 2013, 2017).

The most fundamental difference between traditional methods and new methods based on the AIG framework lies in the conception of development and analysis "unit." The unit of AIG is not an individual item but an "item model" that generates multiple items. This is a paradigm shift from "human writing" to "machine generation" of assessment development (Choi, 2017), and this transition requires, so called, the "unit conversion" from item to item model. An item model serves as a template where content specialists manipulate specific and well-defined elements. The remaining components in the template, once finalized, are not altered during item development. As a result, AIG approach allows subject matter experts (SMEs) to efficiently develop (i.e., create and manage) large numbers of high-quality operational items.

Figure 11.2 illustrates a math item example, adding fractions, to compare the traditional and AIG approach for developing such math item(s). This illustration is based on the wisdom of the Athenian philosopher Plato (428–347 BC). Using the analogy of the divided line, Plato believed there might be a distinction between the "intelligible" world where everything is intelligible (the objects or concepts that have intelligibility) and the visible (or "observable") world where everything is observable. The intelligibility is what can be comprehended by intelligible methods (i.e., metaphysics;

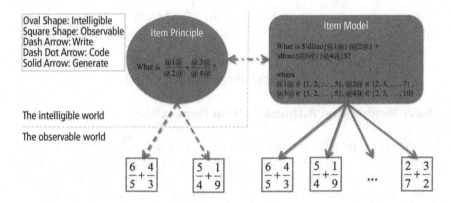

Figure 11.2 Item principle, item model, and item instances.

such as thought thinking itself or the reflection on itself) in contrast to observables which can be observed through the human sensory perception. In this figure, there are three major components: item form (in Greek, idea), item design, or item principle with oval shape represents the intelligible; item or item instance with square shape represents the observable; item model with rounded square shape also represents the observable but links item principle and item instances. Then, these components are connected with three different types of arrows which represent different relationships (dash arrow: write; dash dot arrow: code; solid arrow: generate) between the components (Choi, 2017).

In the traditional approach, an item writer manually "writes" individual items (e.g., math items in Figure 11.2) based on an item principle (e.g., adding fractions task). Because this item principle belongs to the intelligible world where things are not directly observable, one must infer this principle from the item instances and/or from the item writer's additional explanation about the principle, that is, "human writing." In some cases, an item writer may create an item without fully clarifying what the principle is. Therefore, much effort is needed to reduce possible errors that could be in the inference process of understanding, sharing, and verifying the principle.

In the AIG-based approach, based on the same principle, an item developer "codes" an item model (software program or syntax; e.g., an item model for adding fractions task in Figure 11.2) for a machine to generate item instances by varying the element(s) of an item model, that is "machine generation." In this item model example, @1@ ~ @4@ are four elements (or item parameters) to be varied. With the value ranges for each element in Figure 11.2, total 1,350 ($5 \times 6 \times 5 \times 9$) items can be generated without any conditions/constraints for the elements. However, additional constraint(s) may be required to only generate relevant or specific item instance(s). For example, to generate only simplified and different denominator fraction items, an item developer can specify necessary conditions such as @2@ is the mutual prime of @1@; @4@ is the mutual prime of @3@; @4@ is not equal to @2@. By doing so, this item model can generate total 558 items with simplified and different denominators.

Additional digital formatting features can be coded into an item model such as Latex syntax "\dfrac" for displaying factions. Note that an item model is a software program for the AoI environment. Modern standards (e.g., HTML5: the standard for structuring and presenting content on the World Wide Web) to handle multimedia (e.g., graphics, audio, or video) can be seamlessly used into an item model. Furthermore, external digital resources (e.g., text-to-speech module) can also be integrated into item models to implement various types of interactive and intelligent assessments that have not been available in traditional items with static elements. This machine generation method, AIG, will make the most of these digital innovations (Choi, Kim, & Yoon, 2012; Choi & Zhang, 2019). In Lai, Gierl, and Alves (2009) work, 64,260 item instances were generated from 34 parent items for various subjects (e.g., math, literature, science, and social studies) of the 3rd, 6th, and 9th grades. Other AIG projects on math subject (Choi, Kang, & Kim, 2014; Choi, Kang, Kim, Dardick, & Zhang, 2015; Choi, Kim, & Pak, 2018; Choi, Kim, & Yoon, 2016, 2017) also showed that more than two million unique math items can be generated by 350 item models in 6th or 7th grade level.

Using these digital advancements, the AIG item model can support a wide range of assessments (Choi, 2017). Firstly, it supports various item types such as multiple-choice, matching as well as short-answer as shown in the above example. In case of multiple choice items, not only a correct answer and feedback, but also distractor elements can be programmed (i.e., distractor modeling) within the AIG framework. Secondly, it is possible to construct an item model that measures not only simple memorizations, but also various cognitive abilities (e.g., solving complicated math problems) or other cognitive intelligent matters. Thirdly, AIG's efficacy is not limited to simply machine generating items, but it can also integrate other assessment elements (such as scoring, providing feedback, adaptive testing, or equating) to enhance their efficacy and utility. With AIG's digital DNA, the genuine digital assessment innovations can be unleashed.

Due to the characteristics of AIG mentioned in the previous section, AIG has a variety of potential advantages, ranging from economic advantages to theoretical excellence (Choi, 2017; Choi & Li, 2016; Dardick & Choi, 2016). These are summarized as follows:

- *Massive production:* Because an item model serves as a well-defined template where developers can manipulate only specific elements, many errors in item development (such as spelling or formatting) can be avoided. Consequently, one can efficiently create and strategically manage high-quality operational items. Such feature can prevent excessive exposure and increase the fairness and integrity of the assessment, also called "construct preservation" (Embretson, 1983).

- *Manifested principle:* Because an item model is in a standardized form of algorithms that can be read and executed by machine, the new approach technology enables us not only to generate massive numbers of items, but also to help others to understand, evaluate, and clarify the developer's item principle or design, also called "construct representation" (Embretson, 1983).

- *Controlled uniformity:* AIG enables us to control the uniformity (equivalency) of not only structure, but also psychometric quality. For example, we can set an item model to generate isomorphic (e.g., different but same difficulty item) instances. This capability provides many benefits in assessment practices, for example, repeated measure or equating. Wainer (2002) said, "Uniformity of structure and quality that is not possible with hand-built items. When the goal is standardized measurement, uniformity is an often much desired characteristic." Kyllonen (2002) also mentioned that, "Item generation methods can be helpful in stressor studies. Such studies require repeated testing of individuals. In repeated testing, generally speaking, it is not a good idea to re-administer the same test items over and over again."

- *Reduced field-test:* AIG can eliminate or minimize the need for extensive field-test. If an item model is built on a pre-calibrated item, we don't have to field-test the generated isomorphic instances. If one has a strong theory that can fully model item characteristics (e.g., difficulty), the item model can generate pre-calibrated items (e.g., items whose difficulty levels have already been identified).

- *Digitally innovative:* Because of the native digital DNA (i.e., an item model in AIG is a software program code), AIG can seamlessly integrate and take full benefits of other innovative digital advancements such as automatic scoring, computer adaptive assessment, dynamic and multimedia assessment, or gamified assessments, and more.

From Machine Generation to Intelligent Generation

Although the new technology, AIG, has a great potential as mentioned above, AIG is still in its infancy, and its potential benefits have not been fully effective in assessment practices at large. Rather, there are few difficulties that impede the use of AIG in the field. Embretson and Kingston (2018) argued that "the efficiency of AIG will be mitigated if the generated items must be submitted to traditional, time-consuming review processes." Note that the new technique requires the unit conversion from item instance to item model, and this transition may require significant changes over the entire assessment process. Choi summarized the changes required for the new technology as follows.

First, in the new paradigm, note that item developers code item models, the programs (or syntaxes) in which the machine can read and execute. Although most item writing skills are common to item model coding skills, the model development may require additional skills such as debugging skills or problem-solving skills. For these new skills, new human resource development protocol is needed to find, train, or retrain item developers. Second, we need a new computerized system that supports item developers to author (create, review, and test) and store item models. In a new environment where item models are produced, utilized, and managed, the traditional system which treats the item as a unit is not fully functional. Third, we also need a system that validates, uses, and manages the massive number of generated items in various assessment services. Last, the traditional item development reward scheme (e.g., paying item writers at an hourly rate or per item) may not be fully suitable for AIG because it is difficult to quantify the efforts/qualities (e.g., creativity or efficiency in an item model code) of item model developments. The writing of an item and the coding of an item model are quite different intellectual endeavors because item model development additionally requires coding. Therefore, there is a need for a new method that comprehensively compensates for the quantity and quality (e.g., digitally innovative) of the items that item models generate.

Furthermore, Choi (2017) argues that the "automation" in the conventional AIG differs from the concept of smart or intelligence in the 4th industrial revolution, and it is rather "computerized." In order to produce digitally mastered high-quality items, we need "intelligent" generation that goes beyond machine generation. To convert this machine generation into intelligent generation of items, additional efforts and strategies are needed. In the next section, we will discuss the essential elements for the automation and the proposed strategies for the further developments of AIG toward intelligent assessments.

AUTOMATIC ITEM GENERATION FOR INTELLIGENT ASSESSMENTS

Forrester predicts that, by 2025, digital technologies like robots, intelligent software, and related autonomous and semi-autonomous mechanical and digital entities will have replaced 22.7 million jobs in the United States alone, and this number equates to a job loss of 16% between 2015 and 2025. This automation will influence not only jobs operating factory machinery, but also all careers that perform repetitive tasks. Artificial intelligence (AI) and automation will allow us to perform our tasks more strategically by removing the most routine tasks, but they eliminate or reassign human jobs. Automation is already changing many existing jobs. Computers can answer typical questions and refer users to FAQs or knowledge-based articles. They provide access to systems and perform more complex tasks like ordering new equipment. A recent survey by Atlassian, reported that 87% of respondents think that AI will change their job by 2020, 76% believe that at least some of their jobs could be performed by a robot, algorithm, or AI device.

How about assessment industry jobs and tasks? As mentioned earlier, we are already experiencing the transition from PBT to CBT or iBT. However, these CBT and iBT concepts are far from automation or intelligence in the 4th industrial revolution. In particular, the term "automated" or "automatic" of the conventional AIG are better suited to be called "computer-based" or "computerized" (Choi, 2017). Recent digital technologies are evolving into intelligent automation trend that goes beyond traditional computer-based tasks and services across the industries, and the field of assessments should be no exception. Therefore, it is important to understand how intelligent assessments differ from computer-based or computerized assessments and what strategies/options exist to evolve into intelligent assessments.

In the next section, I will illustrate two important digital infrastructure concepts (connectivity and platform) that we can obtain an enormous amount of assessment data. Then, I will introduce the concepts of the machine learning (ML) techniques and/or AI which are the essential elements of intelligent assessments. I will specifically review what history and interrelationships exist between ML and AI. Then, I will introduce a few options for implementing smart or intelligent automation in assessment. In the same section, we will specifically look at how AIG is used as a core component of intelligent assessments in the proposed strategies.

Digital Connectivity and Platform

The Internet of Things (IoT) is one of the main bridges between the physical and digital applications enabled by the 4th industrial revolution. In its simplest form, it can be described as a "maximized digital connectivity": a relationship between things (e.g., products, services, or places, etc.) and people, which is made possible by connected applications, devices, and various platforms. Sensors and other devices that connect things in the physical world (so called the atom's world) to the digital network (so called the bit's world) are spreading at a proliferating rate. Cheaper, smaller, and smarter sensors are being installed in schools, homes, offices, and accessories. Furthermore, there are billions of devices such as smartphones, tablets, and computers connected to the Internet around the world, and these numbers are expected to explosively increase over the next few years. This will radically alter the way in which we manage assessments by enabling us to monitor and conduct assessments to a very granular level. It will have a profound impact in the field of measurement, as it will revolutionize all industries, from manufacturing to infrastructure to healthcare.

Consider assessment systems and applications as widespread applications of the IoT. Any assessment environment and instruments can now be equipped with a sensor, transmitter, or radio frequency identification (RFID) tag that allows us to track where it is, how it is functioning, how it is being used, and so on. The level of assessment security that traditionally relied only on human proctoring or CCTV would be much further enhanced. In particular, through the assessees' behavioral data during an assessment process (so called, process data) observed from the sensors, more accurate and additional assessment analysis becomes possible. By integrating such data into the traditional response data, we can gain more insight into the assessees' thinking processes and strategies. Furthermore, participants can continuously track (practically in real time) the progress of the assessees or the assessment administration itself. The vast amount of data provided by the various sensors over this wide area cannot be compared with traditional response data. The intelligent automation of measurements enabled by this big assessment data will be discussed in more detail in a later section of this manuscript.

The digital technologies will revolutionize the way individuals and institutions engage and collaborate. For example, Blockchain, often described as "distributed ledger," is a security protocol that a network of distributed computers verifies a transaction before it is recorded and approved without centralized intermediaries. The technology behind Blockchain creates network-centric trust by allowing people who do not know one another to collaborate without going through a neutral central organization. In essence, using Blockchain technology, one can develop a shared, programmable, and cryptographically secure system (so called Crypto or Blockchain-economy) which no single user controls but which can be verified by everyone. Immunity, transparency, traceability, and anonymity, which are the inherent characteristics of Blockchain system data, will provide an entirely different data analytic framework. The management of assessment data using this Blockchain technology will also revolutionize the whole assessment process.

Technology-based platforms enable what is now called an on-demand economy (some are called shared economies; Schwab, 2016). These platforms which are easy-to-use on smart devices bring people, digital assets, and data together to create, share, and consume digital goods and services in an entirely new way. The various benefits that these platforms bring can be summarized as follows: Firstly, they lower barriers for assessment services

and individuals to create wealth by altering personal and professional environments of assessments. Secondly, by matching supply and demand in
a very accessible way, and providing consumers with diverse digital assessment services. Thirdly, by allowing both parties to interact and give feedback, these platforms, therefore, foster trust. They enable the effective use
of under-utilized assessment knowledge and skills—namely those belong-
ing to people who had previously never thought of themselves as suppliers
(e.g., assessors or assessment service developers).

Schwab (2016) said, "Digital platforms have dramatically reduced the
transaction and friction costs incurred when individuals or organizations
share the use of an asset or provide some service. Each transaction can now
be divided into very fine increments, with economic gains for all parties
involved." Furthermore, the marginal cost of producing each additional
assessment service approaches zero by using these digital platforms. In the
AoI environment, given the extent to which all parts of assessment can
be digitized, we can gauge how much impact these digital platforms will
have on the assessments. Such digital infrastructures will further drop costs
for creating, processing, duplicating, and delivering digital assessments
(i.e., bits). In the next section, we will look at how the vast and diverse
assessment data provided by these digital connectivity and platforms can
bring about revolutionary changes in the assessment field.

Machine Learning and Artificial Intelligence

ML and AI are currently two very hot buzzwords and are often used in a
similar way. If the topic is a big data analysis or a wave of widespread technological advancements that are sweeping our world (for example, the 4th
industrial revolution), two terms often appear at the same time. However,
they are not quite the same, and the perception that they are similar can
sometimes be confusing. Therefore, before I explain automation and intelligence issues in AIG, it is worth explaining the difference first.

AI is a more conceptual and broader concept of machines (i.e., computers or robots) that can perform tasks in a "smart" or "intelligent" way. This
AI concept has existed for a long time. In Greek mythology there is a story
of "mechanical man" who is designed to imitate our own behaviors. Instead, ML is a computational approach of AI around the idea that machines
can learn for themselves by the data we give. Early European conceived
computers as "logical machines." And, through reproducing functions
such as arithmetic computations, engineers have tried to develop mechanical brains. As technology and theory (e.g., our understanding of how our
minds work) have progressed, the concept of what constitutes AI has also
evolved. Rather than complex calculations or computations, the primary

goal in AI field has been focused on mimicking human decision-making processes and performing tasks in more human-like processes.

Three major breakthroughs have led to the emergence of ML as a tool to develop AI at the current pace. One of them is the realization that we may be able to teach machines to learn for themselves instead of teaching them how to carry out every task. The second is the maturation of the internet infrastructure. By this infrastructure, huge amounts of digital data can be generated by various sensors connected to the Internet and can be collected via the digital platforms. The third, more recently, is the explosive increase of computational capacities such as cloud-computing which can be defined as "an information technology paradigm that enables ubiquitous access to shared pools of configurable system resources and higher-level services that can be rapidly provisioned with minimal management effort, often over the Internet" ("Cloud Computing," n.d.). These developments enable a rapid processing of massive amounts of data which size is not to be compared to the past. With these innovations, engineers realized that writing code to think like humans was more efficient than coding everything for machine to perform tasks. By plug machines into the internet, it is possible to give them access to all of the digital data in the world and to make them learn complex tasks by themselves via ML techniques.

A Deep Neural Network (DNN; also called Deep Learning) is an ML method designed to classify information in a similar way a human brain does. For example, it can be trained to recognize and classify images according to the components they contain. Similar to other ML methods (e.g., logistic regression), a DNN is also essentially a probability model, that is, it can make predictions based on the data fed into it with a degree of probabilistic certainty. However, DNN maps inputs to outputs with, so called, a "universal approximator" because a trained DNN can approximate an unknown function between any input and any output. And, by adding a feedback loop, it can modify the approach it takes in the future by "supervising" whether the previous decisions were right or wrong (i.e., "Supervised Learning," n.d.). The development of DNN plays a key role in teaching machines to learn tasks in a similar way humans do, while holding inherent advantages: speed, accuracy, and lack of bias.

In essence, DNN can be used to determine (predict or make decisions) other data by training a computer system (i.e., neural networks) with a lot of data. DNN can be applied to any form of data—human biological signal, audio, video, speech, written words—to produce conclusions that seem as if they have been arrived at by humans. DNN focuses on developing a logic network which has the complexity of classifying large databases, such as Google's image library. When the data becomes comprehensive and vast, and a logical network is constructed that is sufficiently sophisticated to classify the data, it becomes trivial for the machine to perform tasks that are as accurate as a human being's. Furthermore, the system can "train" itself with new data over time to increase the probability of a correct decision (e.g., classification or prediction). In other words, like a human, it can learn from mistakes. For example, it may incorrectly decide that a particular answer was graded as was a certain score, based on their similar texts and grammatical errors, overlooking another differentiator which it determined had a low probability of being important to the score decision. By learning that this differentiator is, in fact, vital to understanding the difference between two answers, it improves the probability of a correct outcome next time.

Natural Language Processing (NLP) applications, which are based on ML, have been actively innovated in recent years. NLP applications attempt to understand natural human communications in a written or spoken form, and communicate with humans by also using similar natural language. ML technique is used here to help machines to learn how to understand the vast nuances in human language (voice and text), and how to respond back in a way that a person is likely to comprehend. These NLP applications can read texts and figure out whether an answer is correct or not. They can also listen to a person's voice via a voice-to-text engine (which is another ML application) to decide whether it is likely to be correct or not, and select next questions to match the person's learning status. They can even compose their own text expressing the same meaning and context.

There are several NLP applications in assessments. For example, Chen, Liou, and Chang (2006) introduced a method of semi-automatically generating grammar test items based on NLP methods. Liu, Wang, Gao, and Huang (2005) also algorithmically generated reading cloze items on NLP techniques. These are some possibilities offered by assessment systems based around NLP techniques. The idea has also emerged that we should be able to conduct assessments by "interacting" with electronic devices, as naturally as we would with traditional assessment methods (e.g., interview or PBT).

In sum, AI, nowadays ML, certainly has a lot to offer to assessments. Specifically, the promise of automating typical assessment tasks and providing creative insights can provide vast ranges of benefits across the assessment services. The fact that we will eventually develop human-like machines is often deemed inevitable by scientists. Today we are closer than ever and we are moving toward that goal as speed increases. The many exciting developments we've seen in recent years are a fundamental change in the way AI works brought by ML. However, we should also note that the automation and intelligence of assessment services do not fully enjoy the benefits of these technologies. The challenge for us now is to understand how to strategically use these AI and ML in the assessment to efficiently develop and deliver high-quality assessment services in the AoI environment. The following sections introduce these strategies.

Strategy One: Using AI Within AIG

The key point of this first strategy is not to develop new AI, but to use various already developed AI or ML applications with AIG. This strategy is to "inject AI into AIG" to pursue automation and intelligence of assessment item with AIG technology. Large technology companies (such as Google, Microsoft, or IBM) offer cloud AI services that allow a variety of AIs to be used through the API (application programming interface). As seen in Figure 11.3, These cloud-AI services provide various modern ML applications with pre-trained models including text-to-speech, voice-to-text, image search, the voice search, or translate, and so on.

For example, consider the case of applying a "text-to-speech AI" to an AIG item. Using these AI assessment developers can synthesize natural-sounding speech with multiple voices in multiple languages. Using the easy-to-use API, the item model developers can create real-world-type interactions with assessee in many assessment applications and devices. A simple example procedure for integrating such AI in the AIG item is as follows.

a. First, an AIG model is developed to generate texts to be read.
b. Second, prepare to connect the text-to-speech AI API within the AIG model.
c. Third, when an item instance is executed, the generated text is voiced through the API.

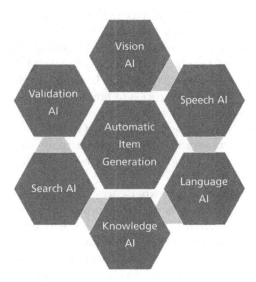

Figure 11.3 Using AIs within AIG.

Some of the advantages of this integration are summarized as follows. First, in this case, it is possible to switch from reading to listening assessment. Reading ability as well as listening ability can be measured separately or at the same time. In other words, the scope of assessments can be widened and deepened by this AI. Second, we can convert the reading text to a listening item without a separate voice actor. With this AI, we can save time and money in recording with voice actors or managing the recorded files. Third, an assessee may select or change the voice that reads the text, thereby reducing potential measurement bias due to a specific voice from a voice actor.

Other AIs can also be included in AIG items to intelligence and automate assessments. For example, "speech-to-text AI" enables assessment developers to convert speech to text by powerful ML models also in an easy to use API. This AI can recognize more than 100 languages to support global assessments with real-time streaming audio. NLP also can reveal the structure and meaning of text by offering powerful ML models. We can use it to extract information mentioned and understand sentiments in the text from the assessee. "Translation AI" provides a simple programming interface for converting arbitrary strings into supported languages. This AI is so responsive that one can integrate with the evaluation application and dynamically convert it from the original language to the target language (e.g., Korean to English).

Strategy Two: Developing AI With AIG

The strategy I'm going to introduce in this section is to build-up AI using AIG. This strategy is described in several steps: First, we will conceptually compare the basic principles of ML with the traditional modeling programming. Second, we will briefly introduce the principle of developing a grading or scoring algorithm using ML. Third, based on the above two explanations, I will also illustrate the process of building problem solving AI using AIG. Finally, we will explain how to use the problem-solving AI in empirical field-testing. Note that the method described here has not been attempted yet and is very conceptual and theoretical in current technology. At the end of this section, I will introduce the requirements for these methods to be realized in the future.

Humans learn through past experiences. The machine performs the indicated operation or task by being programmed to follow the instructions. An important question here is, "Can machines learn from experience?" The answer is, "Yes." This the most important point of ML. Of course, for machines, experiences are replaced by data, and the previous data can be used to train the machine. Let's take "scoring/grading" as an example to illustrate the difference between traditional programming and ML. The traditional

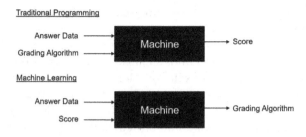

Figure 11.4 Comparison between machine learning and traditional programming for scoring/grading.

programming built the decision-making rules directly into the program. For example, you need to direct for a program to assess grammar, structure, or vocabulary of essay answers. In ML, we wouldn't tell it any of that. As seen in Figure 11.4, in grading from a traditional programming standpoint, the role of the machine is to score the answer by applying a human-developed scoring algorithm. On the other hand, the role of the machine in ML is to build a scoring algorithm using answer and score data. We would build an agent that could look at a bunch of answers and score pair data over time, and the machine can figure out scores for an answer. The execution of very complex tasks such as grading an essay can also be implemented through ML if the essay answer and corresponding score data are very large.

As discussed in the previous section of this chapter, ML has recently been able to process these very large datasets in a computational way. Such computers have finally come along and have become fast enough to be able to handle the kinds of big datasets. In addition, the world relies more on computers and the Internet than ever before, and large amounts of digital data are automatically generated, processed, and stored. So, these things have been combined to make ML a much more useful tool than before. Based on these ML methods, "automated scoring," where machines score on behalf of humans, already occupies an important position in the field of measurement.

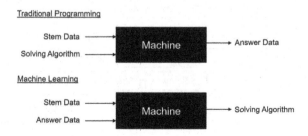

Figure 11.5 Building solving algorithm using AIG and ML.

In this section, I will explain how to use AIG in ML technology to build "solving algorithm." Let's take as an example the process of solving an item. The process of solving a problem is usually the process by which a person reads the stem of an item and finds an answer. Going one step further, let's assume that the machine solves the problem. In traditional programming, the machine reads its stem and finds the answer by a given problem-solving algorithm. Considering the ML situation as in the example above, we conclude that if we have a large amount of stem and answer data, we can build the solving algorithm by learning the machine. Although the problems to solve could be complex and diverse, we could train the machine to solve those problems if there were enough item data, especially stem and answer data. Using ML, we can train a system that can solve problems without specifying and specifying a way to solve specific problems.

Such problem-solving AIs are expanding to a wide range of domains. For example, Noriko Arai, a Japanese AI expert, has developed an AI (called Todai) to take the entrance exam to Tokyo University, the most prestigious university in Japan. And the robot wins 80% of the students who take the 7-section exam, which includes math, English, science, and writing a 600-word essay. As you can see in this example, it is possible to create problem-solving AIs on a very wide and broad level and domain. It is important to note that creating such an AI can be time consuming and expensive. However, if the benefits of creating such an AI are certain, the risk of developing that investment will be reduced. The potential use of these AIs will be discussed later in this section.

By manipulating the number of training intensity or the size of train data, we can develop a set of virtual machines with varying levels of performances (i.e., machine intelligences) as seen in Figure 11.6. In other words, we can conduct tasks of defining, scaling, constructing, and diversifying the problem-solving intelligences of machines by using AIG in ML. Choi (2017) defined this type of study as follows: "Mechmetrics is a field of study

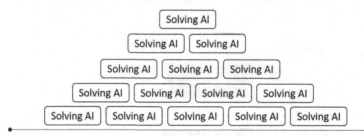

Figure 11.6　Solving AI virtual set.

concerned with the theory and technique of machine, robot, or AI measurement. Generally, it refers to the field in computer science, engineering, psychology, and education that is devoted to assessment, testing, measurement, and related activities for machines."

An important question at this point is, "Where do you use these AIs?" The bottom line is that using these various levels of problem-solving AIs can replace field-tests, some or all of which were done with existing human beings, with machine-performed field-tests. As mentioned earlier, this field-test or empirical-tryouts is a very necessary process to ensure the quality of assessment, but it requires considerable costs such as item exposure concerns, time, and money. By constructing the AIs and using them in the field-test, it is possible to dramatically increase the speed of high-quality item production because we can grasp the characteristics of the new items in near real-time. A situation is presented in which the machine verifies the item generated by the machine. The requirement is that the number of AIG models should be sufficiently big. As the number of AIG item models increases, the AI's intelligence (i.e., solving problem ability) becomes even more enhanced and sophisticated. And as the intelligence of this AI becomes more sophisticated, the quality of machine field-testing increases.

The above-mentioned principle, developing AI using AIG, can also be used in various applications beyond the assessment field. Note that AIG can generate a huge amount of data that takes the question as input and the correct answer as output. And these data can be combined with additional AI, such as text-to-speech and translation AI, to transform into a wider variety of digital variants. If a large amount of expert-designed question and answer data is transformed into various forms again, we can develop even more sophisticated and intelligent intelligence with such data. The requirement is that the number of AIG models should be sufficiently large and the types of the model also should be diverse. As the number of AIG models increases, the AI's intelligence to solve problems becomes even more sophisticated. And as the intelligence of this AI becomes more sophisticated, the quality of AI-based field-testing increases, too.

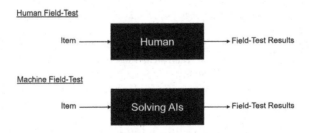

Figure 11.7   Human field-test vs. machine field-test.

CONCLUSION

The conventional AoI face the challenge of maintaining the desired level of quality and security from increasing demands of online applications, which is called the AoI trilemma. Although (AIG has been proposed to address these issues, it is not fully "automated" or "intelligent" yet to provide a variety of high-quality assessment services on a large scale in the AoI environment. In this chapter, we first discussed several important new technological infrastructures (AIG, digital assessment platforms and ML techniques) to better understand them. Then, I proposed few strategies of using AIG with ML techniques to maximally utilize AIG for intelligent assessment services.

The emergence of AIG suggests several very important facts in the assessment field. First, various ML techniques can be injected into AIG to enable high-quality intelligent digital assessments. Second, the assessment theory and practice are not simply about collecting and analyzing data, but also about generating enormous quantities of item data (big assessment/item data) based on theories such as cognitive science and learning theory. Third, in this chapter we also found that we could build various ML applications with such big assessment data generated from AIG. In addition, we have come to a very significant turning point in the assessment from psychometrics into mechmetrics that develop, scale, and measure the intelligence of machines. It is true that such developments including AIG are still in their infancy, and it is unknown when these technologies will be widely adopted. But it is also possible that such a future is already quite close to us.

REFERENCE

Bejar, I. I. (1993). A generative approach to psychological and educational measurement. In N. Frederiskson, R. J. Mislevy, & I. I. Bejar (Eds.), *Test theory for a new generation of tests* (pp. 323–359). Mahwah, NJ: Erlbaum.

Chen, C. Y., Liou, H. C., & Chang, J. S. (2006, July). Fast: An automatic generation system for grammar tests. In *Proceedings of the COLING/ACL on Interactive presentation sessions* (pp. 1–4). Stroudsburg, PA: Association for Computational Linguistics.

Choi, J. (2013). *How google impacts global education.* Retrieved from https://www.youtube.com/watch?v=leOMooSXFwE

Choi, J. (2017). *Assessment engineering: Pathway to digital assessment* [Assessment, Testing and Measurement Technical Report Series]. Washington, DC: The George Washington University.

Choi, J. (2019). Assessment engineering for learning analytics. *Educational Development, 46*(1), 42–45.

Choi, J., Kang, M., & Kim, N. (2014). *Free common core math workbook: CAFA Smart-Workbook user guide.* Retrieved from https://www.youtube.com/watch?v=8Ey4y09FD5I

Choi, J., Kang, M., Kim, N., Dardick, W., & Zhang, X. (2015). A smart way of coping with common core challenges–Introduction to CAFA SmartWorkbook. *Journal of Educational Issues, 1*(2), 70–89.

Choi, J., Kim, H., & Pak, S. (2018). Evaluation of automatic Item generation utilities in formative assessment application for Korean high school students. *Journal of Educational Issues, 4*(1), 68–89. https://doi.org/10.5296/jei.v4i1

Choi, J., Kim, S., & Yoon, K. (2016). *K-Math workbook grade 6.* Clarksville, MD: CAFA Lab.

Choi, J., Kim, S., &Yoon, K. (2017). *K-Math workbook grade 7.* Clarksville, MD: CAFA Lab.

Choi, J., & Li, L. (2016, April). *Automatic item generation: Beyond cost efficiency.* Presented at the Annual Meeting of Korean-American Educational Researchers Association, Washington, DC.

Cloud Computing. (n.d.). In Wikipedia. Retrieved from http://en.wikipedia.org/wiki/Cloud_computing

Dardick, W., & Choi, J. (2016). Teacher empowered assessment system: Assessment for the 21st century. *Journal of Applied Educational and Policy Research, 2*(2).

Drasgow, F., Luecht, R. M., & Bennett, R. E. (2006). Technology and testing. In S. H. Irvine & P. C. Kyllonen (Eds.), *Educational measurement* (4th ed.; pp. 471–516). Washington, DC: American Council on Education.

Embretson, S. E. (1983). Construct validity: Construct representation versus nomothetic span. *Psychological Bulletin, 93,* 179–197.

Embretson, S. E., & Kingston, N. M. (2018). Automatic item generation: A more efficient process for developing mathematics achievement items? *Journal of Educational Measurement. 55(1),* 112–131. https://doi.org/10.1111/jedm.12166

Embretson, S. E., & Yang, X. (2007). Automatic item generation and cognitive psychology. In C. R. Rao & S. Sinharay (Eds.), *Handbook of statistics: Psychometrics* (Vol. 26; pp. 747–768). North Holland, England: Elsevier.

Gierl, M. J., & Haladyna, T. M. (2013). *Automatic item generation: Theory and practice.* New York, NY: Routledge.

Irvine, S. H., & Kyllonen, P. C. (Eds.). (2002). *Item generation for test development.* Mahwah, NJ: Erlbaum.

Kyllonen, P. C. (2002). Item generation for repeated testing of human performance. In S. H. Irvine & P. C. Kyllonen (Eds.), *Item generation for test development* (pp. 251–275). Mahwah, NJ: Erlbaum.

Lai, H., Gierl, M. J., & Alves, C. (2009, June). *Development of an item model taxonomy for automatic item generation in computer adaptive testing.* Poster presented at the GMAC Conference on Computerized Adaptive Testing, Minneapolis, MN.

Liu, C. L., Wang, C. H., Gao, Z. M., & Huang, S. M. (2005, June). Applications of lexical information for algorithmically composing multiple-choice cloze items. In *Proceedings of the second workshop on Building Educational Applications Using NLP* (pp. 1–8). Stroudsburg, PA: Association for Computational Linguistics.

Schwab, K. (2016). *The fourth industrial revolution.* New York, NY: Crown.

Supervised learning. (n.d.). In Wikipedia. Retrieved from https://en.wikipedia.org/wiki/Supervised_learning

Wainer, H. (2002). On the automation generation of test items: Some whens, whys and hows. In S. H. Irvine & P. C. Kyllonen (Eds.), *Item generation for test development* (pp. 287–305). Hillsdale, NJ: Erlbaum.

ABOUT THE EDITORS

Dr. Hong Jiao is an associate professor at the University of Maryland specializing in Educational Measurement and Statistics. She has published and presented on a variety of topics, including testlet modeling, local dependence, integrating product and process data for cognitive diagnosis, computerized adaptive testing for classification and latent class identification.

Dr. Robert W. Lissitz is a professor emeritus at the University of Maryland specializing in Educational Measurement and Statistics. He has published and presented on a variety of topics, including test fairness and validity issues in large-scale assessment.

Application of Artificial Intelligence to Assessment, page 211
Copyright © 2020 by Information Age Publishing
All rights of reproduction in any form reserved.

Printed in the United States
By Bookmasters